POWER, COMMUNITY AND THE STATE

The Political Anthropology of Organisation in Mexico

MONIQUE NUIJTEN

Pluto Press

LONDON • STERLING, VIRGINIA

First published 2003
by PLUTO PRESS
345 Archway Road, London N6 5AA
and 22883 Quicksilver Drive,
Sterling, VA 20166–2012, USA

www.plutobooks.com

British Library Cataloguing in Publication Data
A catalogue record for this book is available from
the British Library

ISBN 0 7453 1947 5 hardback
ISBN 0 7453 1946 7 paperback

Library of Congress Cataloging in Publication Data
Nuijten, Monique.
    Power, community and the state : the political anthropology of
organisation in Mexico / Monique Nuijten.
      p. cm. — (Anthropology, culture, and society)
    ISBN 0–7453–1947–5 (hbk) — ISBN 0–7453–1946–7 (pbk)
    1. La Canoa (Jalisco, Mexico)—Politics and government. 2.
Ejidos—Mexico—La Canoa (Jalisco) 3. Political anthropology—Mexico.
I. Title. II. Series.
    JS2120.L2 N84 2003
    320.972'35—dc21
                                                    2003002322

10   9   8   7   6   5   4   3   2   1

Designed and produced for Pluto Press by
Chase Publishing Services, Fortescue, Sidmouth EX10 9QG, England
Typeset from disk by Stanford DTP Services, Towcester, England
Printed and bound in the European Union by
Antony Rowe, Chippenham and Eastbourne, England

CONTENTS

Contents

ACKNOWLEDGEMENTS

I am indebted to many people who have made this work possible and who have become dear friends. First and foremost, I want to express my gratitude to the people of La Canoa who received me and my family with so much hospitality. I am grateful for their patience and their willingness to cooperate even though they often wondered why I needed so much time to write the 'simple history' of their ejido. The need to protect their identities means that I unfortunately cannot thank them with their real names and that I use the names that I have given them in the book. I am most grateful to Lorenzo Romero and María Lomelí who were 'our family in Mexico'. They and their children helped us in many different ways. Lupe Medina became a dear friend who confided many details of her life to me and helped me understand the importance of land for a mother who saw her children, one after another, leave for the United States. Salvador Lagos was a very inspiring man who enjoyed relating histories of the ejido. He took great interest in the writing of this book and I am sad that he is no longer around to see the work completed. I am indebted to Iginio Núñez and Ramón Romero for their enormous patience and their interest in the problems of the ejido without which I could not have written this book. I would also like to thank Manuel Pradera, Benita Romero, and Iginio Núñez's wife Adelma Godínez for the many pleasant gatherings we had together with them. Alicia Hernández and Joaquin Núñez helped me with the elaboration of a census of La Canoa and genealogies of families and plots of land in the ejido. They were two young people who showed great interest in the history of their own village being written and the many discussions I had with them helped me to develop my ideas. Although I sometimes felt uncomfortable when presenting details of the private lives of several families of La Canoa, I hope that the ethnography expresses the great regard and affection I feel for them.

Gregorio Rivera, a regional historian in Autlán, and his wife Cristina were great hosts and inspiring dialoguers. I am indebted to Ignacio Gómez, the regional historian of El Grullo, and his wife Rosa for their friendship, our pleasant gatherings, and the many insights they offered us into regional politics. I also owe much to many officials of government institutes, with whom I established pleasant relationships. In the region I want to thank especially the officials of the SARH office in El Grullo, of the *promotoría* of the Secretaría de la Reforma Agraria in Autlán and of the Procuraduría Agraria in Autlán. In Mexico City I especially wish to express my gratitude to officials of the headquarters of the Procuraduría Agraria for offering an open dialogue when they had just started their work and were developing new programmes for the ejido sector.

In 1994 and 1995 I worked at the anthropology department of El Colegio de Michoacán, which was a valuable experience. I would like to thank especially Andy Roth for his friendship and his valuable suggestions and critique on my work. With Sergio Zendejas and Gail Mummert I share a fine relationship. Sergio was a great ally in my struggle to approach the ejido and the Mexican state from different theoretical angles. Other friends at El Colegio are Brigitte Boehm, Pepe Lameiras, Rafael and Elena Diego, Marco Antonio Calderón, Eduardo Zarate, Esteban Barragán and Cristina Monzón.

David Myhre invited me to the Ejido Reform Research Project, and in this way offered me a forum to discuss my ideas and enter into debate with prominent academics. A special thanks to John Gledhill, Gavin Smith and Raymond Buve for their continuous encouragement over the years. Their critical comments on several of my presentations and writings were extremely helpful for developing my ideas. The conversations with Rob Aitken have also been very useful.

This book was produced in two stages. First as a PhD dissertation in sociology of rural development at Wageningen University. I thank the Netherlands Foundation for the Advancement of Tropical Research (WOTRO) for the scholarship for the PhD research and for their flexibility in adapting their procedures to personal situations. Second, the dissertation was thoroughly revised for publication. The Netherlands Academy of the Arts and Sciences (KNAW) made it possible for me to continue my research in Mexico and develop the theoretical ideas that are presented in this book.

I want to thank Norman Long for his great inspiration as head of the department of rural development sociology at Wageningen University for many years. If it was not for his stimulating lectures and fresh theoretical ideas, I doubt that I would have continued my career in the sociology of rural development. I specially want to mention Jan den Ouden, who has always been a great support in personal and professional ways. With Gerard Verschoor I share many experiences in Wageningen and Mexico as a colleague and a special friend. Jos Michel was a great support during all those years that she has been a central figure at the administration of the department. I thank Leontine Visser, who has taken over the position as head of the department, for creating a stimulating and supportive academic environment. A special word of thanks to Franz and Keebet von Benda-Beckmann who have been dear friends since they introduced me to the field of legal anthropology. I still remember the visit they made to La Canoa and the long discussions we had at that time. I feel fortunate that our discussions and exchange of ideas have never stopped.

However, most of all, my gratitude goes out to Pieter and our twin daughters Alicia and Liliana. Pieter generously unleashed his critical skills on each version of the book and was the most critical, but also the most enthusiastic reader. I am eternally grateful for the support and encouragement that he has shown me in so many different ways. Our daughters Alicia and Liliana greatly enriched our lives. Born during our years in Costa Rica, Alicia and Liliana then accompanied us to reside in La Canoa and frequently travelled between Jalisco, Michoacán, and Holland. I am afraid that travelling has become part of their identity. I dedicate this book to them and Pieter.

Monique Nuijten
Utrecht, the Netherlands
April 2003

To Pieter, Alicia and Liliana

1 AN ANTHROPOLOGY OF POWER AND THE STATE

INTRODUCTION: ANTHROPOLOGY AND THE STATE

It is remarkable that, at a time when the nation-state appears to be losing influence to global and transnational influences, anthropologists are showing an increased interest in debates about the state (Scott 1998, Trouillot 2001). This increased interest can be seen as a renewed concern with power and rule at a time when traditional structures and boundaries no longer seem to apply. It could be argued that while the state apparatus is being dismantled the notion of the state is becoming central in fantasies of rule, governance and order (Blom and Stepputat 2001). However, both power and the state are subjects that anthropology has been reluctant to theorise about (Nagengast 1994, Trouillot 2001). As Vincent argues, 'political anthropology has never distinguished itself by researching the corridors of power; the challenge to "study up" was not widely accepted' (1990: 400). Or, as Wolf said, 'we actually know a great deal about power, but have been timid in building upon what we know' (1990: 586). To be clear, the aim of this book is not to develop an anthropological theory of the state. The book aims to theorise certain neglected dimensions of power that are central to the working of the state and which are revealed in practices of organisation, rule and governance.

Many students of comparative politics make a fundamental distinction between the way in which state power works in the 'Third World' and in 'developed countries'. In contrast to developed countries, state apparatuses in developing countries are seen as unreliable and corrupt, while power is said to be exercised through extensive networks of patron–client relations and intermediation networks. These mechanisms are seen as expressions of underdevelopment and deviances from western democratic paths of development. In my view, the notion that in developing countries power operates according to logics and rationalities that are different from those in the developed world is seriously

Before elaborating further on the theoretical framework of the research, I will first present the object of study; the agrarian reform and the *ejido* in Mexico.

A STUDY OF STATE PROCESSES THROUGH PEASANT COMMUNITIES IN MEXICO

The ejido form of land tenure was established at the beginning of this century as a result of the Mexican revolution (1910–20) in which masses of landless peasants demanded 'land and liberty' from the state. Large landholdings were expropriated and ejidos were created to receive and administer these confiscated lands. The way in which the land had to be distributed among the landless peasants as well as the organisational structure of the ejido at the local level were all dictated by the agrarian law.[1] The Ministry of Agrarian Reform (SRA)[2] played a central role in the procedures for the establishment of ejidos but also remained heavily involved in the local administration of ejido matters and in land conflicts. This continuing interference by the state made analysts claim that the agrarian insurgents who had fought for *tierra y libertad* (land and liberty), in the end had got *tierra y el estado* (land and the state) (Tutino 1986: 8).

Looking at the Mexican ejido is a good way of studying the themes of governance, rule and state power. Sociologists and anthropologists have above all focused on the effects of local and regional power relations on the operation of the ejido (Bartra 1980a, Esteva 1980, Gordillo 1988, Warman 1976). Regional strongmen (*caciques*) were said to control the executive committees of the ejidos and to use their position to distribute land and other resources among their political 'clients'. As these *caciques* were connected to political networks in the centre, the state managed to keep control at a distance (Bartra 1980b, Warman 1976). The general view is that the regional strongmen or *caciques* 'mediate between the needs of the national state (or private corporations) and the actual on-the-ground situations of peasants and workers, that they derive power from this relation of mediation, and that this power takes on very complex cultural qualities because of the diverse natures of the *caciques*' mediating roles' (Lomnitz-Adler 1992: 297).

This leads to a gloomy picture in which groups of peasants could try to organise themselves independently but 'were generally coopted or repressed by the formidable power and resources available to the various power brokers throughout the system' (Grindle 1995: 42). Although it is often said that this all-pervasiveness of *caciques* enables the Mexican state to exert control over different populations, even in the smallest villages, at the same time this dependence by the state on the *cacique* is seen as a sign of the weakness and ineffectiveness of the Mexican state as it makes it impossible to implement government programmess without giving a central role to regional powerholders.

The ejido has also been analysed in relation to Mexico's political system, which in the view of many authors is characterised by the dominance of the PRI (Institutional Revolutionary Party) through an array of corporatist mechanisms.[3] This has been especially the case in analyses of the rural sector (Esteva 1980, Gordillo 1988, Rincón 1980). For the peasantry the most important official organisation linked to the ruling PRI has been the National Peasant Confederation (CNC) that was created under the presidency of Cárdenas (1934–40). The CNC was set up to represent ejido petitioners and *ejidatarios* in their relations with the state bureaucracies and is said to have provided the bulk of rural support for the PRI. It was argued that, through the machine-like clientele networks of the PRI, ejido commissioners were transformed into brokers between government and peasants, trading their ability to deliver the votes of ejidatarios for special benefits of the regime. This has 'led many analysts to conclude that the agrarian reform – and the ejido in particular – was a cornerstone in the building of Mexico's corporatist and authoritarian one-party regime because it secured the ejidatarios' political submission to the state' (Zendejas 1995: 25).

The tendency in Mexico to adopt top-down models, either of a neo-Marxist or neo-corporatist bent, emphasising the exploitation of the peasantry by the state, has always remained very strong. In fact, 'since the 1970s, accounts of politics in postrevolutionary Mexico have assumed that ongoing domination has resulted from centralised, relatively homogeneous power transmitted outward through corporatist mechanisms' (Rubin 1996: 85). Some authors have recognised the limitations of an analysis based on *caciquismo* as there exist many different types of *caciques* and their basis of control and their style of inter-mediation can vary dramatically. Lomnitz-Adler, for example, argues that 'the phenomenon of "caciquismo" is so diverse – in terms of the kinds of power relations involved, in terms of the economic and ethnic characteristics of *caciques*, in terms of their position in society – that the utility of the term itself can be doubted' (Lomnitz-Adler 1992: 296, see also Tapia 1992). Gledhill (1994) points out that we could better study the complex sets of changing socio-political alignments which structure the relations between people and the state. Following Gilsenan (1977), Gledhill argues that we should explain what particular kinds of social agents fill the gap between local and higher levels and how they do so (Gledhill 1994: 125).

In more recent years attention in anthropology shifted from a focus on powerful people and politics to the many everyday forms of resistance by the peasants (Scott 1985). Attention started to be paid to active manipulation and accommodation of government intervention by the 'clients' of the bureaucracy (Long 1989). In effect, as Long and van der Ploeg (1989) argue, it is at this level that – through negotiations between different producers and officials – significant policy transformations take place. Many ethnographies of state now deal with case studies of bureaucratic projects, state agencies and state workers, elements that were ignored in the past. While in the past many studies argued that peasants lack consciousness of their own situation and processes of exploitation by the state, these theories showed the subtle way in which political consciousness and resistance were expressed. In Mexico, studies also turned towards processes 'from below' (Arce 1993, Joseph and Nugent 1994, Stephen 1997, Zendejas and Mummert 1996).

James Scott has recently offered a larger theoretical framework in which the multiple dimensions of state power are taken into account. In his book *Seeing like a state* (1998), Scott deals with power at higher levels and provides interesting material on the development of modern states. He shows how the state uses governmental techniques, such as maps, procedures and classifications in order to control people and territories. A limitation of his work, however, is that he deals with the state as a uniform monolithic entity 'out there' with intentions, objectives and goals. He does not address the murky and chaotic side of the state, and the different dimensions of power which only become clear when we look at the dynamics within state institutions themselves and when we follow the informal processes of negotiation and settlement. In other words, Scott uses a vision of the state, which is not helpful for the analysis of the different dimensions of state power. In the next section, some examples will be presented of the 'murky' side of state power and the importance of 'imagining'.

A FASCINATION WITH POWER AND CONSPIRACY

The ethnography presented here is based on in-depth research in one ejido, La Canoa in the valley of Autlán in Jalisco, Mexico. In 1938 the village of La Canoa received lands to establish its own ejido. This land was immediately divided into individual plots and distributed among the households of the village. Yet, over the years the number of households has increased substantially and today most households in the village have no access to ejido land. Today there are 196 households in the village La Canoa, while the ejido La Canoa has only 97 members (ejidatarios). Many villagers combine their life in the village with temporary migration to the United States.

I carried out research in this ejido and in several government agencies during several periods of fieldwork from mid-1991 to mid-1995. Since 1995 I have returned to the region several times for short visits. The aim of the research was to analyse how the organising practices in the ejido were related to local power relations and the ways in which they were shaped by interactions with the state bureaucracy. Hence, I studied what had happened with the land since the ejido received it in 1938. How had the individual land plots been distributed at the start of the ejido and how had the use rights been transferred from one generation to the next? How did people organise illegal land sales? How did people protect their land when they illegally rented out the land? How were land conflicts handled, negotiated, settled or not settled? These questions automatically took me to different levels of the SRA, which was especially involved in land conflicts and in the 'legalisation' of illegal transactions. Besides research within the community, critical legal and bureaucratic transformations were studied from within government agencies, based on in-depth interviews with functionaries at different levels of the bureaucracy.

From the very start it was obvious that many matters were not arranged in a legal way and that there was much so-called 'corruption'.

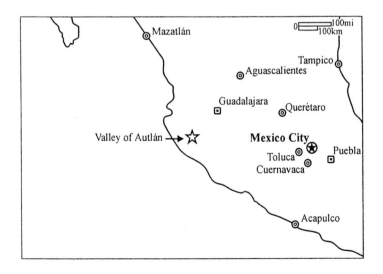

1.1   The Valley of Autlán in Mexico

Despite the strict agrarian law and interference by the Ministry of Agrarian Reform, organising practices developed which were different from what the law prescribed. For example, the agrarian law permitted the division of the arable land into individual plots but prohibited the selling of these plots, renting them out or leaving them unused. In reality, however, these became common practices in ejidos throughout Mexico. With respect to the local administration of the ejido, things also worked out differently. The Agrarian Law stipulated that ejido meetings should be held every month and that decisions had to be taken by a majority of votes of the ejido assembly, in which all ejidatarios are represented. Yet, it became a common phenomenon that no decisions were reached at these meetings and that the head of the ejido, the commissioner, took decisions on his own. Furthermore, in many ejidos the monthly meetings were not held and, if they were held, few ejidatarios attended.

Likewise, the rules were also seldom applied in the resolution of land conflicts by the SRA. It has often been said that the person who can pay the highest bribes or has the best political contacts wins a land conflict. At the same time, land conflicts between ejidatarios and private landowners abound and many have never been resolved. For the foregoing reasons, the ejido system has often been labelled as highly 'corrupt' and the Ministry of Agrarian Reform was seen as a central element in the fostering of such corruption.

The Fantastic Side of the State

While living with the ejidatarios for a long time and following them in their struggles with the SRA and in their fight against private landowners who had invaded parts of their land, many things struck me. First of all, there were many aspects of the ejidatarios' actions that I perceived as contradictory. Although a certain degree of 'contradiction' and 'inconsistency' seems normal, it assumed quite dramatic forms in the field. For example, while ejidatarios could one day theorise about how land conflicts in Mexico were always resolved by elites to their own advantage through political networks, the next day they could spend an enormous amount of energy and money to set in motion the legal-administrative process carried out by the bureaucracy. But why did they spend all this energy on a bureaucratic process when they themselves said that these matters were decided by political influence? I was also amazed to see that in their legal-administrative struggle to recover the land that had been invaded by private landowners, over and over again the ejidatarios paid large amounts of money to intermediaries who in the end always vanished. If one day they had been deceived by one intermediary, the next day they would start working with another who offered his services. I was also amazed by the fantastic stories that were told to them by officials and intermediaries and which they seemed to accept. Was this perhaps a form of false consciousness? Definitely not, for when I talked these things over with them, they appeared to be well aware of the situation. They knew that it was highly improbable that land would be taken from mighty private landowners, they realised that they were paying money to an intermediary who would probably disappear, and they were well aware of the fact that the fantastic promises made by officials were probably lies. However, although they realised that they were being deceived, they still went on working with the same bureaucracy. This phenomenon caused me terrible confusion during the research. At the same time I realised that it was precisely this phenomenon that was essential for understanding the nature of the relationships between the ejidatarios and the Mexican state.

This peculiar relation of the ejidatarios to the state bureaucracy is linked to forms of theorising by the ejidatarios about power and politics in society. Conspiracy theories thrived as many things went wrong in ejidatarios' relation with bureaucracies. These theories provide explanatory schemes for their lack of success with officials and for the fact that their plans always seem to be sabotaged. In particular, in serious conflicts, which occur in an atmosphere of insecurity and opacity, one would hear the most fantastic conspiracy theories. This constant theorising and reflecting is used to rationalise and explain their own actions or those of other people. Through these experiences I realised that this phenomenon of theorising about power and politics in society had to be taken into account as a central dimension of the relation between ejidatarios and the Mexican state. This would take the study 'of the state beyond the apparatus of government to show how the magic and power of the state are formed in everyday discursive practice' (Tsing 1993: 25). It must be added that this theorising and construction of conspiracies is not typical of the Mexican peasantry, but can be found in all social circles and especially within the bureaucracy itself.

I arrived at the conclusion that there are certainly reasons for the 'obsession' with power and the 'almighty state' in Mexico, and therefore these concerns need to be taken seriously. It is related to the feelings of awe and powerlessness of a great part of the population (including academics) towards a bureaucratic machine characterised by opaque politics. Hence, following Abrams, I argue that 'we should abandon the state as a material object of study whether concrete or abstract while continuing to take the idea of the state extremely seriously' (Abrams 1988: 75). Furthermore, although intermediaries indeed played an important role, what was striking during the research was the *lack of effective* intermediaries. In the land conflict between the ejido La Canoa and several private landowners, which I analyse in detail in Chapters 5 and 6, the ejidatarios had great difficulty finding reliable brokers and found themselves in the position of desperately seeking 'the right connection'. Yet, although they invested much energy in this case, they never found the intermediaries who could effectively operate on their behalf. Hence, instead of the gap that can always be filled, we have the image of the gap that keeps people moving but that will never be filled. I argue that we need a conception of the state, which centres on this idea of the unbridgeable gap between people and the state. This entails developing a perspective that takes into account how people's representations of state power are shaped by this continual search for intermediaries.

Naturally, people's representations are not disembodied cultural images but are produced in actual social practices. In order to come to grips with issues of power, without assuming its centredness in the state, I decided to focus on organising practices and what these would reveal about power relations. An important starting point of the research was that we should not assume beforehand the existence of certain power relations and forces in society. As Law points out, instead of assuming that certain powerful positions determine the characteristics of the organising process, it may be more fruitful to study how 'patterning generates institutional and organisational effects, including hierarchy and power' (Law 1992: 380).

ORGANISING PRACTICES AND FORCE FIELDS

Starting from Organising Practices

In my view, the best starting-point for an approach that focuses on the relation between organising practices and power, and that finally leads us to the analysis of different dimensions of the state, is the much-quoted article by Wolf, 'Facing power: old insights, new questions', in which he makes a connection between organising and power. In this article he stresses that 'it is a pity that anthropology seems to have relinquished the study of organisation' (Wolf 1990: 590–1). He argues that we should get away from viewing organisation as a product or outcome, and move to an understanding of organisation as a process. Wolf suggests that we could make a start by following 'Conrad Arensberg's advice (1972:

10–11) to look at the "flow of action", to ask what is going on, why it is going on, who engages in it, with whom, when, and how often' (1990: 591). Yet he adds that, when we study 'the flow of action', we should also ask the questions: 'for what and for whom is all this going on, and – indeed – *against* whom?' (1990: 591, emphasis added). These questions require a conceptual approach capable of analysing 'the forces and effects of the structural power that drives organising processes' (1990: 591). Wolf makes the point that most anthropological studies that deal with issues of power and politics neglect the question of organisation.

In addition to approaching organisation as a process, I argue that we should not define organising in terms of collective action, but rather in terms of different action patterns (see also Verschoor 1997). People often follow fragmented organising strategies, without collective projects ever becoming crystallised. They work with one set of actors and then another, develop strategies and change them in the course of action. Hence, when I talk about organising practices, I refer to the manifold forms of organising, whether they be individual or more collective. Yet my ultimate interest lies not in the isolated organising actions, strategies and performances in themselves, but in understanding their logics in specific socio-political contexts. I ask myself, for example, why ejidatarios, when dealing with persistent problems, operate in changing constellations of people instead of in stable, enduring groups. But I am also interested in organising practices in another way. Besides the action patterns and strategies which we can distinguish when individual people or groups try to achieve certain things, I try to distinguish forms of structuring or patterning in organising practices. In other words, I study the organising practices 'that arise from particular combinations of ideas, material circumstances, and interactional potentials and have patterning as their consequences' (Barth 1993: 4). For example, in the many 'illegal' or 'informal' arrangements with respect to ejido plots, we can distinguish certain regularities. We find a certain pattern in the way in which the sale of ejido plots is settled and that, in these arrangements, other ejidatarios, officials of the SRA, the ejido commissioner and the ejido assembly play specific roles. This patterning of organising practices in unexpected and often 'invisible' ways can also be distinguished in the apparently 'disordered', the 'corrupt' and the 'chaotic'.

Studying the flow of organising also means paying attention to people's ideas and representations. In my view, social theorising, reflexive talk and story-telling by social actors are central to organisation and power. Therefore, I would add to Wolf's point about the importance of following the 'flow of action', the necessity of following the 'flow of ideas'.

It is argued that the creation and re-creation of stories are a way of ordering the world around us and are central to the organising process (Law 1994a: 52, Reed 1992: 114). The continuous dialogues and discussions I had with people on their courses of action, decisions or events were not meant to provide material for a sort of decision-making model. Instead, these reflections were used to show 'how people's consciousness engages with the world precisely within the incomplete processes of everyday social practices' (Smith 1996: 7). This is a point that Rosaldo also elaborates forcefully when arguing that 'not only men and women of affairs but also ordinary people tell themselves stories about who they are, what they care about, and how they hope to realise their aspirations' (Rosaldo 1989: 129–30). In fact, people everywhere are in a critical, reflective dialogue with the world in which they live, with themselves and with the researcher (Pigg, 1996, 1997). An important implication of this perspective is that one does not fear inconsistencies and contradictions in the stories and versions people present. On the contrary, 'shifting, multistranded conversations in which there never is full agreement' may show important areas of contestation and struggle (Tsing 1993: 8). Tsing argues that we should situate local commentaries within wider spheres of negotiation of meaning and power while at the same time recognise the local stakes and specificities (1993: 9). Hence, story-telling, reflective talk, and imagination are essential for the analysis of the force fields in which organising occurs.

Force Fields

I use the concept of force field to refer to wider fields of power without determining beforehand the main actors or the central elements structuring the relations within the field.[4] In a force field certain forms of dominance, contention and resistance may develop, as well as certain regularities and forms of ordering. In this view, the patterning of organising practices is not the result of a common understanding or normative agreement, but of the forces at play within the field. As we will see, in the patterning of organising practices within certain force fields, we can distinguish different social actors with specific roles, different access to resources and differing rights. This is closely related to forms of inclusion and exclusion of socio-political categories. This also explains that organising practices are related to the production of meaning, or in other words to the development of 'structures of feeling' (Williams 1977: 132). The study of the reflective talk and dialogue shows how these express forms of struggle, contention and resistance in relation to existing organising practices and relations of power.

My notion of force field most resembles Bourdieu's notion of a field (Bourdieu and Wacquant 1992: 94–115). Bourdieu (1977, 2001, Bourdieu and Wacquant 1992) developed a practice-oriented approach with attention to creative human agency. According to Bourdieu, the field is the locus of relations of force and not only of meaning. The coherence that may be observed in a given state of the field is born of conflict and competition, not of some kind of immanent self-development of the structure. Every field has its own logic, rules and regularities which are not explicit and which make it resemble the playing of games. However, it always remains a field of struggles aimed at preserving or transforming the configuration of forces. These struggles and activities in the field always produce differences. Bourdieu argues that the active forces which produce the most relevant differences in a field define the specific capital (cultural, economic, social, etc.) of the field. In this way a field cannot exist without a certain capital, and a capital does not exist or function except in relation to a field. In Bourdieu's field, agents and institutions constantly struggle, according to the regularities and the rules constitutive of this space to appropriate the specific products at stake in the game. Those who dominate in a given field are in a position to make it function to their advantage, but they must always contend with the resistance, the claims, the contention, of the dominated.

I modify his notion of field for the purposes of my research. A difference between Bourdieu's approach and my use of the term is that he establishes a direct link between one form of capital and one type of field. In contrast, I do not define one type of capital around which a force field develops but instead try to distinguish the fields of force around certain resources or problems and which have a certain degree of patterning as a consequence. Furthermore, I distance myself from the way Bourdieu deals with culture and from his tendency to conceive of human agents as socialised in unconscious ways. For Bourdieu habitus is the taken-for-granted part of culture. He argues that many of our actions are routine and that practical knowledge organises most of our daily actions. This practical knowledge 'functions like a self-regulating device programmed to redefine courses of action in accordance with information received on the reception of information transmitted and on the effects produced by that information' (Bourdieu 1977: 11). Although Bourdieu leaves room in his analytical framework for improvisation and flexibility, he is above all interested in the regularities of structure and processes of domination and he concentrates on the political culture of the dominant classes.

Criticising Bourdieu's approach Gledhill points out that:

it is surely of some importance that there is communication within social groups about the extended experiences of 'being-in-the-world'. Human beings are not, in fact, windowless nomads, even if the habitus does play a crucial role in structuring the meanings social collectivities ascribe to changing experience. (Gledhill 1994: 138)

I concur with this critique which immediately indicates the limitation of Bourdieu's theoretical framework for the study of 'small politics' and the creativity in 'everyday organising practices'. For these themes we need an approach which leaves room for indeterminateness, fragmentation and the complexity of human consciousness. As explained above, in my approach to organising practices, continuous critical reflections by human agents, their theorising on politics and power in society, and their story-telling are central elements. Organising practices, however structured they may be, are the subject of constant critical reflection.

In talking about the state and the production of meaning in force fields shaped through relations of power and dominance, I come close to notions of hegemony (Gramsci 1971). More recent approaches have 'taken a focus on the partiality, the eternally incomplete nature of hegemony, with its implication of the cultural as a contested, contingent political field, the battlefield in an ongoing "war of position"' (Gupta and Ferguson 1997a: 5, commenting on recent interpreters of Gramsci like Williams [1977] and Stuart Hall [1986]). Roseberry also proposes to 'explore hegemony not as a finished and monolithic ideological formation but as a problematic, contested, political process of domination and struggle' (Roseberry 1994: 358). He proposes to use the concept to understand

the ways in which the words, images, and symbols, forms, organisations, insti-tutions, and movements used by subordinate populations to talk about, understand, confront, accommodate themselves to, or resist their domination are shaped by the process of domination itself. What hegemony constructs, then, is not a shared ideology but a common material and meaningful framework for living through, talking about, and acting upon social orders characterised by domination. (1994: 361)

Although this is an interesting approach to hegemony, we should take into account that the nation-state is not necessarily the only, or the primary, social, political and ideological container of the population living within its border (Trouillot 2001). Mexican peasants, for example, live in a world in which socio-spatial referents are increasingly de-territorialised, transnational and fragmented. Contrary to studies of hegemony, I pay more attention to contradictions, conflicts and conspiracy theories as a central part of relations of power. In this sense I am not only interested in distinguishing a 'common material and meaningful framework' that people use in their dealings with domination, but in explaining the contradictions and inconsistencies that make up the culture of power in different fields of force.

THREE DIMENSIONS OF THE STATE

It will be obvious that I argue against a view of the state as an almighty apparatus with almost total top-down control through corporatism and intermediary structures. Instead of adhering to the notion of state power as a coherent and homogeneous ensemble driven by deliberate projects and strategies, we should conceive of the state as a collection of decentred practices without a central agency, or core project. Here I follow Rubin who in his study on Mexico argues that 'what appears to be ongoing and unchanging domination ... is the overall result not of an all-controlling centre of particular structures of political bargaining and rule but of numerous changing forms and locations of domination and resistance' (1996: 88). This does not mean that power elites do not have projects of domination, but that we should not assume their effectiveness in advance, nor their centrality for understanding the working of state power. Starting from these decentred notions of power we then have to develop an analytical framework in which the state is conceptualised at several levels and in different dimensions (Trouillot 2001). Hence it is important to take into account the cultural dimension of power relations. In this book I develop three dimensions of the state.

The Idea of the State

Following Abrams, the belief in the existence of a strong, coherent state system is what I call the 'idea of the state'. According to Abrams, the state-idea is 'an ideological artefact attributing unity, morality and independence to the disunited, amoral and dependent workings of the practice of government' (Abrams 1988: 81). This belief in the state 'conceals the workings of relations of rule and forms of discipline in day to day life' (Alonso 1994: 381). The widespread belief that there is a centre of state control in which power is concentrated is illustrative of how this 'idea of the state' is reproduced. These are misrepresentations that lead to forms of state fetishism (Taussig 1992). I argue that it is in this context that the search for brokers has to be analysed. Hence, contrary to traditional approaches to intermediation, I argue that brokers do not necessarily have a role in effectively connecting communities or peasants to the state, or in effectively 'filling the gap', but play a role in the fantasies of state power. By searching for the 'right intermediary' and by presenting themselves as the 'right connection', ejidatarios as well as brokers are implicated in the construction of this 'idea of the strong state'.

The Hope-Generating State Machine

Obviously, there exist governmental institutions made up of diverse sets of practices linked to the political system. Abrams calls this the state-system, 'a palpable nexus of practice and institutional structure centred in government and more or less extensive, unified and dominant in any given society' (Abrams 1988: 82). Because of the specific characteristics of the Mexican bureaucracy I decided to call it the hope-generating machine. Ferguson (1990) talks about the 'anti-politics machine' referring to the depoliticising effects of 'development' institutions in Lesotho. Yet, as we will see, in Mexico one of the most remarkable aspects of the bureaucracy, rather than its tendency to depoliticise the relationship between people and the bureaucracy, is its hope-generating capacity. In part, this generation of hope is related to a presidential system in which a new president takes office every six years, heavily criticises former programmes and introduces new projects often together with new institutions (see Chapter 7). But this hope-generating characteristic of the bureaucracy is also based on the fact that the bureaucracy offers endless openings, and that officials are always willing to initiate procedures. The bureaucracy as a hope-generating machine gives the message that everything is possible, that cases are never closed and that things will be different from now on. The bureaucracy never says no and creates great expectations. On the other hand, many promises are never fulfilled. Rather than producing a certain rationality and coherence, the bureaucratic machine generates enjoyments, pleasures, fears and expectations.

The Culture of the State

The state system in terms of a set of institutions and procedures acquires significance by reference to cultural categories, which are also used in government propaganda, schoolbooks, national festivities, etc. We should not then view the state as a set of institutions and procedures whose political significance is obvious without reference to cultural categories. This points to the cultural dimensions of domination (see Dirks et al. 1994). It places 'culture and everyday experience squarely within discussions of power' (Rubin 1996: 90, see also Aitken 1997, Gledhill 1994, 1995, Joseph and Nugent 1994, Lomnitz-Adler 1992,

Pansters 1997a). For that reason I introduce the notion of the 'culture of the state'. With the culture of the state I refer to the practices of representation and interpretation which characterise the relation between people and the state bureaucracy and through which the idea of the state is constructed. It is present in the 'reading' and interpretation of speeches, official acts, programmes, and documents by the ejidatarios. Thus in Chapters 5 and 6 I refer to 'the lost map', which becomes a fetish in a land conflict, and to official stamps and documents which acquire symbolic meanings beyond their administrative functions. The culture of the state is expressed in the numerous letters written every day to the Mexican president. An important aspect of the culture of the state is the atmosphere of opacity, distrust and conspiracy, which always surrounds conflicts, negotiations and dealings with the bureaucracy, especially in conflictive cases. The practices of 'impression management' in which officials and brokers exaggerate their importance in order to convince the ejidatarios that they have the necessary 'access' and connections to make the bureaucracy work are also elements of the culture of the state. In sum, the culture of the state is the construction of the idea of the Mexican state through techniques of mapping, fetishisation, interpretation and speculation or, in other words, it is 'the cultural inscription of the idea of the state' (Alonso 1994: 381).

In this context, it is important to discuss the relevance and limitations of studies of governmentality in which the power of the state is said to rest in the creation of subjectivities and identities by the 'routines' and 'rituals' of state (Corrigan and Sayer 1985, Rose and Miller 1992, Rose 1999).[5] Although practices of 'governmentalisation' are certainly important, we should not assume their effectiveness beforehand. The point is that governmental techniques always encounter populations that have already been integrated within political systems in a variety of ways (Thomas 1994). In other words, state rituals and discourses recombine with representations of the state that are already in circulation (Pigg 1997: 281). So they do not necessarily constitute an effective means for controlling and disciplining populations. On the other hand, although governmental techniques sometimes are not really effective in controlling people, they can generate side effects that are central to the reproduction of the bureaucratic system. For example, in Mexico, maps, stamps, and documents are all extremely important, even though it is not their official meaning that matters. In the relation between 'clients' and the hope-generating bureaucratic machine, all these artefacts acquire different meanings, leading to a 're-enchantment of governmental techniques' (cf. Comaroff and Comaroff 1993).

It must be stressed that my notion of 'the culture of the state' differs strongly from the way in which 'political culture' is used by political scientists (Almond and Verba 1980, Camp 1986, 1996, Cornelius and Craig 1988, 1991). In the studies of political scientists, the notion of political culture refers to the cultural elements that are characteristic of a certain political system. The analysis of a political culture is related to political processes such as elections, faith in the government and the legitimation of the state. In contrast, recent works on political culture focus less on the legitimacy of the political system and distance themselves from a one-sided focus on political culture as a study of attitudes. Instead they focus more on political practices (see the volume edited by Pansters 1997). Although this latter approach is more interesting, my focus is a different one. My central interest is not the legitimacy of a political system, nor the working of a political system. In my use of the concept of the culture of the state, I am concerned with the role of symbolism in the everyday interactions between people and state bureaucracies.

In the Mexican context, Lomnitz-Adler's work is interesting as he sets out to analyse 'the cultural heterogeneity that arises in spaces of hegemony' (Lomnitz-Adler 1992: 4). He defines regional culture as an internally differentiated cultural space with both a common regional cultural framework and distinct sets of understandings that are specific to the groups that compose the region. Lomnitz-Adler uses the term 'intimate culture' 'to represent the real, regionally differentiated mani-festations of class culture. Intimate culture is the culture of a class in a specific kind of regional setting' (1992: 28). He claims that this way of dealing with culture will stop the endless literary publications on the Mexican character, or *lo Mexicano*, as it will show how culture is actually produced in different spaces. The work is interesting for several reasons. First of all, Lomnitz-Adler pays attention to the enormous diversity in regional power structures and the cultural manifestations that go along with it. This is an important contribution to discussions on regional politics in Mexico and on the relation between power and culture. He shows well the diversity in the forms of articulation between different social groups, as well as the cultural heterogeneity that results from these relations. His concept of intimate culture is appealing, as it does not define beforehand the dominant groups in a certain region. In that sense, it is a flexible concept that can be used to study different situations. However, the work can be criticised for several reasons.

One of the limitations of his approach is the fact that he only focuses on the interaction between the state bureaucracy and regional elites. What about the daily dealings between thousands of government officials and thousands of peasants? How do we analyse the interactions between ejidatarios from the state of Jalisco and officials of Mexico City and what sorts of intimate cultures interact in these situations? When we study the interactions of ejidatarios with officials we certainly notice specific cultural practices, but should we call this the distinct intimate culture of the agrarian bureaucracy? It is here that I introduce the notion of the culture of the state. I differ here from Lomnitz-Adler who uses quite different concepts of the state and the culture of the state. According to Lomnitz-Adler the state represents national society and as such is a major player in the construction of the culture of social relations. In this line of thinking, the culture of the state is the 'intimate culture' of the state apparatus. In opposition to Lomnitz-Adler, I do not conceive of the state as an actor or entity with its own culture. In my analytical framework, the culture of the state is the way in which this 'mighty actor' or 'neutral arbiter' is imagined through administrative procedures, stamps, maps, theories about power and the belief in the 'right connection'.

THE CREATION OF A MULTI-SITED, REFLEXIVE ETHNOGRAPHY

It would be impossible to present here all of the many methodological choices made during the research but I wish to pay special attention to a number of them. In the different chapters, other methodological issues are discussed. As I explained above, I had specific reasons for not studying the ejido from the perspective of official models and of instead working 'from the ground'. I avoid a conceptualisation of the ejido merely in institutional-legal terms. As Barth puts it, 'I am in no way arguing that formal organisation is irrelevant to what is happening – only that formal organisation is not what is happening' (Barth 1993: 157). Barth points out that

it is by attending systematically to people's own intentions and interpretations, accessible only if one adopts the perspective of their concerns and their knowledge of the constraints under which they act, that one can start unravelling the meanings *they* confer on events, and thereby the experience they are harvesting. (1993: 105)

Yet, this working 'from below' had the consequence that I arrived at an image of the ejido that was rather unusual. This became particularly clear during presentations of my research material in academic circles. While I presented the dynamic of ejido practices which I had found during the research, the audience always referred to the official and established academic views of the ejido and wanted to divert the discussion towards the role of the CNC, the *caciques* or the nature of the political system, in what was, in fact, a search for a particular kind of theoretical closure. However, working 'from below' more often than not, means postponing such closure, and often searching for other modes of interpretation and explanation which do not privilege key actors or structures such as the CNC, the *cacique*, capital or the state.

Considering the detailed material I wanted to gather and the fact that agrarian issues in Mexico are a rather politicised theme, I decided to study only one ejido. La Canoa is in no way a special ejido or village. I had lived in this ejido for a short period in 1987 when I participated in a research project on the relation between irrigation organisation and peasant strategies.[6] La Canoa is one of those many small places which do not attract the attention of academics because of some special form of political struggle, well-known revolutionary history or agrarian problematics. However, the study of these 'ordinary' places may give us important insights into the working of state power. As Scott argues:

One might ask: why are we here, in a village of no particular significance, examining the struggle of a handful of history's losers? ... The justification for such an enterprise must lie precisely in its banality – in the fact that these circumstances are the normal context in which class conflict has historically occurred. (Scott 1985: 27)

It must be recognised that the scope of the study is not defined by saying that the research concerns one ejido. For example, different offices of the SRA in Mexico City, Guadalajara and Autlán are involved in 'local' transactions of ejido land. Furthermore, the dynamics in the village and ejido can only be understood by taking into account migration to the United States and the increasingly transnationalised lives of ejidatarios. In other words, the relations that affect the production of locality are fundamentally translocal and we should try to find the means to study the production of locality in a world that has become deterritorialised, diasporic and transnational (see Appadurai 1997: 188).

From the start of the research I tried to find areas of contention, struggle and conflicts in the ejido or the village. The critical importance of conflicts for anthropological studies was developed explicitly by authors in legal anthropology (Comaroff and Roberts 1981, Gulliver 1979, Nader 1969, Starr and Collier 1989). In contrast to several of these authors, however, I focus on conflicts not because I am interested in the constitution of normative orders, or the study of mechanisms of conflict resolution, but because in my view conflictive situations give insights into the central issues at stake, and the power struggles and practices which develop around them. The study of conflicts shows how social actors organise themselves, what is important for different categories of people, and how they talk about this. In this way, it provides a point of entry for the study of organising practices, ideological processes, power relations and forms of ordering which develop in certain force fields. An additional reason to study conflictive situations was that they offered me the possibility of studying in more detail the role of agrarian procedures and 'how individuals and groups in particular times and places have used legal resources to achieve their ends' (Starr and Collier 1989: 2). In this way I could 'analyse the relationship of the law to wider systems of social relations' (1989: 2). The fact that conflicts were an important part of the research does not mean that I only studied the visible, the crucial, and most dramatic events. In reality, most of the organising around serious land conflicts was 'invisible', in the sense that it was done in small groups outside formal arenas, and at places and moments that most people were not aware of.

Specific case studies (Mitchell 1983, Walton 1992) and situational analyses (Long 1968, van Velsen 1967) were elaborated during the research. These detailed studies of conflicts, people and events are central for the research as only in this way can the complexity of different organising processes and power relations be revealed. I agree with Scott when he says that 'any carefully detailed empirical case is always far richer than the generalisations that can be extracted from it' (1994: ix). Among other things, detailed studies were made of one big and several smaller land conflicts in the ejido; and of the implementation of a new government project for the ejido. Obviously, the cases should be chosen on the basis of their importance for the theme of the research. The choice and presentation of case studies and situational analyses 'require theoretical judgements about causality, necessary connections and abstraction. Consequently they are not a rationale for naive empiricism and make great demands of analytical rigor' (Rogers and Vertovec 1995: 10–11).

Another focus of the research was public events. I realised that important questions and conflicts were hardly ever spoken about or settled at the official meetings and that most issues were resolved in private settings. However, although official meetings may have little to do with their formal function, they may be illuminating in other respects. First of all, formal meetings may give important clues about what is happening 'behind the scenes', from the ironic remarks, the conversations and discussions in the back of the room, and the discussions afterwards. Furthermore, these public meetings show the ways in which matters are formalised. They may show how issues that have been resolved informally are formally presented, challenged and negotiated. Public debates also give an indication of the most powerful political or administrative discourses (see Bloch 1975 and Parkin 1984 on political language). A central aim was to study these official events in relation to other kinds of gatherings and encounters. I wanted to find out what the role of formal meetings and gatherings was in the organising practices at the local level. Did people organise these formal events in order to attain certain ends? Did they use these meetings for other purposes? Or had these meetings perhaps attained certain unintended characteristics and roles through time? Were there different types of public meetings?

The interactions between officials and ejidatarios formed a different object of study. Long (1989) introduces the notion of the interface in order to analyse the encounters between different groups and individuals involved in the processes of planned intervention. The interface reflects different types of power relations and different patterns of negotiation between, for example, peasants and government officials. According to Long, such interactional studies offer a middle-ground level of analysis, and reveal specific aspects of state–peasant relations. Long argues that 'development interface situations are the critical points at which not only is policy applied but at which it is "transformed" through acquiring social meanings that were not set out in the original policy statements' (Long 1989: 3). The study of direct interactions between bureaucrats and 'clients' can be especially interesting in situations of new government programmes and changing institutional contexts, such as the transformation of Mexico's Agrarian Law. These interfaces reveal, for example, the role of institutional discourses, the expectations and perceptions of officials and ejidatarios, and the different contexts and processes of negotiation. In these interfaces we can also study the role of professional jargon and whether, for example, legal language indeed 'renders powerless the ordinary language of the uninformed' (Parkin 1984: 360).

Talking to people and getting information through interviews or informal conversations is one of the main sources of anthropological fieldwork. Yet in this study talking with people has not only been used to acquire 'information', but also to study story-telling, reflective talk and the use of certain discourses. As Cohen points out, 'we could begin by paying attention to the ways in which people reflect on themselves, and then see in what ways these reflections are indicative of social and cultural context, or require such contextualisation to be intelligible to us' (Cohen 1994: 29). I looked for theories people construct about history, society and the things that happened around them. I analysed the way in which villagers and ejidatarios tended to express themselves about themselves, the ejido, their society, the history of their community, and other topics they came up with themselves. Attention was also paid to expressions which were frequently uttered, standard ways of talking about certain themes, and distinctions and categories people employed. I also tried to pursue the more difficult task of distinguishing differences in expressions people used in different settings, topics which were avoided, and parts of reality which were made invisible by their way of talking (see Alasuutari 1995, Silverman 1993). It is important to stress that the significance of certain ways of talking can only be determined in relation to other research material. For example, only in relation to the rest of the research material may one draw conclusions about, why ejidatarios always mention certain ejido rules and not others, why officials always start talking about corruption in the institutes they work for and at the same time stress the importance of formal procedures, and why officials and ejidatarios use completely different languages when they talk about the same land conflict.

The manifold conversations I had with the same people over the course of several years were the most important source for my research. With these people I entered into elaborate debates as I became a sort of discussant for them, 'someone who was not party in the petty and hard struggles ... but who was, nevertheless, to some extent part of the picture' (de Vries 1992: 70). Especially towards the end of the fieldwork period, these interviews took on more and more the character of critical dialogues. I challenged people on certain ideas they held and deliberately confronted them with what I saw as contradictions in their statements and actions. I myself had also developed certain ideas about the ejido and the difficult relation of the ejidatarios with the state bureaucracies and I discussed these ideas with the ejidatarios. It was interesting to see how they reacted to my theories and doubts, but they themselves also started asking me questions about my personal views on the matter. This resulted in interesting research material that helped me to develop further my ideas about the most striking phenomena I found during my fieldwork. With officials I discussed my ideas about the workings of the Mexican bureaucracy. While with some people this resulted in interesting discussions, with others this kind of dialogue was not possible at all. Some officials liked to be challenged on their views and they themselves liked to discuss what they saw as problems of the agrarian bureaucracy and the rural sector, but others held on strongly to their official role and formal discourse and gave standard bureaucratic answers.

Towards the end of the fieldwork period, I myself became actively involved in ejido matters. This active participation had not so much been a decision on my part as a decision on the part of some ejidatarios who thought that I could be of use to them in their troublesome relation with the agrarian bureaucracy. In this way I became enrolled in their 50-year-old fight to recover a piece of land that is in the hands of private landowners (see Chapters 5 and 6) and I became a member of the local committee that had to formulate internal ejido rules (see Chapter 8).

During the research I worked on three databases: a census of the village, genealogies of families of the village and genealogies of land plots of the ejido. The decision to work on these three databases was taken during the research. For this part of the research I worked with two young people from the village: a girl whose father is landless and a boy whose father is ejidatario of La Canoa. The census was a relatively easy endeavour. On the other hand, the genealogies of land plots and the genealogies of families were an enormous investment of time. Yet there were several reasons for making this investment. First of all, kinship relations seemed to be very important but at the same time extremely confusing to an outsider. Everybody seemed to be related to each other in different ways. I felt that genealogies could help me to disentangle these webs of kinship relations and to estimate the role that kinship relations played in social life and politics. Second, with respect to the ejido plots I wanted to find out more precisely what had happened with the land over the years. In the end, the more quantitative material, which was the result of the genealogies of land plots, was crucial for the contextualisation of some parts of the qualitative field material. An additional methodological advantage of working on genealogies is that it proved to be an excellent way to make people talk about things that happened in the past, and about people who had disappeared or were never mentioned but who appeared in the genealogy. During more than two years I worked on the genealogies of land plots and families. Although these genealogies were very labour intensive, they gave invaluable insights about movement of people, kinship relations and land histories.

The process of writing in general, and of anthropological writing in particular, goes together with many doubts, frustrations and decisions during the creation of the text. One of the most difficult decisions for me during the writing process was when to write in terms of generalisations and when to let in the richness and diversity of social life; when to talk in a summarising way, presenting only my own analysis and when to leave out my analysis and let the reader judge for herself from the material presented. When one decides to present more detailed ethnographic material the danger always exists that the reader loses sight of the theoretical or analytical points one wants to make. On the other hand, the ethnographic material presented should not be so thin as to become pure illustration either. I finally made the decision to present a lot of ethnographic material in the book in order to substantiate the points I want to make. Several of my own doubts, surprises and theoretical struggles during the research are also included, since this gives insights into the creation of the ethnography. As Smith argues, we should try to 'self consciously defamiliarise particular moments in the social world we are studying – a life history, a dispute, an element of panic, humour or despair – in order to bring into focus the work of interpretation, not just the actors' but also our own' (Smith 1996: 6).

2 FACTIONALISM AND FAMILY AFTER THE AGRARIAN REFORM

INTRODUCTION: *CACICAZGO* AND FACTIONALISM IN MEXICO

This chapter engages in the discussion on *cacicazgo* and factionalism, which are both widely used to explain political processes in rural areas in Mexico. To that end, the history of land reform in La Canoa is presented and an analysis of the ways in which relations in the village developed after land reform. Particular situations obviously varied greatly, but the phenomenon of the local bosses who arose after land reform and combined political and economic control is very common in rural Mexico (Tapia 1992). In the literature it is claimed that many rural *caciques* actually

find their origin in the process of agrarian reform, which they were the initiators of and which they obtained their power from through a complex network of compradazgo (ritual kinship), friendships, debts, favours and threats which made it possible for them to control the agrarian communities. (Bartra 1980a: 29, own translation)

Many authors have argued that in most ejidos the *cacique ejidal* controlled access to ejido land and that, through the renting out of ejido land and monopolisation of plots, an illegal land market developed which formed the basis of accumulation for the *cacique* (Gordillo 1988: 231). As factionalism and the role of powerful political families form such a rich tradition in the anthropology of rural Mexico (Friedrich 1986, Schryer 1980, Zárate 1993), it was an important theme during my research.

As a background to this discussion, first a short history is presented of the agrarian reform in Mexico in general and in the region of La Canoa in particular. As we will see, the success of the village La Canoa in establishing its own ejido is accompanied by conflicts, struggles and new forms of dominance, leading to a 'situated community of kin, neighbours, friends, and enemies' (Appadurai 1997: 179). After this historical overview, the chapter sketches an image of present-day life in La Canoa.

26

Attention is paid to migration to the United States and the impact this has on life in the village. The chapter especially focuses on the role of kinship and *cacicazgo* in the analysis of relationships in the village. Among other things, it is shown that, in La Canoa, by no means all local divisions can be reduced to family politics or fixed loyalties. Divisions in the village change frequently according to the problems involved and interests at stake. It is shown that hospitality and kinship relations are highly valued, but that these are only cultivated within a small circle of close relatives and friends. This means that instead of taking the role of these relations at face value, more attention should be paid to the political use of the kinship idiom.

AGRARIAN STRUGGLE AND LAND REFORM IN THE VALLEY OF AUTLÁN

The Mexican Revolution, which began in 1910, has been extensively documented and discussed. New versions and analyses of the years of revolution (1910–20) and its consequences still appear with great frequency (see Buve 1988, Knight 1986, 1994, Meyer 1991, Tutino 1986). This makes any general summary of these events a tricky endeavour. The same holds for the background and implications of the agrarian reform, which was implemented from 1915 to 1992. The common – although contested – view of the Mexican Revolution, is that it was a broad popular movement with strong agrarian demands. It is generally presented as a reaction to the authoritarian regime of Porfirio Díaz (1876–1910) during which the process of concentration of the land in the hands of a small group of large landowners had intensified. The Indian communities which had been granted communal property rights in colonial times by the Spanish Crown, saw their properties gradually diminished by the expansion of the *haciendas* and by agrarian laws issued in the second half of the nineteenth century.[1] In this way a process of land concentration that had already started centuries before, was carried to extremes. As many rural communities were robbed of their lands the majority of rural people were forced to work on the large landholdings under dreadful conditions. Economic crisis and severe food shortages between 1908 and 1910 intensified agrarian grievances of the masses of landless peasants. So, in 1910 the regime of Porfirio Díaz was finally overthrown with mass support from the rural population.[2]

The Agrarian Law of 1915 formed the legal basis of the agrarian reform programmes. In 1917 this law was turned into the famous Article 27 of the Mexican Constitution. The Constitution of 1917 defined the three principal forms of land tenure in Mexico: small private property (*pequeña propiedad*), ejidos and agrarian communities. Large landhold-ings could now legally be expropriated and the land granted to peasant groups. The peasant groups who received land were organised in ejidos. Violent seizures of haciendas also took place, which were later legalised by official agrarian procedures.

In the 1930s, the situation calmed down. During the presidency of Cárdenas (1934–40) the greatest amount of land was expropriated and the greatest number of ejidos established throughout Mexico. Today there are 28,000 ejidos, occupying more than half of Mexico's arable land and including over 3 million ejidatarios (INEGI 1990). However, agrarian reform has been full of irregularities and many large landholders have been able to avoid the expropriation of their lands.

Land Reform in the Valley of Autlán

The valley of Autlán, in Jalisco, western Mexico, covers 22,300 hectares. It lies at an altitude of 900 m above sea level and is surrounded by mountains. The valley has fertile soils and the several rivers that cross the valley have made the construction of small irrigation systems possible in certain parts. The town of Autlán has 34,073 inhabitants (INEGI 1991) and is 180 km from the state capital Guadalajara. At the other end of the valley lies the village of El Grullo.

The agrarian structure of the region of Autlán at the beginning of this century was dominated by a large number of small haciendas or land-

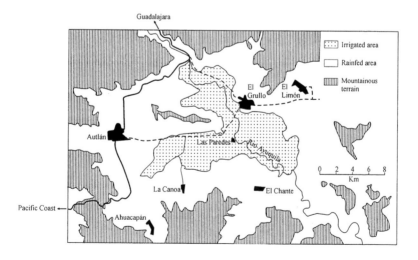

2.1   Irrigated areas and mountainous terrains in the valley of Autlán in 1993

holdings. There were 33 haciendas in the Autlán region with an average size of 2,500 hectares (Muriá 1982: 110). Although several haciendas were known to have irrigation systems, most arable land was rainfed and most landholdings depended on one, insecure rainy season a year (from May to November).

The hacienda La Canoa was small and poor. The village, which had 258 inhabitants in 1921 (Departamento de Estadística Nacional 1921), fell within the limits of the hacienda property. As La Canoa did not have enough work for the villagers during the whole year, people were allowed to work on other haciendas, as labourers or as sharecroppers. Only in the rainy season did they have sharecropping arrangements with the *hacendado* of La Canoa.

The man who initiated the agrarian struggle in the region of Autlán in the years of the revolution was Casimiro Castillo. He was a vegetable seller in the marketplace and organised secret meetings in Autlán. People from the surrounding hamlets also joined his group and came to the meetings. Among them were several men from La Canoa. In 1916 Casimiro Castillo started the official procedures to request land for the establishment of the ejido of Autlán, the way having been opened by the law of 1915 and later the Constitution of 1917. The ejido of Autlán was established in 1924. Several men from La Canoa received a plot of land in the ejido of Autlán.

One of the most important and remarkable men in La Canoa at that time was Filomeno Romero. He is the great grandfather of the majority of the people who live in the village today. Don Filomeno was a very rich man and well known in the region. He did not own lands in the village but he rented lands. Don Filomeno supported the men in La Canoa who worked with Casimiro Castillo. Among other things, he paid for their trips to the offices of the agrarian authorities in Mexico City. La Canoa residents requested the establishment of their own ejido in 1923. However, as a large number of people from La Canoa were included in the group of beneficiaries of the ejido of Autlán, the people of La Canoa were denied the possibility of establishing their own ejido.

The two most important men of La Canoa in the continuing struggle were don Filomeno's son, Miguel, and Juan García. In 1932, the residents of La Canoa again requested land to form their own ejido and the decision again went against them. Times changed with the presidency of Cárdenas, when throughout Mexico an unprecedented number of haciendas were expropriated and ejidos established. In 1937, after 14 years of administrative struggle, the SRA finally recognised that the village of La Canoa was separate from the town of Autlán and that the inhabitants needed land to make a living. It was decided to award an endowment grant to La Canoa and expropriate land from the hacienda La Canoa and three other large landholdings nearby. At last, the people of La Canoa could establish their own ejido. Villagers of La Canoa who had been ejidatarios of the ejido Autlán left that ejido and now became ejidatarios of La Canoa. The ejido Autlán yielded the land held by these ejidatarios to the newly established ejido.

As the land they received in the endowment grant was not nearly enough for all the people with recognised agrarian rights, the ejidatarios of La Canoa made a request for an expansion grant two weeks after the ejido was formally established in 1938. This request was acceded to and in 1942 the ejido received a small expansion grant. Most heads of family in La Canoa had received a plot of land by 1942.

The creation of the ejido of La Canoa was full of irregularities. By presidential resolution La Canoa was granted 1,843 hectares of which 20 per cent (396 hectares) was said to be suitable for agriculture. The remaining part was mountainous terrain. However, during the execution of this presidential resolution in 1938 when land was measured and formally handed over to the ejidatarios, the surveyor only came up with 1,770 hectares. This might seem strange, but this was a common phenomenon during the execution of resolutions, as the provisional projects for the establishment of ejidos often did not have very detailed maps or information. For this reason, during the execution, some land 'appeared' that was not on the maps, or vice versa – there was less land than officially registered. In the case of La Canoa the executing surveyor decided to take 230 hectares from other landholdings that were not officially affected in the presidential resolution. Afterwards, the SRA decided that the ejido could keep these 230 hectares and that the SRA would indemnify the owners of this land.

Nevertheless, according to the ejidatarios they never received this amount of land. First of all they did not receive all the 20 per cent of 1,843 hectares that was suitable for agricultural use. A large part of this land was sold or given away at the very start. Second, they only received 90 of the 230 hectares that were additionally given to them. Chapters 5 and 6 deal in detail with this land conflict and with the struggle of the ejidatarios of La Canoa to get the land they are officially entitled to. Throughout the book I will use the term the 'lost land' when I refer to this land conflict.

At this point I should introduce the man who was without doubt, the most influential person in the region for several decades, General Marcelino García Barragán. The General came from Autlán and derived regional power from successfully pacifying the region. In the 1940s he became the Governor of Jalisco. In 1947 he was removed as state

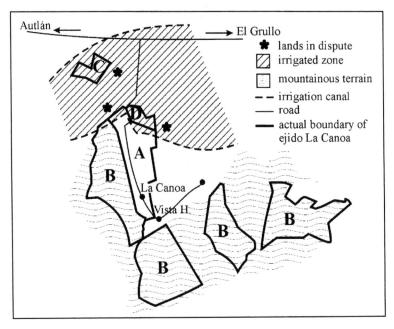

2.2   Lands in dispute of the ejido La Canoa

Key
A = Lands the ejido of Autlán received in their endowment grant of 1924 and
    which they ceded to people from La Canoa.
B = Lands the ejido of La Canoa received in their endowment grant of 1937.
C = Lands that were erroneously given to the ejido La Canoa by the surveyor of
    the SRA during the execution of the endowment grant in 1938.
D = Lands that the ejido La Canoa received in the extension grant of 1942.

governor and for a long period lost influence in national politics.
However, he made a political comeback and in 1964 became Minister of
Defence. The General has had considerable influence in the region of
Autlán even when he held positions in Guadalajara or Mexico City.
Torres describes how the General appointed the candidates for the
presidency of Autlán and how he visited the region every month to talk
to his followers about necessary regional projects and public services,
such as drinking water and roads (Torres 1997). The role of the General
in land reform was variable. He supported the establishment and
extension of ejidos in the region of Autlán when he was Governor of
Jalisco in the 1940s. However, he was not really interested in agrarian
issues and his position on specific land conflicts depended on the people
involved. Although he agreed with the expropriation of landholdings for
the establishment of ejidos, he also helped friends who were private
landholders in their efforts to keep certain lands. One of the most famous

cases in which he was involved concerns the ejido of Autlán where he opposed the expropriation of lands that were necessary for the extension of the ejido of Autlán.

Although opinions about the General differ, the common image that is conveyed is that of an impressive man who was more held in awe than loved. There were always rumours going around about the General and his people. The lack of transparency about what was going on only strengthened feelings of caution. Although many people talk in negative ways about the General and his politics, some also glorify him as a symbol of Mexican revolutionary *machismo*. He had allies in the ejidos and villages whom he supported in different ways. However, the General was more willing to support followers personally than to comply with the collective demands of their agrarian communities. 'For example, when someone approached him with an ejido problem, he would inquire instead about their personal needs' (Torres 1997: 116). Although nobody will deny the General's influence in the region, views and opinions about his operations and specific interventions differ. In Chapter 5 I will discuss speculations as to the role of the General in the conflict over the 'lost land' of La Canoa.

Today there are 37 ejidos in the municipalities of Autlán and El Grullo and 3,906 ejidatarios in the region as opposed to 441 private landowners. Of the total amount of arable land, 75 per cent is in the hands of ejidatarios and 25 per cent in the hands of private landowners (SARH 1985). Since the beginning of the 1960s there has been a government irrigation system in the region. In La Canoa half of the arable ejido land falls within the irrigated zone. A sugarcane refinery was brought to the region in the 1960s and sugarcane is now the dominant crop on the irrigated lands.

LAND, POWER AND PARTY POLITCS

Although people received their own plot of land, life after the establishment of the ejido remained hard. As a result of the difficult situation caused by the scarcity of land and the insecurity of the harvest (dependent on the rains between May and November), many people migrated to other regions in Mexico or to the United States. Some ejidatarios left the village and were never heard of again, in particular after three consecutive dry years from 1938 till 1941.

The richer men, who had initiated the establishment of the ejido, began to take control of several village and ejido matters. Their dominant position was based, first, on control of the maize market. They provided expensive credits for the sowing of the ejido plots and, after the harvest, bought the maize at a low price. Cattle were another important factor in socio-economic differentiation. Only the richer families could afford cattle; they let the cattle graze on the abundant commons and on the plots after the maize harvest. Furthermore, drinking water was also a problem in the village and private wells distinguished the rich families from the poor. Some of these wealthier men in La Canoa became money-lenders who confiscated houses and plots when people could not repay their loans. Don Miguel (the son of Filomeno) and some others had built up relations with the state bureaucracy through their efforts to found the ejido. They also maintained relations with influential PRI men in Autlán.

There are many things the men who helped establish the ejido are criticised for in the village. Several villagers loathe them and use a discourse of *cacicazgo* and exploitation when they discuss the practices of these men. Although it would be too strong to talk about factions in the village, I broadly distinguished two political networks: the 'establishment' and the 'opposition'. The 'opposition' consists of the men who express very negative views about the old bosses and who have been very active over the years to recover the 'lost land'. They have been members of different political opposition parties. Others in the ejido call them the 'opposers', 'troublemakers' or 'leftists'. The 'establishment' is a broad network of people who feel close to the old bosses and who maintain relations with PRI circles in Autlán.

People from the 'opposition' in La Canoa would agree with the analysis that local *caciques* monopolised the land and made sure that all their sons acquired a plot of ejido land. However, my own study of land distribution since the start of the ejido shows a different picture.[3] After the extension of the ejido in 1942, almost all 71 households in the village had access to at least one plot of land. In the first years after the establishment of the ejido, the official rule which prohibited the renting out or abandoning of ejido plots was used to take land away from ejidatarios who left the ejido for a long time. These dispossessions and the redistribution of these plots were indeed influenced by local power relations. Especially don Miguel influenced the redistribution of several plots. At that time the value of the land was low, and people had no resources to fight a powerful ejido commissioner. Several migrants were dispossessed without a struggle. However, with land becoming more valuable because of the irrigation in the 1960s, and with ejidatarios acquiring more resources and experience, the practices changed. Land became a scarce resource in a region with hardly any other sources of income and ejido land gradually turned into a valuable commodity. Nobody let the land be taken away from him or her anymore without a fight. This meant that, in order to dispossess an ejidatario of his or her land, a long and dirty struggle had to be undertaken in which the SRA would become involved and the outcome was never assured. This was not a pleasant prospect even for local powerholders. Land became more scarce and ejido land possession became more and more a form of private property and land was no longer taken away from ejidatarios who had migrated.

Table 2.1   Distribution of land in the ejido La Canoa in 1942 and 1993

	1942	1993
Ejidatarios with land	77	94[4]
Total number of ha	422	438
Number of plots	118	136
Average number of plots per ejidatario	1.5	1.4
Average size of plot in ha	3.6	3.2
Average number of ha per ejidatario	5.5	4.7

Although the figures are not dramatic, Table 2.1 shows that succeeding generations work ever-smaller plots of land. An important subdivision of plots has taken place due to the transfer of plots to more than one child and to the sale of fractions of plots. Many ejidatarios have more than one plot of land. Some ejidatarios possess up to five different plots. The seven ejidatarios who possess the largest area of irrigated land in the ejidos possess 6–8 hectares.

Over time there was no land available for the majority of sons of ejidatarios and they could only hope to inherit their father's land. Also, several sons of these local bosses never received land. In this way a category of landless households was created that would grow steadily with the years. In La Canoa ejido land tenure is the most common form of land tenure. Only a few families bought land as private property, but they are all ejidatarios.[5] Today, many landless people are sons of ejidatarios for whom there was no land available anymore. However, with the exception of some of the bigger entrepreneurs with irrigated land, most households with an ejido plot cannot possibly live off the land and have several other sources of income. Property is mostly inherited by one of the sons. People who possess several plots of land, often divide their property between several sons by passing plots over to them during their life.

EJIDATARIOS AND THEIR LANDLESS NEIGHBOURS

According to the government census of 1990, La Canoa has 837 inhabitants (INEGI 1991). According to official statistics the village grew from 258 inhabitants in 1921 to 837 in 1990 (Departamento de Estadística Nacional 1926, INEGI 1991). My own research suggests that the figure of 1990 is an overestimate. This means that many sons and daughters who live in the United States or elsewhere in Mexico were still counted in the census. In 1993 my figures were as follows. When I only counted the people present in the village at that time there were 690 inhabitants. When I included the unmarried migrant children I arrived at approximately 803 inhabitants. If we define the household as the co-residential domestic unit, today 138 of the 196 households in the village do not have access to an ejido plot.[6]

The commons have been an important resource for the growing group of landless families in the village. Most of the lands that the ejido La Canoa received were common land, namely approximately 1,800 hectares, as against only 400 hectares of arable lands. Unlike the arable lands, the agrarian law did not allow the division of the commons into individual plots. All members of the ejido had the right to an individual plot of arable land and to the use of the commons. Although officially the commons belonged to the ejidatarios, nobody complained if other families collected fruits and vegetables or hunted on these extensive terrains. Many landless families were even allowed by the ejidatarios to take a part of the commons for a *coamil*: an extensive form of maize cultivation. For the landless families the *coamil* can make a difference to the household economy. It makes it possible for them to produce their own maize and have some animals that they feed with the waste of the crop. Many of the landless families cherish their *coamil*. This also has to be seen in the light of the fact that many landless men are sons of ejidatarios, who did not inherit the plot of their father. Hence, the *coamil* is their only remaining link with the land. Although the commons the ejido La Canoa received in 1938 were abundant, over the years almost all the common lands have been brought into use.

As the regional economy depends so much on agriculture, changes in agriculture are directly felt in household economies. When agriculture is in crisis, the whole region is in crisis and when agriculture is booming, the regional economy is booming. During periods of crises there is a tendency for people to leave the region and during boom periods, people from other regions come to look for work. Hence migration, especially to the United States, is an important source of income in the village. Migration to the United States is not a new phenomenon. The state of Jalisco is characterised by a long-standing and extensive migration to the USA. Many men from La Canoa went to work in agriculture in the USA in the 1940s and 1950s. This was augmented by the *bracero* programmes (1940–63), introduced by the United States in order to get

Mexican labourers for the harvest in American agriculture. In this way peasant farming in Mexico was combined with wage labour in the USA. However, since the 1970s a new form of migration has developed in which not only the men go to the USA but complete families leave the village (see Massey et al. 1987).

An indication of the extent of the migration to the USA is the fact that, of all people born and registered in La Canoa between 1946 and 1986, and who were still alive in 1993, 23 per cent lived in the village and 31 per cent in the United States.[7] Many ejidatarios have also left the village. Today many ejidatarios even have their permanent residence outside the village. My research showed that of the 97 officially recognised ejidatarios of La Canoa, in 1993, 37 lived outside the village. Ejidatarios with small plots of rainfed land, as well as ejidatarios with large irrigated plots have left the village. The ejidatarios who have moved to Autlán, remain actively involved in the ejido and work the land themselves. Ejidatarios who have moved farther away, are less actively involved in local ejido matters. Some regularly return to till the land, others rent the land out or leave it to a son or other relatives. Most of the ejidatarios who live outside the village, still show great interest in their land and would not think of selling it.

Strong support networks exist between the households in La Canoa and the households of relatives in the United States. Despite the money coming in from the USA in the village the 'peasant' or 'ejidatario way of life' remains important for a large part of the population. Several authors have argued that remittances from migration is precisely what permits the continuation of (unremunerative) ejidal farming and the maintenance of a 'peasant culture and mentality' (Gledhill 1991, Kearney 1996: 16).

LAND AND LOCAL POLITICS

What struck me from the beginning in La Canoa was that, among the local people (ejidatarios as well as landless people), land was considered to be a central asset in life. Other authors have also described this strong value attached to the possession of land in rural Mexico. Luís González, writes that many consider this obsession with possessing land that produces very little and is the source of thousand quarrels and pains a foolishness. However, 'in the rural environment almost the only way to stand out, to be taken seriously, to become a respectable and respected person is to be the owner of arable and pastoral lands' (González 1988: 56, own translation).

At first, this glorification of land seemed understandable in a region that is characterised by agriculture and animal husbandry. However, among the ejidatarios there are also many people who possess only a very small plot of rainfed land and who cannot possibly live off the land. Many landless families these days are richer than their ejidatario neighbours are. This can primarily be explained by migration to the United States, which has reduced the importance of the land as the main factor in socio-economic differentiation.

In order to understand the value attached to the land, we have to look at the many different meanings that are attached to the possession of an ejido plot. Obviously, land is not only valued as a source of income. When I talked to Aurora García, an ejidataria in La Canoa, about the many conflicts over land in the village she commented:

All this fighting over land, while it does not produce very much. But for the people it is important to have land even it does not produce very much. It is the idea of having something; the security that the land provides.

Besides security, the land is also important for the production of maize for home consumption. The production of one's own maize has a strong cultural significance and is also important for people who have enough income to buy the maize. People try to be at least partly self-supporting in their annual maize consumption.

A clear social distinction exists between ejidatarios and landless families in the village. In the village, the ejidatarios are the independent and proud people. The richer ejidatarios are very aware of their position and feel superior to landless labourers. They refer to their fathers who fought for the land. Another topic, around which the distinction between ejidatarios and landless villagers is strongly felt these days, is the commons. The commons have become scarce and have started to become a source of serious tension in the village. Many ejidatarios have started asking questions about non-ejidatarios possessing *coamiles*. The landless people in their turn, recognise that the ejido only lent them the land, and that the ejido remains the real owner but at the same time they are very angry with, what they call, the selfish and egoistic attitude of the ejidatarios, who are better off and yet are claiming lands that landless families have been working peacefully for many years. Among the landless families themselves, divisions are also created: landless sons of ejidatarios claim that they have more rights to the commons than landless people in the village who are not even related to the ejidatarios.

The ejido is also a dominant factor for other reasons: the ejido provides the necessary land and money for village projects. Many of these projects need a plot of land for the construction of buildings and ask for the financial participation of the village. As the ejido owns all the land, it is the ejido that has to decide on the gift of a plot of land. By renting out the pasture of the commons, the ejido also has the possibility of generating money for some of the projects. The ejidatarios are very conscious of the fact that the ejido provides many services to the landless families. Even the football field and the bullring are situated on ejido land. Whenever problems arise in the village, the ejidatarios are eager to stress that landless families only have access to school (built with ejido money and on ejido land) and to many other privileges because of the benevolence of the ejidatarios.

Apart from the elements mentioned above which give the possession of an ejido plot all kinds of values besides economic ones, being an ejidatario also means that one can participate in government programmes for the ejido sector: credit programmes, subsidy programmes and so on. Landless families are excluded from most of these programmes. So, the membership of the ejido gives access to many different resources. Some ejidatarios are also capable of appropriating resources that are meant for the whole village, including the landless families. As a woman of a landless family said after expressing herself very negatively about ejidatarios: 'The government only helps the people who already have things; government support is directly taken by other people, the poor do not get anything. The government only helps the farmers.' This comment illustrates the view of landless people that the ejidatarios are not only better off, but also monopolise other resources and support that may come from outside. The point is that, several ejidatarios did indeed control projects that were meant for the entire village. The offices of the municipality in Autlán administer government projects and political networks are crucial for gaining access to these municipal resources. Different ejido commissioners with good political connections in Autlán managed to bring government projects to the village, such as electricity, a housing project for poor families, a piped water system, a nursery and a small clinic.

Yet, the prevalence of socio-political relationships and bureaucratic opacity mean that gossip, scandal and criticism surround all these projects. The people who organised these projects are criticised for giving houses to friends instead of poor families, for not listening to the needs and wishes of the villagers but deciding on their own what the village needs, and keeping part of the money to line their own pockets. A well-known characteristic of Mexican government projects in the rural areas is that participation by the village itself is demanded in the form of labour or money. This only gives rise to more negotiations between officials and local organisers. This leads to a situation in La Canoa where many villagers stress that local leaders always enriched themselves from these projects, while the leaders and their children feel frustrated that the villagers have never appreciated their efforts for the development of the village.

Hence the importance of the ejido as an organiser of local projects also derived from the fact that some ejidatarios had the necessary political contacts to get things arranged. In the beginning, these contacts were based on their experiences with agrarian reform and, over time, they developed on the basis of personal political networks with influential people in Autlán.

Although the number of landless families grew over the years, ejidatarios still dominate local village politics today. The landless villagers naturally benefit from projects for the village, but, at the same time, these projects stress their dependence on the ejido and some of its influential members. All these processes explain the frustration of the landless families and the ideology which surrounds ejido land at a time when land is not the most important means of production for most households anymore.

In administrative terms, a separation exists between village and ejido. The ejido is an agrarian institution, which falls under the responsibility of the Ministry of Agrarian Reform, while the village is an administrative unit, falling under the municipality of Autlán. While in the beginning there was no real difference between ejido and village as almost all households received land; this situation obviously changed over time. The official administrative term for the village La Canoa is *delegación*. The administrative head of the *delegación* is the *delegado*. He is responsible for village affairs and has two local assistants, who operate as armed police officers at public events and other occasions that require their intervention. Unlike the ejido commissioner, who does not receive a salary, the *delegado* receives a small salary for this work.

The most important activities of the *delegado* are the organisation of local projects and the coordination of government programmes for the village. Another important responsibility according to the villagers (although not an official one), is the organisation of the village parties in November and December. The villagers do not see the position of *delegado* as one of much influence but more one that gives opportunities to line one's own pocket through the administration of government projects. The management of resources and organisation of these projects always gives room for negotiation and some enrichment. Until recently, the influential ejidatarios always decided who would be the *delegado* in the village through their political networks in Autlán. Until 1983 they always appointed an ejidatario, while the majority of villagers had become landless. After 1983, the influence of other villagers grew and landless people have been appointed.

So, the 'ideology' around ejido land in the village can best be analysed in relation to the development of a force field in which the ejido dominates landless villagers. This also explains the bitterness and frustration in the way landless people talk about their poverty and explain this in terms of a lack of land. Landless people often reacted with amazement or irritation when I asked if there were any differences between ejidatarios and other villagers. It was as if I was asking something very obvious and was blind to what was going on. The landless families not only feel frustrated about not having land, but also because of their second-rate position in the village. The ejido not only means access to land, but also control of political projects. The ejido is more that a land tenure institution or a means of agricultural production (see also Goldring 1996, Stephen 1994). Other authors have also written about the phenomenon of the ejido dominating the village in local government. Jones points out that in many municipalities it is the ejido that has traditionally functioned as the local government, and that the non-ejidatarios are excluded from the decision-making process even when they are in the majority (Jones 1996: 195).

Much has also been written on the distribution of government resources and 'the selective distribution of material benefits (agrarian reform, agricultural credit, titles for squatter settlements, low-cost medical care) which have been delivered as particular favours through clientelistic channels' (Foweraker 1994: 3). Carlos points out that peasant hierarchies 'are the principal conduit through which the Mexican state transfers economic and political goods to the peasantry' (Carlos 1992: 93). Yet, although relationships are crucial for all forms of organisation, the question remains to what degree and in what ways organisations are shaped by them. The fact that resources are distributed through personalised channels does not necessarily lead to strong forms of top-down control. As discussed in Chapter 1, it has often been suggested that the Mexican state kept control over the villages through the PRI apparatus with ramifications in the village, but on the basis of my research material I would not agree with this conclusion. In fact, the influence of state institutions on local practices has been very limited. The PRI party networks certainly played a role in local-level affairs, but not in the form of control from above. It was much more an instrumental network to get access to government resources. This also explains the instrumental outlook ejidatarios tend to have on party politics. The common image that corporate party structures and patron–client relations have led to a strong form of top-down control does not seem to

apply. I would rather say that it might equally well lead to the fragmentation of local and regional power as the resources are distributed through
different institutions and persons. Nobody controls more than a fraction
of the resources and the outcome is often unpredictable (de la Peña 1986).

A GLIMPSE OF PRESENT-DAY LIFE IN LA CANOA

La Canoa is very much a rural village. From any house, one can walk
directly to the fields, the *cerro* (hills) and the river. There are a large
number of cattle and in the street one often comes across herds of cows,
which are on their way to the field or on their way back to the stable.
Many men ride horses but this is considered to be more a sign of wealth
and leisure than of work. Today, machines do most ploughing on the
arable land. The houses used to have large *corrales*. In these *corrales*
people have their fruit trees, plants, chickens, goats, a pig and so on.
People do not grow their own vegetables, but buy vegetables in the shops
in the village. Some fruits and vegetables are freely collected in the
commons of the ejido. There are several small shops and one telephone
in the village, a public telephone in the shop of Lupe Medina. The village
has a large school complex for kindergarten, primary school and
secondary school (by television), a small clinic and a football field.

The gendered division between private and public spheres in Latin
America and the relation with the patriarchal ideology is well known
(see Gledhill 1994: 198–206, Rouse 1989). In this view, men are
thought to be oriented primarily to honour and the public domain of
bargaining and negotiation, while women are associated with unity and
the domestic realm of nurturance. As a general image this applies well to
the situation in La Canoa. While the house in general is very much a
woman's place, the street is a man's place. When women go out, it is
only to do the shopping and then they have to be back. On the other
hand, men often stay the whole day outside the house. They work, come
home to eat, and then leave again to talk or drink with other men.

Village life is very rich in all kinds of social gatherings. Religion plays
an important role in the life of the people and almost everybody belongs
to the Catholic Church. It is important to pay some attention here to
compadrazgo (ritual coparenthood) as a central institution for the creation
of social ties. During the rituals of the Catholic Church a man and a
woman may be invited to become *padrino* and *madrina* of a child and
accompany the child in the church ceremony. In the life of every person
there are many occasions when these relations are established. Children
address their godparents with much respect. The godparents not only
assume certain responsibilities towards their godchild, but also establish

a special relationship with the parents of the godchild. The godfather (or godmother) of a child, becomes *compadre* (or *comadre*) of the parents of this child. *Comadres* and *compadres* have a special bond and help and support each other whenever necessary. *Compadrazgo* relations are highly valued.

The many Catholic celebrations during which relations of *compadrazgo* are established are the occasion for big parties. However, any event may serve as an occasion for a big party if the family has money to spend. The most important festivities are those of each village's saint's day. Around this day, a whole week of festivities is organised which is intended to attract people from the neighbouring villages and the *hijos ausentes* (the absent children) from the United States. In the beginning of November, La Canoa celebrates its saint, the Virgin of Guadalupe. Although the official date of the Virgin of Guadalupe is 12 December, according to the villagers they have always celebrated this day in November as otherwise their festivities would coincide with the national celebration of the Virgin and then nobody would visit their village. During the twelve days of festivities in honour of the Virgin a fair is brought to the village, dances are organised for the evenings, and bull riding takes place during the day. The festivities end with a display of fireworks on 12 of November.

Another important event takes place at the end of each year. In the last days of the year and the first days of the New Year bull riding and *rodeos* take place in the village. This is a common form of diversion in rural villages in which young men try to stay as long as possible on the back of a bull. The villagers cooperate in the costs of organising these festivities. The organisers of the bull riding sell tickets to people who want to watch the spectacle and sell beer and food. The idea is that if money remains after the payment of all costs, it is used for village projects. For that reason the organising committee is called the *Junta de mejoras* (committee of improvements), but as one woman remarked: 'The only point is that they do not do the *mejoras* anymore. The money stays with the organisers.'

There is always a lot of gossiping and talking going on in the village around these events. It is often said that the organisers keep the profits in their own pockets, or that they drink all the beer that is left over. So every year it is said that this time there will be no bull riding as the people refuse to cooperate any longer. But in the end, it is always organised.

FACTIONS AND THE KINSHIP IDIOM

Although it is common in studies on rural Mexico to read about village factions, and the importance of kinship and *compadrazgo* relations in local politics, I found that reality is more complex than these views would have us believe. Although the villagers themselves also like to talk in terms of clear-cut divisions in the village, we have to be very careful in our interpretation of these statements.

The division between the 'PRI-establishment' and the 'opposition', which I mentioned above, was the clearest form of division in the ejido during the research. However, the dividing lines were not clear-cut and most ejidatarios did not belong to either of these two 'camps'. The 'establishment' which was a network formed around the Romeros, had most characteristics of a 'political family' in the sense of persons who share the same name and which develop into a group with political purposes (Friedrich 1986: 106–7). However, although they had some characteristics of a 'political family' this group had nothing like the power of the mighty political rural families described by other authors.

This was not a 'political family' that had monopolised land or other resources, nor had they tried to make political careers through the ejido and PRI networks. The 'opposition group' was less based on kinship ties and more on political sympathies. Their main political project was to counter the influence of the 'establishment' and at times it seemed that they were principally fighting the influence that this 'political family' had had in the past. Memories of past injustices played an important role in the motivations of this group. In reality, the 'opposition group' was more a loose network of allies in which different people participated over the years. Their activities were focused in particular on the struggle for the 'lost land'.

It also proved impossible to define interest groups according to central problems and conflicts in the ejido and mobilisation around certain leaders. Interest groups could be distinguished around problems during specific periods, but next time different interests were at stake. There were enduring problems in the ejido, as we shall see, but it was impossible to distinguish more or less stable interest groups of ejidatarios or villagers on the basis of these problems. Positions were never fixed, and nor were the groups around certain problems. As Tapia points out:

In the social web of power, political relations do not develop in a single direction nor are they produced within socially homogeneous groups. They generate alliances and oppositions; they become more diverse or homogenous, and are repeatedly reorganised according to strategies dependent on interests at stake, the actors present, the resources available and the social forces that as a whole determine the local political context. (Tapia 1992: 385, own translation)

Furthermore, all divisions in the village and ejido are cross-cut by other quarrels and relationships. This is very well expressed by Barth in his study of an Indonesian village:

Certain factional cores of persons can be identified who, for the moment, share positions and interests; but most persons have their particular networks of friendship, kinship, sympathies, conflicts and enmities, which for each one of them covers less than the village as a whole. Therefore, linkages do not add up to larger factional groups, and few longer sequences of events can be identified as resulting from the systematic strategies of such groups. (Barth 1993: 119)

Hence, several times, when I thought that I had more or less captured the central divisions in the ejido, new problems came up and new configurations of people became visible which did not fit into my model. Ejidatarios could work together for some time and then split up and continue the work with others. Alternatively, they could start working with someone with whom they had been in a conflict shortly before.

Although I often felt disturbed by these changing coalitions and networks, the people in the village always found logical explanation for these shifts in loyalty. Without exception these explanations took the form of kinship relations. They could say, for example: 'It is logical that he has changed his position as he is a nephew of the ejido commissioner and therefore wants to support him.' Or they could say: 'His loyalty to Pedro can be explained by the fact that his wife is a sister of Pedro.' After some time I also realised that when villagers talked about *the* Romeros or *the* Garcías they only referred to one or two of these men and not to entire families with this surname. For example, when villagers talked in a disapproving way about the Garcías, they always referred to Ricardo García and not to his brothers Tomás and Juan, who never played a prominent role in local affairs.

The fact that villagers in La Canoa tend to use kinship relations to explain divisions in the ejido is similar to what Bailey experienced in the Indian village Bishara. He noticed that there were two factions in the village and when he first enquired about this, it seemed as if the two groups were recruited through kinship.

The two leaders represented different lines of descent and were each, so it seemed, supported by close kinsmen and opposed to more distant kinsmen. Closer investigation showed that this was not quite the case, and there were several examples of people changing sides and of close kin (an uncle and his nephews) being in opposed factions. (Bailey 1969: 47)

Friedrich describes the same experience in the village Naranja, in Michoacán, where people tend to speak of village factions in terms of political families. However, he found out that in reality factions were not so strictly based on family lines as 'each faction included at least one person from every political family' (Friedrich 1986: 107). This is similar to the situation in La Canoa. While there was always considerable activity in the village and ejido it was difficult to talk about long-lasting coalitions, factions, or family networks based on political projects, common interests or shared histories.

This is not to deny the importance of kinship relations. Kinship relations and 'the family' are indeed highly valued in the village and many support networks exist among relatives, *compadres, padrinos* (godfathers) and *ahijados* (godchildren). However, as Sabean points out, 'in a certain sense, where everyone is kin, no one is kin; that is to say, all the connections between kin could hardly carry the same meaning, moral exigency, or attitude' (Sabean 1998: 3). Although it is clear that kinship relations are very close, after some time one realises that not all kinship ties are valued. In Barth's words 'becoming more familiar with the community, the anthropologist discovers that there are also close kin who do not visit each other, and that people are aware of strands in the relations of close kin that are not so positively valued' (Barth 1993: 127). For example, after some time I noticed that in some families that I regularly visited they maintained close relationships with several brothers, sisters, uncles and other relatives but there were also relatives who never visited the house and who were never commented upon.

In the same way as with kinship relations, one discovers after some time that bonds with some *compadres* are stressed and developed but others are not. The 'banned' relatives and *compadres* tend to become 'invisible' and 'inaudible'. They do not visit the family any longer, do not attend birthday parties and are not talked about. There is not even much gossiping about these people, they are ignored. The selection of only a small number of kinspeople for close relations, means that there is no such thing as an exclusive kinship domain. We should be sensitive to the 'political' use of the kinship idiom and the ways in which it can bring people together but also separate them (see also Bailey 1969, Barth 1993, Bloch 1971).

There have been a large number of serious conflicts within and between families in the village. For example, there were several murders that influenced relations in the village for decades. Many resentments exist about inheritance problems within families, and there have been several conflicts over land. As kinship and ritual kinship are so highly valued, people try to avoid commenting upon conflicts with their next of kin or *compadres*. Yet, long-standing relations of real and fictive kinship connect the majority of people in the village to each other, and they share histories of tensions, conflicts, cooperation and joyful events.

All these intrigues also explain the highly exclusive 'visiting' and 'socialising' circles in the village. For all families in the village, visiting other houses is restricted to a small circle of very close relatives and friends. Only within these circles do we find the ideology of the 'hospitable open house' where everybody can enter and will be well received. Most villagers will never enter a house if they do not have close relations with those living there. This means that 'the house' as a locus of socialising is not only a form of inclusion but also of exclusion. Within these visiting circles people are very hospitable, eat together and help each other in many different ways. Contacts with people who do not form part of this small intimate circle may take place in the street, in the church group or in the bars. These contacts may concern exchange of information, working arrangements, the latest gossips, etc. Here also circles can be distinguished of people who often talk to each other and people who will never exchange a word. Hence, besides being a central organising principle, kinship relations and bonds of *compadrazgo* are also part of a discourse which is used to stress and honour certain relationships, while making others invisible.

CONCLUSION: A GLOBALISED SITUATED COMMUNITY

The establishment of the ejido La Canoa cannot be analysed in terms of the struggle of a corporate community that successfully fought against the *hacendados*. Smith rightly argues that 'when peasants ... rebel, we are often tempted to slip back into stereotypical and decontextualised notions of the peasant community as one of tradition and homogenous solidarity' (Smith 1991: 182). La Canoa was a diversified village before land reform and new forms of dominance developed after the founding of the ejido. The founders of the ejido La Canoa developed into authoritarian local bosses and a lot of hard feelings exist in the ejido about these men. Some people tend to use a discourse of *cacicazgo* when they talk about them. However, even though some ejidatarios like to recall the terrible practices of these *caciques*, the degree to which these powerful men used the ejido for enrichment and political control was limited. No concentration of land in the hands of local leaders has occurred.

Yet the fact that the ejido did play a role in local politics and distribution of resources explains the importance of the possession of an ejido plot and of membership of the ejido. As F. and K. von Benda-Beckmann (1999) point out, property has functions other than the merely economic. In La Canoa, many elements constitute the value of ejido land: the fact that the land is related to the agrarian struggle and establishment of the *comunidad*; that it gives one the identity of being an independent peasant;

that it is the provider of maize, the central ingredient of the rural diet, and that the ejido has been central for local politics.

In the same way as the discourse of *cacicazgo*, we should be careful with the use of the kinship idiom for the explanation of political practices. Family and *compadrazgo* relations are ideological constructions that should be analysed as such. These normative bonds are highly valued and developed with some relatives, but ignored with others. Hence, we should be sensitive to the 'political' use of the kinship and fictive kinship idiom. In La Canoa, village dynamics and ejido affairs are intricately related, with varying degrees of tension. Different categories of villagers (ejidatarios, non-ejidatarios, sons of ejidatarios and outsiders) are defined, who claim differing rights, especially around conflicts.

The village can best be defined as a situated community (Appadurai 1997) in which people are connected to each other by different types of experiences and in which differing forms of dominance and various mechanisms of inclusion and exclusion exist. I argued before that situated community refers to feelings of belonging to certain groups or networks, but always is related to processes of domination (Sabean 1984) which implies that distinctions are made between different social categories, and between insiders and outsiders. Gupta and Ferguson also argue that community 'is premised on various forms of exclusion and constructions of otherness' and that 'it is precisely through processes of exclusion and othering that both collective and individual subjects are formed' (Gupta and Ferguson 1997a: 13).

3   POLITICS AND LOCAL ORGANISATION

INTRODUCTION: ORGANISATION AND ORGANISING PRACTICES

This chapter is concerned with the organisational characteristics of the ejido. The organisation of the ejido at the local level is laid down in detail in the Agrarian Law. Since the change of law in 1992, ejidos have more freedom in their local regulation. Yet, the ejido is a formal organisation with officially recognised members, resources and responsibilities. The ejido has an executive committee for daily management and a general assembly of all ejidatarios, which is the highest authority at the local level and takes decisions by majority of votes during the monthly ejido meetings. The executive committee also represents the ejido in relation to outside agencies and government programmes for the ejido sector. Like most other ejidos, La Canoa has a special ejido house (*casa ejidal*) where the meetings are held and ejido materials are stored.

Many ejidos in Mexico do not really function according to the above-mentioned model. To give you a better idea of the situation in La Canoa; ejido meetings are seldom held, few ejidatarios attend the meetings and few matters are discussed on these occasions. On the other hand, although ejido meetings are seldom held and decisions are seldom taken on these occasions, things are always going on in the ejido and suddenly seem to have been decided somewhere by some people. In a similar fashion, information concerning the ejido always seems to circulate in small undefined circles. Thus, there is a lot of organising taking place in – what appear to be – informal and changing settings. In this chapter I analyse the organising practices in the ejido and pay much attention to the ways in which the local people themselves reflect upon the logics behind the organisational dynamics.

Although it is quite common that organisations do not operate according to formal models, anthropology offers few conceptual tools for the analysis of these situations. There is a strong tendency in the literature to label organisations that do not operate according to the principles of so-called 'accountable' management, as corrupt. However, the label 'corruption' still does not explain what is going on. Furthermore, there is a general belief that if the rules are not followed it must be because some powerful agents are behind it and determine what will happen. However, even 'powerful people' with 'influential connections' and 'wealth' are based in a force field which operates according to certain 'rules of the game', 'implicit agreements' or 'customs'. This puts certain limits and conditions on their actions.

For example, the study of La Canoa shows that while the ejido commissioner has developed a high degree of autonomy in his decisions, at the same time he has little power and authority. The autonomy of a leader does not necessarily mean that he is 'in control'. This is caused by the fact that his autonomy only refers to a limited field of action that leaves little room for abrupt changes of established routines. It will also be shown that, although the ejido commissioner may not be asked publicly to render accounts of his actions, other effective forms of accountability exist outside the formal channels. There are several ways in which ejidatarios control their leaders. This dynamic has led to a situation in which official procedures do not fulfil their official roles. On the other hand, the formal structure and official administrative rules can become important again in serious ejido conflicts. Then the 'official game' is played in combination with informal ways of exercising pressure.

Hence, instead of using bi-polar models of the 'democratic, transparent, accountable organisation' against the 'clientelistic, corrupt organisation', more attention should be paid to a wide variety of organising practices. In fact, nowhere do organisations operate according to these two stereotypes. Instead of labelling organisations in simple ways, we should study specific organising practices and find out the implications with respect to governance, control and accountability.

EJIDO ADMINISTRATION AND THE ROLE OF THE COMMISSIONER

Every three years the general assembly of the ejido, which includes all ejidatarios, elects the executive committee. The president of this committee is the *comisario ejidal* (ejido commissioner). The executive committee is responsible for the daily administration of ejido affairs but the highest authority at the local level is the general assembly. The ejido administration concerns a broad range of activities. Besides the administration of different types of land (the individual plots, the commons and the urban zone), the ejido acquired additional administrative tasks when government programmess started to use the ejido as an intermediate organisation to channel resources, such as agricultural inputs and credits. The income of the ejido consists above all of the money earned from the renting of pasture in the commons. The ejido expenses can include travelling costs of members of the executive committee, maintenance of the ejido building, payment for meals and other expenses to officials, and fencing of parts of the commons. The executive committee of the ejido (president, secretary and treasurer) is called *comisariado ejidal.* The members of the executive committee do not receive a salary for their work.

In La Canoa, as in many other ejidos, the ejido commissioner is the central figure in the ejido administration and sometimes almost eliminates the role of the general assembly. In addition, the ejido archive is very incomplete and there is no registration of land possession of the individualised land, the urbanised area, nor the commons. There is no information on the organisation of ejido projects under the different ejido commissioners, or minutes of ejido meetings. The whole organisation seems to congeal around the person of the commissioner. The commissioner takes many decisions which should be taken by the general assembly on his own. He often validates documents with his signature and the stamp without consulting the general assembly. He decides on his own to lend parts of the commons to ejidatarios or landless villagers. He decides to whom he sells the ejido pasture and how the ejido will spend the money. It is common that in the case of conflicts between ejidatarios, the commissioner reaches an agreement with one of the parties and interferes on behalf of this party.

Explanations for the fact that the role of the commissioner extends far beyond his formal competence can partly been found in agrarian history. In the previous chapter we saw that the men who made the most efforts to establish the ejido La Canoa had developed good political contacts in the bureaucracy, whereas the other ejidatarios lacked contacts, information and resources. In the first decades of the ejido, these 'founders' had great influence in the village and the ejido. Elections in the ejido at that time were a public event and people just had to queue up for the man they were voting for. The position of ejido commissioner automatically seemed to correspond to these local bosses. Furthermore, the idea of demanding that these men publicly render accounts of their actions was out of the question.

However, the embodiment of the ejido in the figure of the commissioner has also been stimulated by another characteristic of the Mexican bureaucratic machine, namely the fact that officials always try to establish personalised relationships with formal representatives of organisations. It is a common phenomenon in Mexico that formal representatives of organisations or leaders of movements never act only in their capacity as official spokesman, but also in their capacity as a person who operates in different personal and political networks. Hence, for the officials of the agrarian bureaucracy, ejido commissioners were not only important because they were formal representatives, but also because they were influential people at the local level, and through them they could get important information and open space for negotiation in conflicts. Hence, a combination of local socio-political differentiation in the context of agrarian reform and the importance of personal relations in the Mexican bureaucratic system led to the expansion of the role of the commissioner at the expense of the general assembly.

MEETINGS AS ARENAS OF BICKERING AND INDECISIVE CONFRONTATION

During the time of the research meetings were convened whenever the executive committee felt there was a reason for it or when officials called a meeting. Meetings were normally held on Sunday afternoons. The meetings were announced by sticking posters on the walls of certain houses in the village and sometimes by a car driving around with a loudspeaker. Still, many ejidatarios were often not aware of meetings that were planned and only found out afterwards that they had taken place. The ejido meetings always took place in the *casa ejidal* in the centre of the village.

The first time an ejido meeting is called, half the number of ejidatarios plus one need to be present for the voting. If fewer ejidatarios are present, no decisions can be taken and the meeting has to be called a second time. At the second meeting decisions are valid irrespective of the number of ejidatarios. This is also the reason why few ejidatarios attend a meeting the first time it is called, as they know that a second meeting almost always has to be called. More people may attend this second meeting, but during the time of my research, the attendance at the meetings was generally very low.

Ejidatarios themselves often say that they feel that they should go to the meetings, but immediately give several reasons for not wanting to go. First of all, the real decisions are taken outside the meetings. If somebody has to arrange a matter, he or she goes directly to the ejido commissioner or to other people of importance. Second, ejido meetings can be unpleasant and sometimes result in an aggressive atmosphere in which problems and conflicts become worse instead of being resolved. Long-standing conflicts between ejidatarios or things that happened long ago are often dug up. Finally, many affairs the meetings deal with are of no interest to the ejidatarios.

Naturally, the type of meeting determined the attendance of the ejidatarios. For the meeting at which SRA officials arrived to check on the use of the individual ejido plots (see next chapter) even ejidatarios who lived in the United States came over. These IUP (Investigación de Usufructo Parcelario) meetings, although chaotic, followed the agenda set by the official. Other meetings, which were convened by officials to inform ejidatarios about new government programmes, for example about deforestation, met little enthusiasm and often had to be cancelled. Many ejidatarios had other channels, which provided them with relevant information.

The ejido meetings did not remotely correspond to the image of a public gathering of people in which information is given, arguments are presented, debates take place, voting occurs and decisions are taken. The ejido meetings were characterised by many ejidatarios talking and quarrelling at the same time. There was seldom a central discussion and, when there was, it soon dissolved into side-discussions in which old fights were recalled and often the same people started criticising each other again. One thing that became very clear during these meetings were the areas of contestation in the ejido. The same conflicts about the 'lost land' and the commons, for example, always came up, and, without exception, ejidatarios accused each other of things that had gone wrong. However, these were loose accusations, in the sense that no central discussion would follow in which attempts were made to resolve these issues. None of the three commissioners I knew over the years had any authority at these meetings. They were just like the others, talking, giving an opinion, or quarrelling. Minutes were hardly ever kept, nor were acts drawn up.

Although sometimes meetings were held to discuss important ejido matters, collective decisions were never taken and voting never took place. Different people expressed their opinion and that was it. When accounts of income and revenue were presented they were always quickly passed. Certainly, there were always people complaining about these accounts, but the commissioner was never obliged to give a public explanation. Many asides were made during the meetings, along the lines of: things should be different, more ejidatarios should attend the meetings, people should learn to listen to each other, the rules should be followed, and so on. During the meetings, ejidatarios used to walk in and out of the building. Outside the building small groups discussed what was going on inside. When they thought they had heard enough, the ejidatarios left the meeting.

Although Bailey (1969) describes a very different situation in the village of Bisipara, India, there are some similarities. Bailey nicely describes how in the village council people publicly accused each other of failure to contribute to common tasks, of embezzling of village funds, and other matters and how this always led to heated debates. Yet, decisions were never reached on these affairs and after these open confrontations the affair would slip back to the more covert competition of gossip and backbiting. 'Then sooner or later, there would be another confrontation of just the same kind, followed by another period of gossip and slander' (Bailey 1969: 89). The interesting similarity is that, in Bailey's study as in La Canoa, public meetings have become an arena of 'bickering and indecisive confrontation' and not of decision-making and resolution (1969: 90).

The ejido meetings and acts drawn up at these meetings only become important as the 'formal game' has to be played towards outside agencies. Then, meetings are convened, more ejidatarios attend and acts are drawn up. The acts are signed by the ejidatarios and stamped by the commissioner. The executive committee then goes to several offices in Autlán with the official document. This shows that for the struggle in a different arena – in this case the arena of public offices in Autlán – the official ejido structure and official procedures can play an important role again. Although, at the same time, the playing of the formal game is only part of the struggle in these wider arenas and political influences and personal networks have also to be mobilised.

It is obvious that ejido meetings in La Canoa do not follow the official formula in which the executive committee presents the problems and issues in the ejido to the general assembly which then discusses the points and takes decisions by voting. There is no question of publicly accounting for one's actions either and the commissioner can take several decisions on his own. However, there is no concentration of power in the position of the commissioner either. The commissioner is bound by many restrictions and when he goes too far or damages the interests of certain people, they will let him know and he will be stopped. Very effective means of accountability exist outside the formal structures. Although many things are not discussed at ejido meetings, people find out what is going on in the streets and other places. Commissioners can be criticised by fellow ejidatarios and called to account for the spending of the ejido money in many other settings. He is not asked to render account by people speaking up at a meeting, but by their talking to him in private. Effective ways of controlling the commissioner and stopping him abusing his power include, for example, the use of regional political networks, gossip, and the exclusion of his relatives from other village activities. The politics of honour also plays an important role in the room for manoeuvre that people create for themselves and in the way others judge them. So, although meetings are often not held, and although the general assembly is not the decision-making body in the ejido, there are other ways in which the ejidatarios check on what is going on and keep control over the executive committee.

The facts that no decisions are taken at ejido meetings, that the executive committee is not asked to render accounts and that many ejido affairs are arranged in small loose constellations of people, are often seen as signs of an undemocratic form of organising in which some people can abuse their position at the expense of the other ejido members. Yet, in my view, such conclusions cannot be drawn without a study of the distribution of and access to ejido resources and forms of control and accountability outside the formal setting.

THE FORCE FIELDS OF EJIDAL ORGANISING PRACTICES

In Search of the Action

If we know that official organigrams give little insight into what is going on, but on the other hand do not want to start from a one-sided focus on bossism and leadership for the study of organising practices we have to think of alternative ways to approach the ejido administration. This is not always an easy task. At first, I felt frustrated that things had happened in the ejido that I had not been aware of. This experience closely resembled John Law's experiences during his study of organising practices in a nuclear laboratory in Great Britain. Law describes it in the following way:

I had a terrible anxiety about being in the right place at the right time. Wherever I happened to be, the action was not. Sometimes people would say: 'Did you hear what happened at such-and-such meeting?' ... 'Did you hear what happened to so-and-so?' Always it seemed to me, that the *real* action was going on somewhere else. (Law 1994a: 45–6)

I was slightly comforted when I realised that many ejidatarios found themselves in the same position. They had not heard anything about a meeting or about the visit of an official. They had not been aware of decisions that had been taken either. However, while most ejidatarios did not seem to be bothered by this phenomenon, it certainly did disturb me. The ejido was my research object and I felt it necessary to know what was going on and to 'follow the flow of action'. During the research I gradually found out to whom I had to go in order to find out what was about to happen. Towards the end of the research, when I myself became actively involved in several ejido projects (see the following chapters), I felt that I had finally 'gained control' over my research object. The odd thing was that, in the same way as Law describes for his study, 'other people, those excluded from these meetings, sometimes assumed that where I was, *there* was the action, and they'd ask me questions – questions that I'd have to deflect – about what had happened at "important" meetings' (Law 1994a: 46). In La Canoa it was not so much a question of being present at 'important' meetings but more of being part of a network in which ejido affairs were discussed and decided.

However, even though being present at important meetings or having access to central networks gives interesting insights, it only explains part of the organising practices. As Law points out, 'since there are disconti- nuities in place, and discontinuities in ordering, it follows that the largest part of the action is always generated elsewhere' (Law 1994a: 47). This is certainly true. In fact, a locus or centre of control, which directs the ejido, does not exist. Actually, this belief in a centre of control prevents us from seeing the complexity of the historical force field in which the organising practices and forms of ordering have developed.

Following Wolf's (1990) suggestion that we should follow the flow of action, I decided to study organising practices around concrete resources, projects, areas of contestation and overt conflicts. Such studies of a variety of projects can throw light on the forms of governance, rule and accountability that exist in the ejido. In this section, three examples are presented which make it clear that the force field in which organising practices in the ejido have developed, are composed of many different elements. This also shows that the influence of the commissioner is restricted and contested.

Punishment of the abuse of power by an ejido commissioner
When Ricardo García (son of Pedro García, one of the founders of the ejido) was commissioner of the ejido (1970–73) a serious conflict arose the effects of which still can be felt today. The central actors in this conflict were Ricardo and the treasurer of the ejido, Inocencio Romero. Both were then among the biggest farmers in the ejido.

At that time there was a government programme for the construction of school buildings, which asked for a financial contribution from the village. La Canoa already had a small school but needed a much larger building. The ejidatarios of La Canoa decided to rent the pasture from 600 hectares of common lands for five years in a row. This resulted in a large amount of money, which could be invested in the school project. The executive committee of the ejido took responsibility for the school project. However, Ricardo convinced Inocencio Romero, who as treasurer of the ejido had received the money, to use this money for equipment Ricardo needed for his farm. At a later stage, he would return the money.

When meetings about the building of the school were organised, Ricardo did not turn up any more. He withdrew from active involvement in the school project. The other ejidatarios started to get angry and suspicions mounted about the use of the ejido money. Not only was a lot of money involved but the building of the local school was also endangered. When they realised that the whole project could fail because of the actions of the commissioner and secretary of the ejido, several ejidatarios took measures. They looked for help from important PRI politicians in Autlán, among others, Héctor Romero. Héctor informed the Mayor of Autlán, who made Ricardo call a meeting in the ejido and return the money to the ejido. Ricardo held the meeting but he could not return the money as he did not have it. The conflict continued and Ricardo and Inocencio were sent to jail for several days. In the end Inocencio managed to borrow enough money to pay back the ejido. Later on he settled the matter with Ricardo. The school was built in La Canoa. Ricardo García declared that he would never send his children to this school. He kept his word and, despite the practical troubles, all his eleven children went to school in Autlán.

This incident, together with the way in which Ricardo, as a very rich farmer, exploited the labourers working for him, made him a man disliked by most people in the village. Today many villagers still do not talk to Ricardo or his wife and children. They remain very isolated from activities and festivities in the village. In his turn, Ricardo feels that the efforts he and his father made for the development of the village never were appreciated. He recalls the troubles he went through to have water and electricity installed in the village.

This example is interesting as it shows how political networks with people in Autlán may be used to influence dynamics in the ejido La Canoa. Several ejidatarios contacted Héctor Romero and the Mayor of Autlán to stop Ricardo. However, the interesting point here is that Ricardo himself maintained good relations with this political group. The fact that he was punished despite his good political contacts, meant that he had gone too far in his manipulation of ejido funds. The opposition to him in the village had grown so strong that the people in Autlán had to interfere and stop him. This shows that even well-placed powerholders have to know how to 'play the game' and should not enrich themselves too much.

Ricardo's position was also weak, as he had never created groups of loyal followers in the village. More than anyone else, he is criticised for the unpleasant way in which he treats the villagers and ejidatarios who work for him, and for not keeping his promises. This position clearly limited his room for manoeuvre. In the end, Ricardo came out as the most damaged person in terms of political networks and his status in the village.

Finally, this example makes clear that ejidatarios use different ways to get somebody to render accounts. When the normal methods – directly addressing the person in question – do not work, they look for other ways to put pressure on him or her.

The next example shows another common aspect of organising practices, namely the appropriation of resources through personal networks.

The appropriation of resources through personal networks

The BANRURAL credit programme for maize was one of these government programmes in which the ejido was used as an intermediary structure to channel resources. For several years the credit programme of BANRURAL was automatically connected with a governmental crop insurance programme through the insurance company ANAGSA. This meant that part of the credit for the ejidatario was immediately used by BANRURAL to pay the fee for the crop insurance. In the case of the loss of a crop, ANAGSA repaid the loan to BANRURAL and the ejidatarios were let off their debts. The ejidatarios could receive new credit the next year.

Although this system made the credit rather expensive (because of the high fee for the crop insurance) ejidatarios with rainfed land liked the remission of debts in the case of bad harvests. However, this remission of debts only took place if the loss of a crop was due to bad weather and not to the neglect of the crop by the ejidatario. So, inspectors of the ANAGSA and BANRURAL offices in Autlán would come and visit the ejido in order to see if the crop was well taken care of. At the last visit of the season, the ejidatario as well as the ejido commissioner had to be present as an assessment of the harvest was made by the inspector. The ejidatario had to sign that he or she agreed with this assessment. The assessment of the total harvest of a plot was important as it determined the percentage of the loan the ejidatarios had to repay. With a high production they had to repay a higher percentage of the loan than with a low production. The ejido commissioner would mediate in case of problems between the ejidatario and the inspector.

As will be clear, these field inspections offered interesting possibilities for negotiations between field inspectors, commissioner and ejidatarios. However, although some negotiations took place, by the beginning of the 1990s all ejidatarios, except for some close relatives of one of the officials of the BANRURAL office in Autlán, had got into serious problems with BANRURAL and ANAGSA. This official, Marcos Vargas, who was born in La Canoa, always made sure that his mother and brother, who are ejidatarios in La Canoa, were treated generously by BANRURAL and ANAGSA. His mother always obtained the best arrangements. Her crops were always assessed to be a total loss due to bad weather even if the crops were not lost. She also received credit and remission of debts for many more hectares than she possessed. However, Marcos did not help other ejidatarios in La Canoa.

Ejidatarios complained that BANRURAL did not pay the fee for the crop insurance to ANAGSA and that for that reason they were not indemnified by ANAGSA when their crops were lost. Other problems were the late payment of the credit and the excessively high assessments of harvests by inspectors. At the beginning of the 1990s, most ejidatarios had stopped working with BANRURAL and complained bitterly about corruption at the institute. The problems with BANRURAL and ANAGSA were a problem at the national level and the government credit system for the ejido sector was changed.

For a certain period BANRURAL also provided credit for tractors to groups of at least ten ejidatarios. As most ejidatarios in La Canoa prefer to work on their own and be the sole owner of a tractor, they found an easy way to buy a tractor with credit from BANRURAL. They asked several good friends and relatives to sign the credit contract with BANRURAL and in this way, they bought the tractor officially as a group. In reality, only one ejidatario took the credit and owned the tractor. He was the one who was responsible for the repayment of the credit. As the whole group was officially responsible for the repayment, this was a relation of trust with the tractor owner. Several tractors were bought in this way by ejidatarios in La Canoa. Naturally, it was the richer ejidatarios with irrigated land who bought these tractors (Amador García, Rubén García, Ignacio Romero, Inocencio Romero). Also for these arrangements the signature and stamp of the executive committee were needed. No problems occurred with these arrangements.

In these examples of BANRURAL, we see the appropriation of resources through personal networks. In the credit programme for maize close relations between an official and some ejidatarios in La Canoa proved to be more important than negotiations between the executive committee, ejidatarios, and officials. In this case, most appropriation of resources took place by the officials of BANRURAL and ANAGSA and their relatives in the ejido. However, in the case of the BANRURAL credit for tractors, the appropriation took place by a select group of richer ejidatarios. So, depending on the circumstances and the other actors that play a role, the appropriation of resources may take different forms. Yet, it is notable that in both cases the commissioner did not play a central role.

In the next example different aspects of ejido organising practices are shown. This example illustrates how conflictual situations may linger on for many years without resolution. However, in the end a group of ejidatarios may join forces and tackle the question. The reason why so many conflictual situations linger on for a long time without anything being done about it is that the 'resolution' or 'ending' of conflictual situations is accompanied by hard fights, family quarrels and violence. The following conflict evolved around a part of the urban zone of La Canoa.

The ejido retakes control

A famous local conflict around the urban zone is the conflict of '*las Malvinas*'. This concerned a tract of land within the urban zone of the ejido, near the commons. As in former times nobody used this land, the ejido gave Elías Romero, one of the richest ejidatarios, permission to use it for the cultivation of maize. However, the land was lent to him on condition that it would be returned to the community when more land was needed for the construction of houses. According to the ejidatarios, an agreement was drawn up which was guarded in the ejido archive. Elías used this land for many years. When he passed away, his wife Petra Sánchez and their sons continued to use this land. However, the pressure of the population on the urban zone was growing and, in the 1970s the ejido decided to ask for the land back from Petra.

Petra said that the ejido had given this land to her husband and she refused to return the land. The conflict dragged on for many years and Petra and her sons tried to keep the land by all possible means. The agreement, in which Elías declared that he would return the land when the ejido would ask him for it, had disappeared from the ejido archive. For many years Petra refused to give in and the ejido did not get the land back. Since at that time the war between England and Argentina about the Falkland Islands (*las Malvinas* in Spanish) was taking place, the ejidatarios started referring to this part of the village as *las Malvinas*, a name it retains today.

Francisco Romero was the ejido commissioner (1982–85) who decided to make a real effort to recover this land. Besides lodging an official complaint at the SRA, he hired a lawyer. The majority of ejidatarios supported Francisco. Francisco and several ejidatarios had to go on many trips to the SRA offices in Guadalajara and Mexico City. Petra and her sons also hired a lawyer and tried to get several ejidatarios on their side. However, apart from some close relatives of Petra, all the ejidatarios supported the commissioner in his efforts. Manuel Pradera remembers that one of Petra's sons visited him to make him sign a letter which said that he, as ejidatario, agreed to Petra possessing this land:

But I did not sign. I told him: as far as I know the ejido only lent your father the land, they did not give it to him. I do not have a personal interest in this matter. You can try and see what you can get out of it, but it is your fight. Later on I had to sign the papers of the ejido that said that I agreed that the land should be taken away from her.

During this period the ejido meetings were well attended. Although the majority of ejidatarios supported Francisco, for him personally this fight was not a pleasant one. He was threatened by Petra's brother and one day he was even put in jail, accused of illegally invading Petra's terrain. The ejidatarios immediately reacted and got him out of prison in one day. Rumours went around that one of Petra's sons intended to kill Francisco. Finally, after many incidents and much tension in the village, the SRA reached a decision, which said that the land had to return to the ejido. The conflict was formally won by the ejido, and the ejidatarios took the land. The recovered land was immediately divided into *lotes* for the construction of houses. As the ejido had spent a lot of money on lawyers, trips to the cities and on officials, the people who received a *lote* had to pay an amount of money to cover these costs. The widow was offered two *lotes* for her sons, but she refused. Many villagers stopped talking to Petra and her sons for years. Shortly afterwards Francisco Romero left with his family for the United States.

These three examples show very different aspects of organisation and practices of control in the ejido. They make clear that a simple analysis in terms of *cacique* families who arrange everything in their own favour by monopolising relations with the bureaucracy is highly inadequate as a general explanatory model for the organisation of the ejido. One of the aspects which, in my view, is much more central to the management of the ejido, is that illustrated in the last example. Namely, the fact that the costs that are involved in the resolution of conflicts and in 'retaking control' over certain ejido matters may be extremely high in personal and social terms. Retaking control often means quarrels, tensions and fights. This is precisely the reason why there is no interference in many ejido matters.

THE UNPOPULARITY OF FORMAL POSITIONS

In relation to the flow of action, attention now turns more to the 'flow of ideas' and to the way in which ejidatarios themselves reflect on organising practices in the ejido. As we saw, all ejidatarios are related to each other and this means that every project may soon become embedded in a dense web of socio-political relations. This explains why many people choose not to take action, and why even issues that, in the opinion of most ejidatarios, should be dealt with are not tackled. While many ejidatarios have clear opinions about what is going wrong in the ejido and what should be changed, at the same time they feel powerless or are afraid to do anything about it. They know that they will get into problems with their neighbour, uncle or *compadre* and that is something they want to avoid. In addition, most ejidatarios are old people who have already had many experiences with conflicts and murders in the village and they do not want to become involved in these problems any more. So, several people told me that the best strategy is not to do anything. As somebody said, even the politically most innocent act will in the end annoy someone. Rubén Romero, gave a nice explanation of this phenomenon of 'not doing anything' being the best strategy, when I asked him how the *delegado* was doing:

The one who doesn't do anything is good (*es bueno el que no hace nada*). The people don't talk about the delegado we have now. He doesn't annoy anybody. He is a bad worker (*para trabajar es malo*). But the point is that whatever you do, you will always have opponents. For example, if you want to make a street you will annoy the people who do not want a street near their house or through their land. If you want to prohibit the cows from walking in the street you will have problems with the cattle owners. If you want to let the people pay their water according to the quantity they use, you will also have problems with cattle owners, etc. Everything good he is doing, is bad for someone else. And then he has his friends, his compadres and his relatives whom he doesn't want to harm ...

As a consequence of this situation, most villagers do not want to take any formal responsibility and most ejidatarios do not want to stand for a post in the ejido. Some people are very explicit about their wish to stay away from an official position. For example, Manuel Pradera is a very capable and much respected ejidatario who never gets into trouble with anyone. On many occasions he has been asked to become ejido commissioner or *delegado*, or to take a position in special committees. He is asked to fill formal positions especially when conflicts are going on, as nobody will doubt his integrity. However, so far he has always refused because he does not want to get involved in all kinds of problems and, as he says, he does not 'want to be used in the political games of other people'.

Besides the fact that one can easily get into conflicts with other people, the leaders of organisations and projects are always criticised. As there is always a lot of uncertainty about what is going on, there is always room for rumours, complaints and gossip. The executive committee of the ejido is always held responsible for everything that goes wrong. If they do not go on trips for the ejido, they are blamed for not working on behalf of the ejido or it is said that they have been bought by the *caciques*. If, on the other hand, they go on many trips, they are blamed for spending ejido money on nice trips, hotels, restaurants and other amusements.

In addition to all this criticism, the commissioner may become involved in delicate matters that he would like to avoid. He can be asked to negotiate on behalf of the ejidatarios with inspectors of BANRURAL. In the case of serious problems in the ejido, the commissioner is often held responsible and, on several occasions, the commissioner of La Canoa was put in jail. The commissioner also has to deal and negotiate with a range of officials. Officials from the Ministry of Agriculture often come to explain new programmes, inspectors from the forestry police can come by and fine people who burn the commons, the judicial police occasionally invade the ejido to check on marijuana production. In 1994, for example, the ejido commissioner was summoned to accompany the judicial police to a part in the commons of La Canoa where they had found marijuana. Although the commissioner was not personally held responsible, this was not a very pleasant experience for him as exchanges of gunfire often take place between the judicial police and marijuana producers.

For all these reasons the positions in the executive committee are not very popular among the ejidatarios. The position of commissioner is especially unpopular. Most ejidatarios have no interest in a position which implies little authority, possible involvement in a series of conflicts and continuous accusations by fellow ejidatarios. Ignacio Romero, who had been commissioner from 1985 to 1988, told me: 'I would not like to stand for the post of commissioner again. You do not gain anything from it and there are always a lot of problems in the ejido.' During his own administration, Ignacio was very active campaigning for the 'lost land'. However, it was said that he suddenly stopped working on the 'lost land', when he was really making headway. It was rumoured that he was given a plot of private land in exchange for abandoning the case. Ignacio himself said that he bought the land, but others assured me that he was bribed with this land.

To a certain degree, the executive committee and the commissioner can decide themselves how active they want to be in the ejido, how fairly they want to carry out the administration and how much they want to get involved in conflicts. There have been different executive committees with different agendas.

Formal Positions and Views on Corruption

This view of the close relation between formal positions and personal relationships is directly connected to villagers' reflections on corruption. It is very common for officials to receive payment for whatever task they do for ejidatarios. Even simple administrative tasks such as the registration of inheritance papers often have to be paid for. Naturally, these payments depend on the kind of work or 'favour' done and the parties in the negotiation. Standard compensation for a surveyor who visits an ejido is the payment of his petrol and hotel bill, and they are often taken out for dinner and to any place the official wants to go. Although these kinds of services or payments may be called 'bribes' or 'corruption', by the people involved these are considered to be logical forms of reciprocity and seen in terms of the development of certain types of relationships and even forms of friendship. Besides certain immediate benefits, the different parties also make an investment for possible arrangements in the future. Officials, as well as ejidatarios, can be interested in establishing relationships with people who may be of help in future arrangements. These 'strategic alliances' are often established between influential ejidatarios and functionaries, and can eventually develop in many different ways.

Hence, although the ejidatarios pay for many services of the bureaucracy, they will not easily use the term corruption when they talk about these practices. They see them as normal transactions in which an exchange of services or favours takes place. Furthermore, the ejidatarios do not mind paying when they feel that they are treated well and get what they want. On the contrary, these successful transactions make them feel very pleased and give them the feeling that they are capable of dealing with the bureaucracy. If the transaction was successful, they will try to continue their relationship with this same official. These transactions often take place in a pleasant atmosphere of partying and abundant meals and may strengthen useful relationships. So when ejidatarios pay the official at the SRA office in Autlán to register the inheritor of their land in the SRA office in Guadalajara, they do not call this corruption. When they invite officials to big meals in exchange for all the paperwork they did, this is considered to be a normal compensation and an act of gratitude. The bribe (*mordida*) which is paid for help with illegal actions, such as the legalising of illegal land sales, is also seen in the same light.

'That is the way we are used to it in Mexico', is a usual expression. All people pay money to get things arranged, documents changed, etc. It is part of life. The ejidatarios themselves also try to use the influence of their relatives, *compadres,* or friends in bureaucratic positions if necessary. In this sense, no distinction is made between, for example, corrupt people and honest people, or between the honest ejidatarios and the corrupt officials. In this view, everybody in Mexico is to a certain degree corrupt, or can be made corrupt, and this is the way the system and society works.

On the other hand, these same favours or compensations may be called corruption when they take place in unbalanced exchanges; when ejidatarios feel that there is no balanced reciprocity. Hence, ejidatarios use the label corruption when they pay money or do favours and this does not bring them the services they expect in exchange. When, for example, they pay a lawyer and nothing is accomplished, or when they pay a surveyor who never finishes the work, or when amounts of money are asked for which are considered to be too high for the favour done, they may talk about corruption. However, no fixed rules can be given about what are considered to be acceptable transactions and what are not. This very much depends on the situation and the people involved. Furthermore, as it is often not clear to the ejidatarios what exactly is going on or what exactly officials or intermediaries are doing for them, they tend to be careful in their judgement. Hence, corruption is not so much seen as a personal characteristic, but above all as a characteristic of society in general. Ejidatarios know that all officials will be confronted with different kinds of pressures. Some will yield more easily to these pressures than others, but all are moving within certain limits and conditions set by wider influences.

However, the ejidatarios use the term corruption above all in a general way, to refer to the 'way in which the system works' and to refer to the fact that 'justice is never done'. So they tend to use the term as a form of social criticism, referring to the accumulation of experiences in which they have been deceived, promises made that were not kept, and money accepted while nothing was done in return.

CONTRASTING DISCOURSES OF ORGANISATION

Ejidatarios reflect a lot on the organising characteristics of their ejido. In some organisation theories it is argued that the creation and re-creation of stories is a way of ordering the world around us and is central to the organising process (Czarniawska 1997, Reed 1992). Law (1994a,

1994b) talks in this respect about the many organisational narratives that can be found in every organisation. He shows how participants in an organisation may present very different and contradictory narratives about what the organisation is about and/or should be about. These narratives can be contrasting and inconsistent as they deal in different ways with conceptions of agency, self-interest, opportunism and performance. According to Law, these manifold narratives of organisation show the decentred nature of organisations, since no narrative can completely capture the dynamic of the organising processes. All narratives are true and incomplete at the same time. In this approach, the forms of discourse available to and used by social actors in assessing their organisational situation are a central object of study.

Yet I would take this position a step further. In my view, different views or images of the organising process not only show different sides of the same organisation; they also reflect areas of tension and conflict. We should situate commentaries within wider spheres of negotiation of meaning and power, recognising at the same time the local stakes and specificities (Tsing 1993: 9). Hence, the study of organisational stories and discourses, and the manifold contrasting views we may find, should be used for the analysis of organising practices in relation to the broader setting.

In La Canoa the ejidatarios often reflect on the organisational characteristics of their ejido and struggle with the contradictory nature of their own reflections. Discussions of this kind, about the organisational characteristics of the ejido occur at the ejido meetings but also in private circles. To a certain extent, outsiders induce this dialogue. Officials always say to the ejidatarios that they should accept their responsibilities, follow the formal rules and organise themselves better. This places the ejidatarios in a dialogue between their 'practical knowledge' and a 'modernist organisation discourse'. For example, many ejidatarios say that they know that it is their duty to attend the ejido meetings but at the same time they can explain to you why they often prefer not to go. They argue that important decisions are not taken at the meetings anyway. This illustrates that they are in a critical, reflective dialogue with the world in which they live, with themselves and with government officials.

These reflections also play a role in the construction of the self in relation to the wider force field. The works of Pigg (1992, 1996) offer important insights on these issues. Following Pigg, I would say that the activity in which I found myself participating when the ejidatarios were reflecting on and theorising about the organisation of the ejido, 'involved representations of self and other' (Pigg 1996: 161). In the same way as Pigg busied herself 'documenting people's beliefs for purposes of scholarship' and 'came across many people who were questioning their own and other's beliefs in the name of science' (1996: 161), I busied myself documenting people's organising behaviour and came across people who were questioning and reflecting upon their own and other's organisational actions. That this was a debate with 'modernity' became particularly clear when ejidatarios apologised to me for what they said was a total lack of organisation in the ejido. After ejido meetings, they used to come up to me and say that they felt ashamed about the way that these meetings evolved, adding that I was probably startled by this chaos. Although I tried to convince them that it was not my aim to evaluate these meetings, they saw me as an 'exponent of modernity' with whom they entered in debate. They knew what 'modernity' looked like and government officials had often instructed them about it.

Since the ejidatarios themselves are struggling with ideas about how the ejido should work, we find contrasting discourses at the local level. To begin with, we find the 'accountability discourse'.

The accountability discourse
This discourse presents the way in which the ejido should function as a modern bureaucratic organisation. According to this discursive model, every ejidatario should assume a position in the executive committee and take responsibilities if he or she is asked to do so. The executive committee should organise meetings and the ejidatarios should all attend these meetings. At the meetings, decisions should be taken about the important affairs in the ejido and the implementation of decisions should be open to inspection. The executive committee should render accounts of their actions at the ejido assembly and defend the interests of the entire ejido at the different institutions. Ejidatarios who do not follow the official rules should be punished, fined or even deprived of certain rights.

This accountability discourse is especially used by the ejidatarios when things are happening in the ejido that they do not agree with. In situations like this, some ejidatarios would prefer the ejido to retake control. However, most of the time the ejidatarios do not mind the lack of management and control. Nor do they care that outsiders view their ejido as 'disorganised'. The fact that the ejido does not function according to the official model gives them a lot of freedom in their operations and means that nobody interferes with their illegal land transactions. Furthermore, they have considerable security of land tenure. So, most of the time there is no reason for the ejidatarios to want the ejido administration to work differently or in a so-called modern, democratic, accountable way.

Another discourse, which is very strong in the ejido, could be called the 'personal politics discourse' of organisation. The personal politics discourse of organisation provides a language for reflecting on the workings of power within organisations. It stresses that power is concentrated by corrupt politicians at the top and that people take formal responsibilities only for the sake of personal enrichment.

Personal politics discourse
According to this discourse, people in official functions always use their position to favour themselves and friends. It is argued that there is always a lot of *favoritismo* (favouritism) and politics in the organisation and that, in the end, everything is determined by money and relations. The people with the most money or with the most influential relations will always come out on top. Within this discourse, it is said that personal enrichment is the main reason for people to take an official post. This discourse is an illustration of the fact that politics and organisation are seen as intricately related.

The personal politics discourse of organisation is directly related to the ways in which ejidatarios talk about corruption. Complaints about corruption and the related 'personal politics discourse' of organisation is above all used when people want to express their frustration about the outcome of specific conflicts. It is also used as a general critique about how things work in the ejido, the government bureaucracy and society at large. It is also often used as a justification for not taking initiatives to change situations or for not assuming formal responsibilities. The ejidatarios have a double attitude towards this image of organisations as being determined by personal politics. They may complain about favouritism in the ejido management but at the same time will acknowledge that they themselves make use of these mechanisms when they need their own affairs to be settled. They may explain that this is a weakness in themselves, and say: 'As Mexicans, we ourselves are to blame for it' or 'It is hard to change these things as they form part of our life, of the way we are.' At the same time they are proud of the fact that they as Mexicans know how to support friends and relatives when necessary.

The model of organisation, which is presented in the personal politics discourse, is more a fantasy of power and politics than an accurate representation of organising practices. Although organising processes in the ejido are definitely influenced by power relations, these are not the only or even the most important factors. For example, although the ejido commissioner takes many decisions on his own, he has very little room to operate. In the same way, the model of the modern democratic organisation is an ideological construct that does not relate to the real workings of organisations. In fact, the 'accountability discourse', as well as the 'personal politics discourse' of organisation present images of organising which do not exist in reality. Yet, they do express different, partial dimensions of the same organisation and are used in conflicts and struggles in the ejido.

Hence, the ejidatarios' theorising and reflecting may partly be analysed in terms of a dialogue with 'modernity' but also has to be seen in relation to preoccupations with control and power. These reflections and contrasting discourses on organisation in the ejido played a role in conflicts, in efforts to change situations in the ejido and in attempts to retake control over ejido resources.

CONCLUSION: ALTERNATIVE FORMS OF GOVERNANCE AND ACCOUNTABILITY

Someone approaching the ejido La Canoa from a formal organisation perspective would easily arrive at the conclusion that the ejido administration is a mess. Rules are not applied and most ejidatarios do not seem to know the rules nor are they interested in them. Very few people come to the meetings and the meetings are not held very regularly. Most ejido affairs are arranged informally and the ejido commissioner seems to have taken over the role of the general assembly. From a formal organisation perspective this is labelled as a lack of transparency and public accountability which is symptomatic of undemocratic, traditional organisations. This modernist development discourse is often used by government officials who say that ejidatarios lack certain skills and should be helped to organise themselves (see Chapter 8). In this line of thought, the ejidatarios should be better educated in their tasks as community members with collective resources and interests.

Yet, in this chapter it was shown that there is only a 'mess', 'apathy' and 'disorganisation' when we approach the ejido from a modernist organisation perspective. On the other hand, when we study the ejido from a practice approach of organising, we see considerable patterning and ordering with respect to the access to resources and forms of control and accountability. I studied the organising processes around these different resources, and also looked at specific projects, and areas of conflict.

It is true that in the everyday context of ejido management, matters are organised in small groups in private spheres. On the other hand, although the ejido commissioner and the people around him take decisions on their own they have very little room for manoeuvre. Little scope exists for abrupt changes of established routines. Their decisions may concern to whom they rent the pasture in the commons, or how many trips they have to go on to Mexico City, but they cannot decide to evict somebody from an individual ejido plot or to take land back from

4   ILLEGALITY AND THE LAW

INTRODUCTION: A SHADOW WORLD OF ILLEGAL PRACTICES

This chapter follows the development of land transfers in La Canoa in the period between the establishment of the ejido in 1938 and 1992, the year that the agrarian law was changed. Many illegal transfers of ejido plots have taken place in those years. Many ejido plots have been sold and others have been divided into several plots and were passed to several children. The renting out of ejido land by migrants was also common practice. The majority of these illegal arrangements were never brought up in the official arena. In fact, the ejidatarios developed considerable autonomy in land transactions and a high degree of security in land tenure without formal registration and protection by government agencies.

The aim of this chapter is twofold. First, it analyses the force fields in which these practices became established. It is shown that many different elements are important in land transactions: the different values attributed to ejido land, the ideology of the family, local politics, wider social networks, and bureaucratic rules and processes in government agencies. Notions of individual responsibility and honour in the striking of deals all play important roles. As Sabean points out 'property is not a relationship between people and things but one between people about things' and 'all social transactions take place within a field of rights, duties, claims, and obligations, which taken together comprise the system of property holding' (Sabean 1990: 17–18).

Second, the relation between these illegal practices and the law is investigated. In other words, the ways in which these illegal arrangements were protected from the official law. It is shown that many illegal practices are in fact organised in cooperation with officials and the state bureaucracy (Heyman 1999). In many cases, official rules and procedures are used to 'hide' illegal activities in formal categories. Hence, official rules and procedures acquire new roles in a shadow world of illegality. Actually, control by the SRA over ejido land use and interference in dispute settlement culminated in a widespread set of relations and spheres of influence encompassing the local ejido level and different institutions belonging to the state bureaucracy (Ibarra 1989: 21). Consequently, studies from 'below' of the way in which ejidos and ejidatarios become involved in the juridical structure and the state apparatus are necessary to arrive at a full understanding of these processes (1989: 23).[1]

A BASIC CONTRADICTION IN THE AGRARIAN LAW

The Mexican agrarian law has been the object of much criticism and debate. It is well known that 'post-revolutionary states are especially prone to enacting laws of high ideals which come up against an intractable reality' (Harris 1996: 9) and the case of Mexican Agrarian Law is no exception. Here I will discuss one fundamental contradiction that worked through all the procedures. The reason for discussing this point in detail is that it greatly influenced the practices around land transactions which developed over time. This central contradiction consisted in the fact that on the one hand the Agrarian Law allowed the 'individual' possession of ejido plots, while on the other hand the use of the ejido plot was restricted by many 'social' rules. The Agrarian Law not only provided procedures for the division of the arable land into individual plots but also allowed the ejidatarios to choose their own heir. This individual possession and inheritance of plots made ejido land tenure very similar to private landownership. However, the Agrarian Law also expressed a more 'revolutionary' aim of land reform by presenting the ejido as an agrarian community with important social duties. This was apparent, for example, in the official terminology, which said that the ejidatarios only received 'use rights' to the land and not property rights. An important general principle derived from the Mexican Revolution was: *land to the tiller*. This principle underlay many of the rules in the Agrarian Law, for example, the rule that the ejidatario had to work the land himself and could not leave it unused or rent it out. Ejido land was meant to provide a subsistence basis for peasant families and should not become an economic commodity. Furthermore, the rule that ejidatarios were not allowed to possess more than one plot was an indication of the social character of ejido land tenure. As they only possessed use rights to the land the ejidatarios obviously could not sell the land either. The use rights to the land could be taken away from the ejidatarios if they infringed the Agrarian Law and the ejido assembly could then 'transfer the use right' to somebody else.

This tension between the 'individual' and 'social' character of ejido land tenure became especially clear in the registration of ejido land. Although almost all ejidos made use of the opportunity to divide the land into individual plots, the law never provided the procedures for the registration of ejidatarios in relation to a specific plot of land. Hence, maps of the individual ejido plots were seldom made. In this way, the Agrarian Law never carried through the individualisation of land tenure which it had set in motion. At the SRA ejidos were registered with their name, a map of the total ejido (if the ejido was lucky) and a list of ejidatarios (members of the ejido). On the basis of this list, numbered certificates of agrarian rights were issued. These numbered certificates accredited ejidatarios as members of the ejido and provided them with certain rights. The first and most important right was the usufructuary right to an ejido plot and the right to designate the heir of the land. However, it also gave them rights to use the common lands and the right to receive a free *lote* within the urbanised zone of the ejido.

In terms of the law, the numbered ejido certificates referred to a specific plot of land (*unidad de dotación*) and protected the ejidatario in his or her agrarian rights. However, as individual plots were never measured, the link between a plot and the number of the certificate was never formally established. Nevertheless, for the ejidatarios these certificates acquired a very important, even symbolic value. It was their proof of land rights. The certificates were issued after a long delay (some ejidatarios had to wait for more than 30 years) and were cherished and well guarded by most ejidatarios. Although ejidatarios acknowledged that the basis of their security of land tenure was not so much official registration at the SRA, but recognition by the other ejidatarios, the ejido certificates had an important legal-symbolic value. However, enormous formal complications and bureaucratic discrepancies were raised by the fact that the government wanted to keep control over ejido land use and in this way tried to guarantee the 'social use' of the land.

In order to keep control over the 'social use' of the lands, the Investigation of Use of Plots (Investigación de Usufructo Parcelario, IUP) was introduced. The aim of the IUP was to check whether ejidatarios used their land in a legal way. In cases where they did not, the land could be taken away from them and the ejido assembly had to decide to whom the land should be given. There were several steps involved in this. The first step was for an official of the SRA to visit the ejido with the official list of ejidatarios and their certificate numbers. An ejido meeting was convened in which the official named one ejidatario after the other. Ejidatarios who had ceased to till the land themselves for two or more years would lose their agrarian rights and the ejido assembly had to say who had been working these plots during this time. These persons would then officially be proposed as the new ejidatarios with the agrarian use rights to the plots. The dispossession of an ejidatario from his or her agrarian right was seen as a serious issue and the ejidatarios who were to be dispossessed of their rights were given the opportunity to defend their position at the office of the SRA. After the final decision was taken by the SRA, the dispossessions were published in the *Gazette of the State*.

In practice, the IUP functioned in a way that had very little to do with control over land use. Instead it became a way to disguise legally permitted transactions that had not followed the formal procedures, as well as many illegal manoeuvres. This was encouraged by the fact that the ejido assembly had the decisive vote at the meeting of the IUP. As an ejidatario in La Canoa told me: 'If we ejidatarios did not want to let the functionaries interfere, they had no way of knowing what was going on here.' The point is that the assembly could 'hide' every type of land transfer under the category of ejidatarios who had abandoned their plot, which was being tilled by someone else.

Illegal land sales were practices 'covered' by the IUP. The official who visited the ejido for the IUP was often uncertain whether the changes in ejido members concerned inheritances, sales, dispossession or what, nor was he particularly interested. Officials had to cope with procedures that did not offer them any instruments of control and which did not bear any relation to what was going on 'on the ground'. Ejidatarios often tried to strike a deal with the official before or after the meeting of the IUP. As the SRA official who regularly attended La Canoa, explained to me:

We often became aware of the illegal sale of ejido plots at the meeting of the IUP. Or people themselves came to talk to us before the meeting took place. We helped them by making the transfer of the agrarian right to the new name easy, by not asking questions. In return we received money from them.

In this way, these sales could also provide some room for negotiation and an extra source of income for the officials of the SRA.

Both officials and ejidatarios knew that they were dealing with procedures that did not bear any relation to reality. Hence, during these meetings officials deliberated with the ejidatarios about the best way to formalise the many illegal situations. At one of the IUP meetings in La Canoa at which I happened to be present, the official himself suggested an ejidatario put one of his plots in the name of his son, as he was not allowed to possess more than one plot. In quite an open atmosphere during these public meetings, officials and ejidatarios together tried to squeeze 'illegal' practices into 'official rules and categories'.

This awkward registration of ejido plots also led to an interesting dynamic in the case of land conflicts. In the official documentation around land conflicts reference is always made to the number of the ejido certificate and the related plot (*unidad de dotación*). Yet, because of the active land market the numbers often no longer bore any relation to the original plots that were handed over at the first land distribution. However, the ejidatarios had clear maps of ejido land distribution and trajectories of plots in their head. So, for the people involved in the conflict it always was very clear which plot they were fighting over. When they were fighting over a plot that was referred to by a certain number in the SRA documents, they knew exactly which of the (for example) five plots of the ejidatario was in dispute.

Although the official settlement of land conflicts says little about what really happened to the land, the official administration remains very important as it provides the legal language and categories according to which deals have to be formalised. Many people prefer to 'play the official game' as far as possible.

MIGRATION AND THE RENTING OUT OF LAND: A RISKY ENDEAVOUR

The renting out of ejido land by migrant ejidatarios is particularly interesting since the agrarian law prohibited the abandoning or renting out of ejido plots for more than two consecutive years. Yet, migration became increasingly important in the lives of the ejidatarios and many rented out their land for many years in succession. As renting out the ejido plot was a risky situation migrants used to take several precautionary measures.

One precautionary measure was the payment of the ejido land tax. This tax was collected by the ejido treasurer and written down in a book. The ejidatarios received a receipt of payment. Although the amount of money paid was negligible, this tax acquired a different and very important role. It became a 'proof of land use'. People who rented out their land, insisted on paying the tax themselves as this was considered to be an important proof of their being in the ejido and working the land themselves. If, instead, the leaseholder paid the tax and had the receipts in his name, he could try and claim rights to the land at the SRA. Furthermore, in the case of an official investigation (for example, during an IUP), the payment of the land tax by the leaseholder would weaken the position of the migrated ejidatario. In addition to paying this land tax every year, the migrant ejidatarios also tried to be present at the IUP meeting in the ejido. When an IUP meeting was announced by the SRA, migrant ejidatarios in the United States were immediately informed by their relatives in La Canoa and, if possible, they would return from the United States. The migrant ejidatarios also tried to remain good friends with the ejido commissioner and paid officials if necessary. In this way, they would not make problems about their case.

For the official the migrant ejidatarios provided an interesting way to raise some extra money. They tried to strike deals with these ejidatarios in the sense of not making problems about the fact that they lived in the United States if they paid some money. However, the power of the official was limited. He depended on other ejidatarios and often on the ejido commissioner for information about ejidatarios who were living abroad. The following example illustrates this dynamic well.

Pedro Bautista
M: Did you never have problems with your land because of your residence in el Norte?
P: I never rented my land to others and never had problems. Only on one occasion. But I always paid the land tax. They could not take the land away from me. When there was an IUP meeting the commissioner always warned me and I came over from the USA. On one occasion I was warned by Pedro Montaño, who was commissioner in Vista Hermosa at that time. He said that this time things looked very bad for migrated ejidatarios with the IUP. He told me to be present at the IUP meeting in Vista Hermosa [a neighbouring ejido] in order to be better prepared for the meeting in La Canoa. I went to the IUP meeting in Vista Hermosa and heard all the problems there. After the meeting we went to Pedro's house together with the SRA official. The official asked me: 'How long have you lived in the USA?' I said: 'Five years.' He said: 'Don't you know that that is prohibited?' I said: 'Yes, but I also know that we have the obligation to maintain our family.' The official said that he could arrange the matter if I gave him 10,000 pesos. I told him that I did not have that amount of money. He said: 'How can I believe that, after five years in the US, you do not have this money?' I answered him that even if I did have the money I would not give it to him, as there was no reason to do so. When I left to go home, the official followed me and told me where I could leave him the money. But I did not pay.
M: And what happened finally when he arrived at the IUP meeting in La Canoa?
P: Nothing, I thought that he would cause me trouble, but nothing happened. The same happened when Davíd [an official of the assistance office of the SRA in Autlán] came to do the IUP.
M: When was that?
P: That was when Ignacio Romero was commissioner (1985–88). At the meeting in which they checked the land titles Davíd did not say anything about my case. But after the meeting Davíd told Ignacio to tell me to come to Autlán on a certain day and time. Ignacio said that they were threatening to take the land away from me. I did not go to see Davíd. Three days later Ignacio and Davíd visited me at my house. I said that I did not want to talk to Davíd as he only wanted money and I did not intend to pay any money. Davíd said: 'You don't live here.' I said: 'No, but that is something that cannot be avoided. I am still a Mexican and was never nationalised in the USA.' We were quarrelling like that for an hour. Then I said: 'Is it money that you want?' Davíd said that he did not want money. I said: 'I have been ejidatario for more than 50 years. I always paid my tax. If you think you can take the

land away from me, try it. But in that case I will lodge an official complaint about what you are doing here.' I was already retired from my job in the USA then. I have never heard anything about it. I know they cannot do anything against me. I have my ejido certificate.

Although Pedro likes to stress that he never paid anything to avoid trouble, other ejidatarios told me that Pedro always paid the ejido commissioners to keep him informed about what was going on and to support him at the IUP meetings. Pedro's situation was less risky than that of other migrated ejidatarios as most of the time he himself came over to till the land in La Canoa or his sons managed the land. Also, the fact that he always came over to be present at the IUP meetings made his position much stronger.

The renting out of ejido plots by migrants was not only a risky endeavour because the migrant infringed the law, but also because the leaseholder was building personal rights to the plot. The person who rented and tilled the same ejido plot for several years, legally acquired rights to this plot (the land belonged to the person who tilled it). Hence, these renting arrangements could turn the leaseholder into a personal enemy of the migrant ejidatario. This becomes clear in the following example.

A leaseholder tries to acquire the rights to an ejido plot
In the 1960s Daniel Fábregas started renting 2.5 hectares of rainfed land from Ignacia Hernández, a widow who lived in the United States with all her children. When Daniel died, his sons continued renting Ignacia's land. Before dying Daniel had told his wife Aurora García: 'That land is yours, don't let anybody take it away from you!' Every year Ignacia came to the village to agree on the renting arrangement and pay the land tax. However, Aurora had twice paid the tax before Ignacia arrived in the village and Ignacia had been furious about it.

When Ricardo García, Aurora's brother became commissioner (1970–73), Ricardo told Aurora that he could easily dispossess Ignacia of her land rights and pass these to Aurora or one of her sons. They decided to start a formal procedure at the SRA to start this process. Aurora found herself in a good position. She had worked the land for many years, she had paid the tax several times, and she had the support of the ejido commissioner. However, Ignacia was not prepared to lose the land and she fought back. Among other things, she claimed that she had been living in the village all these years. As tensions between the families in the village rose and things seemed to get out of hand, Aurora told her sons not to put any more efforts into the case.

By not putting any more efforts into the conflict, and by stopping their dealings with the SRA bureaucracy, it was most probable that Aurora would lose the case, especially as Ignacia actively negotiated with the SRA officials. In 1973 the SRA issued an official decision in which Ignacia was indeed recognised in her rights to the plot. So, Ignacia kept the land.

After having won the case Ignacia and her sons worked the land themselves for three consecutive years. They obviously did not want to run any more risks with renting arrangements. Later Ignacia sold the land to another ejidatario. As will be discussed later on, sale of ejido land was a safer option than renting the land out. Aurora regretted the affair very much as she would have preferred to continue renting the land or, even better, buy the land. For several years the two families did not speak to each other. However, now relations have been normalised and they even visit each other again.

The migrated ejidatarios were well aware of the danger presented by the leaseholder and, for that reason, they were very careful to whom they rented their land. They often left a relative in charge of the land. The other ejidatarios followed the strategy of not causing problems. As long as they were not involved as a potential beneficiary and knew that it was very improbable that the land of the migrated ejidatario would be allotted to them, they would not start any trouble. So, no objections were ever made in the majority of renting arrangements by migrants.

THE INHERITANCE OF LAND AND THE LAW

The Agrarian Law left the ejidatarios relatively free in the choice of their heir and only made the restriction that the plot could not be divided and that the right to use the plot had to be left to one heir from amongst their partner and children. What happened is that inheritance practices developed which are strongly embedded within the ideology of the family. Ejido land tenure is seen as a form of private property, but also as family patrimony within patriarchally organised families. There is a strong feeling that the 'owner' of the land has certain moral obligations to take good care of the land and make sure that it will be there for his or her children. Land and the inheritance of land are used to keep continuity in the family.

The fact that so many factors influence inheritance decisions and that no fixed inheritance pattern exists, is reflected in the inheritances between 1942 and 1993. Although many people tend to give a common rule for inheritance – such as: 'The custom here is that the youngest son inherits the land' – the study showed a great variety in types of inheritance. Eighty-one per cent of all inheritances were not from father to youngest son! So taking this as a general rule would give a very distorted view.

Mutual obligations of care between parents and children influence the choice of the heir and ensure that there is no fixed person in the family with a 'natural right' to inherit the land. This can make the inheritance of land a long-lasting process in which any new development may lead to a change of the heir. As Sabean points out, 'property can focus attention and create expectations, provide opportunities to exhibit skill and character, and establish connections and co-operation or points of resentment and disruption' (Sabean 1990: 33).

Inheritance is a sensitive subject, which is often not openly discussed within the family. Although there may be a lot of speculation and gossip, it is considered to be a decision of the ejidatario him or herself which is not open to discussion among siblings and their parents. Although inheritance decisions may cause tensions, expectations, frictions, disappointments and joys among 'would-be heirs'; we may find the same feelings among testators. Many ejidatarios have great difficulties in deciding on the heir of their property. When I asked people about inheritance customs in La Canoa, many said that the custom was that the youngest son inherits the land except when he could be described by the phrase '*no sirve*'. Then another son inherits. This '*no sirve*' generally means that the man in question does not work and spends his money on women and alcohol. In other words, men who are considered to be irresponsible. People are afraid that they will sell the land and prefer another heir instead. The increasingly transnationalised lives of ejidatarios and their children only seems to make the inheritance question more complex.

The notion that the land is family patrimony and that it should be used to maintain and support the different members of the family and not just one means that many ejidatarios want to leave their plot to more than one child. So, the official rule that only one person could inherit the right to use a plot causes certain tensions. If the land is left to one son, he is often made to promise that he will look after the other brothers and sisters once the parents have passed away. For the same reason, the land is also often passed from the husband to the wife, who can continue looking after the land for the benefit of the whole family. F. and K. von Benda-Beckmann talk in this respect of 'the social continuity function of inherited property' which 'instils a sense of responsibility to guard and maintain the property' (F. and K. von Benda-Beckmann 1998: 18). Inheritance by a wife may be seen as the postponement of the transfer to the next generation. Often it is not clear yet who will be the most appropriate heir to the land in the future and then the land can better remain with the longest-living partner. This explains why the number of women ejidatarias has grown considerably between 1942 and 1993. Of the first group of 77 ejidatarios, 5 (6 per cent) were women, whereas of the 97 ejidatarios today, 21 (22 per cent) are women. Most women have become an ejidataria by inheriting the land of their husband. At the transfer to the next generation, the land normally returns to a man, as parents prefer a son to inherit the land.

Before 1992 the ejidatarios had to go to the offices of the SRA to register or change the designated heir. There they had to deliver a letter, which had to be signed by the majority of ejidatarios, and signed and stamped by the ejido commissioner. Although this was an easy procedure, many officials tried to make it more complicated and asked money from the ejidatarios. One of the officials of the *promotoría* (regional office of the Ministry of Agrarian Reform) in Autlán, Davíd, was always prepared to help ejidatarios with their inheritance papers in exchange for large amounts of money.

In the case of ejidatarios who possessed several plots, these were often transferred to different children and this transfer often started when the ejidatario was still alive. This happened when the ejidatario was warned that the Agrarian Law prohibited the possession of more than one plot and that plots might be taken away from him. Some plots were then put in names of one or more sons.

Through these practices, land could be divided among different sons from one generation to the next. This partly explains the growth in the number of ejidatarios in La Canoa from 1942 to 1993 (see Chapter 2). I will illustrate this with the example of an ejidatario who left part of his land to two of his sons during his life and left his remaining land to another son. This case also gives insights into the many elements, which influence the choice of an heir, and the problems the change of heir may cause within the family.

Julio Pradera: building up inheritance rights by looking after the parents
Julio Pradera possessed two plots of land, one of 1 hectare and another one of 3.5 hectares. Julio had seven sons and two daughters. His two oldest sons received land themselves at the founding of the ejido. However, the other five sons remained landless. At a certain moment Julio decided to give the 1 hectare to two of his landless sons. Federico, another landless son, would inherit the remaining plot of 3.5 hectares and was registered as the heir of his father's land.

All sons married and the youngest son Manuel stayed with his parents, working their land. Manuel married and his wife came to live in the parental house. When Julio fell ill, he told Manuel that he wanted him to have the land as he was taking care of him and his mother. So, Manuel went to the SRA office in Autlán and arranged the papers to change the heir from Federico to himself. The papers were signed by Julio, a majority of ejidatarios and were to be signed and stamped by the executive committee of the ejido. Then the papers were sent to Guadalajara. Federico, who heard that he had been removed as heir of Julio's land, was furious.

When his father died, Manuel continued working the land as he had been doing for many years already. Manuel was well aware of the fact that now that his father had passed away, he could recover the 1 hectare that his father had given to two other brothers, as this formed part of the possession of his father. But Manuel said that he would not act against the will of his father. These two brothers in the end sold their land. Yet the buyer of the land realised that Manuel was the legitimate owner of the land and could cause him problems in the future. So he went to Manuel and asked him if he agreed to the sale. Manuel told him that he agreed to it because their father had given them this plot of land and it was their responsibility. Manuel did not sign any document concerning the land. It was very much a question of trust between Manuel and the buyer. If Manuel later claimed that the land had been his and that he had not agreed to the sale, the buyer would have had a difficult time trying to keep the land. As in the majority of land sales, no problem was ever made about it.

However, other problems came up. The ejido commissioner at that time told Federico that he could easily take the land away from Manuel and pass it to Federico. He told Federico to pay the ejido contribution for his father's land. He suggested that this would help him in the struggle to get the land transferred to his name. Federico started procedures to get the land and paid the commissioner and an official who was helping him for their efforts. Manuel went to see the ejido treasurer. He managed to get the name on the tax payment changed and from then on he paid the tax. Federico was angry and stopped speaking to Manuel for years. Federico let the case rest. After a time, Federico started talking to Manuel again and relations have been normalised.

In the case of Julio we notice several considerations that play a role in the choice of heirs and the transfer of land rights to the next generation. The fact that Manuel had looked after his parents for a long time up to their death, gave him certain rights to his father's land. Although it is logical that his elder brother was very disappointed at being removed as the heir of the land after having been registered as the heir all those years, he did not have a strong case. Moral principles played a role in the decision of Manuel to respect his father's decision to give part of the land to two of his brothers. This division of lands had already taken place a long time before his father's death, so everybody had been used to this situation and accepted it. For the same reason, out of respect for his father, Manuel accepted the fact that his two brothers decided to sell this land. Although he did not agree at all with their decision. The one who took most risks at this land sale was the buyer. However, he accepted Manuel's word that he would not make problems about it. Manuel is a very respected man in the village and this oral agreement offered enough security to proceed with the purchase of the land. What we find here is a complex combination of moral rights and obligations, locally developed inheritance practices and the influence of formal rules and procedures. This complex combination of elements can be found in many inheritances and can lead to different outcomes.

The following example also illustrates expectations and quarrels around an inheritance. Here the inheritance from grandfather to grandson is cancelled by the interference of a father who wants to secure the future position of a disabled son. The aggrieved son decides to accept his father's decision even though he knows that his father is acting illegally and he could easily win a formal case against his father. In this example, elements of care among relatives also play a central role in inheritance decisions.

Claudio Núñez: assuring the future of a disabled son

After Claudio Núñez became a widower, he went to live with one of his four daughters in Autlán. Hence, this daughter expected to inherit Claudio's land. However, Iginio, Claudio's only son, insisted on his father coming to live with him in La Canoa, and Claudio spent his last years there. During the last years of his life, Claudio was an invalid and needed a lot of care. Iginio's wife caringly looked after him. In 1992 Claudio died and a delicate situation arose about the inheritance of his land: almost 7 hectares of irrigated land and 4 hectares of rainfed land.

Years before his death Claudio Núñez had made his will. He had told his children that Joaquín, one of Iginio's sons, would be the heir to his land. Another arrangement was made as well. An oral agreement was made between Claudio, Joaquín, a daughter of Claudio, and a nephew that, although Joaquín would officially inherit all the land, he would leave 1 hectare to this aunt and nephew. Joaquín, who inherited his grandfather's land when his grandfather died in 1992, was 23 years old, single and preoccupied with the establishment of a workshop in the village. The land his grandfather left him was very welcome to him. Joaquín started to develop a serious interest in ejido affairs and started attending the ejido meetings.

However, it soon became clear that Iginio had other intentions for the land that Joaquín had inherited. Iginio wanted this land for another of his five sons, Antonio. Antonio is ill and has always helped his father in the field. Iginio and his wife know that Antonio will never be able to do anything other than work on the land and that he will probably never marry. Hence, they wanted Antonio to inherit the land as a form of insurance. In this way he would at least be able to maintain himself when his parents passed away. So, Iginio decided to change the papers and make Antonio the heir to Claudio's land instead of Joaquín. Joaquín's dreams of becoming an ejidatario vanished. Although Joaquín felt bad about his father changing the inheritance papers, he also understood his father's concern for Antonio. Furthermore, he decided not to challenge his father's authority. However, he did not agree with the way his father was operating:

My grandfather left the land to me, but there was more. We had made a promise to leave 1 hectare or more of this land to my aunt and nephew. My father was against this, as my aunt always behaved very badly. But, to be honest, my cousin never did anything bad, only my aunt. This agreement was made between my grandfather, my father, my aunt, and me. I loved my grandfather very much and always listened to him. He liked that very much; somebody who listened to him. Perhaps that was the reason that he left the land to me. If I was another type of person I could claim the land and my father could not do anything about it. But if this is the way my father wants it ... if my brother needs it ...

Although Joaquín accepted his father's decision, he felt extremely frustrated about the whole affair. A short time later, Joaquín suddenly left the village and found work in Las Vegas.

We saw that property 'marks periods of transition between generations, demarcates areas of competence, and creates bonds of dependence' within the family (Sabean 1990: 33). The different principles that guide inheritance practices offer flexibility but also cause difficulties and tensions for ejidatarios as well as their children. In conclusion, in the inheritance practices ideas about the land as family patrimony, and mutual care and obligation between parents and children, are most important. These notions, which guide the inheritance decision, can lead to many different outcomes in the ultimate choice of an heir. Family relations are complex and can change over time. In an increasingly transnational context, sometimes contradictory consider-ations are taken into account in the choice of an heir (trying to get children back to the village through inheritance or, on the contrary, favouring children in the village). Thus inheritance is a source of tremendous tension within families and can strongly influence relations between different family members.

ORGANISING PRACTICES WITHIN AN ILLEGAL LAND MARKET

Between 1942 and 1993, 29 plots have been sold in La Canoa. Many of these sales concern only parts of ejido plots. As yet, ejido plots have always been sold to people within the community, that is to say to sons, brothers or sisters of ejidatarios. Hence, it was an internal land market. People 'from outside' have never bought land in the ejido.

According to the Agrarian Law, the ejidatario who sold his plot, as well as the person who bought the plot, would lose the right to the land. Although this certainly was a threatening prospect, the fact that both parties infringed the law and could lose their rights meant that they would be careful not to make problems about the issue. This is in contrast to renting arrangements, in which the leaseholder was building up rights to the land at the expense of the migrant ejidatario.

Many ejidatarios had mixed feelings about the sale of ejido plots, mainly because land was considered to be family patrimony. The ejidatario as the official 'owner' of his or her plots was not considered to be the only person with rights to the land. According to most ejidatarios, the other members of the ejidatario's household – his wife, his children and even grandchildren – had certain rights to the land. For that reason, the ejidatarios and other villagers heavily condemned ejidatarios who sold their land without any urgent need for money, especially when they left their partner or children without land. In the same way, people often felt ashamed about the fact that they had sold a piece of land in the past.

However, despite this moral judgement on ejido land sales, ejidatarios did not interfere in the transactions of others. A strong sense of individual responsibility reigned and if somebody wanted to sell, the others would not make it impossible. They would gossip about it and criticise the ejidatario who had decided to sell his land, but they would not interfere. This attitude of the other ejidatarios was very important for the people involved in the land sale, for they needed the approval of the ejido assembly for the transfer of the ejido land right from one person to another. Notions of honour also played an important role with respect to land sales and the support of the other ejidatarios. The common view was that if people had agreed on a transaction they should not go back on it later. So people who later on tried to recover land that they had sold in the past could not count on the support of the other ejidatarios. As we will see, this support of the majority of the ejidatarios could be crucial in a land conflict.

Nevertheless, because of this ever present 'menace' of the Agrarian Law, which prohibited land sales, people tried to 'formalise' their illegal arrangements in a way that made it look like a permitted transaction. In this way they hoped to be safe in the future if someone created problems. Land sales were formally presented as a 'voluntary transfer of use rights' from one person (the seller) to the other (the buyer). The majority of ejido members had to agree to the 'voluntary transfer' of the land and signed a document. (They always knew that it concerned a sale.) There were additional ways to protect the sale. One was to put the new owner down as the successor of the one who was going to sell. In this way, one avoided officially registered heirs claiming their rights at a later stage.[2] Likewise, it was important that the partner of the ejidatario who sold the land signed his or her agreement with the 'transfer of rights', as well as their children. This was important since if an ejidatario 'transferred his rights' without the permission of the rest of the family, the sons or wife could later on try to claim the land. The above-mentioned elements were all very usual but there were no fixed common rules in this respect. There are for example, people who sold ejido land without informing the ejido assembly or asking permission, or without putting the buyer down as their successor. Others sold land without the permission of their wives. These arrangements were more risky and led in some cases to problems at a later stage.

Apart from these formal precautions, it was helpful to assure the favourable attitude of officials of the SRA, so that they would not make problems about the sale. Therefore, they were often paid a certain amount of money 'to keep quiet'. These functionaries of the SRA often were actively involved in the sales, as they knew the working of the bureaucracy better than anyone else, and the best way to arrange and formalise these transactions. When we look at what eventually happened with land transfers in La Canoa, we see the following. The great majority of illegal transactions was never mentioned or reported in the formal arena. Ejido land sales in La Canoa were never cancelled, although on several occasions people have tried to cancel them in a formal procedure.

I will now relate in detail the history of a sale of an ejido plot in the 1960s in La Canoa. The case illustrates how people bypassed the law, how ejidatarios and officials were all involved in these arrangements, and how disagreements were fought out. Although several ejido plots have been sold in La Canoa, this case is the one most commented upon by the ejidatarios, as it is one of the few cases in which the former owners tried to cancel the sale at a later stage.

A FAMOUS LAND CONFLICT IN LA CANOA

In the beginning of the 1960s there were serious problems in La Canoa. One of the Sánchez men had killed a son of Juan García in a conflict over cattle that had damaged crops in a field. People in La Canoa were disconcerted by the murder and a hostile attitude developed towards the Sánchez family. Speculations circulated about possible revenge by the influential García family. In this atmosphere of hostility Mario Sánchez, a brother of the murderer, decided to sell his ejido land, leave the village with his wife and children, and establish himself in another region. Gustavo Romero, who was ejido commissioner at that time, wanted to buy the land. The sale of the ejido plot took place in 1962. The fact that Gustavo was commissioner obviously helped him in the purchase of the ejido plot. However, what was more important than his being ejido commissioner was the help he received from his uncle Miguel Romero. Miguel knew how the SRA functioned and had several influential contacts.

As usual with the sale of ejido plots, the sale was formally presented as a voluntary transfer of the right to use the plot. As the law does not allow the possession of two use rights by one person, Gustavo decided to register the plot he bought in the name of his son Raúl. To 'play safe' Gustavo furthermore asked Mario to put Raúl formally down as the heir of his agrarian right. As Mario had no successor registered for his land, this was easy to arrange. At the ejido meeting where the transfer of the ejido right from Mario to Gustavo had to be approved, all the ejidatarios knew that the 'transfer' concerned the sale of an ejido plot. A majority of ejidatarios was present at the meeting and signed the document. Mario and his wife both signed their agreement to the transfer of Mario's agrarian right. After the meeting the papers were sent to the offices of the SRA in Guadalajara and Mexico City. Gustavo was the new 'owner' of the land, which was registered in his son's name. Mario left with his family for the coast of Jalisco.

Years later Mario and his wife separated and Mario's wife, Angela and their sons tried to recover the land. They came to Gustavo's house several times to talk about it, but Gustavo made it clear to them that nothing could be done about it anymore. Angela and her children then decided to go to the SRA in Mexico City. The efforts of Angela at the different offices of the SRA had had some results as became clear at the IUP that was held in La Canoa in 1974. Mauro, the functionary of the SRA who came to La Canoa to carry out the IUP, had Gustavo listed as the illegal invader of the land that he had bought. Mauro told the ejido commissioner Rubén García this, the day before he was to come and do the IUP. Rubén immediately informed Gustavo about it and Rubén and Gustavo decided to go straight away to Autlán that evening to talk to the functionary.

Rubén and Gustavo arrived at the *promotoría* of the SRA in Autlán. They were told that Mauro had gone to the movies. Gustavo and Rubén went directly to the cinema and told the girl at the entrance to go and get the functionary. This act is significant as it shows a particular style of dealing with the bureaucracy and gives an indication of Gustavo's status. Gustavo is a self-confident entrepreneur, conscious of his position and prepared to strike a deal. His attitude contrasts with that of many ejidatarios who characteristically display a frightened, over-respectful attitude, and would not do anything that might disturb a functionary. By this act it also immediately became clear to Mauro that Gustavo had the support of local powerholders, such as the ejido commissioner, who accompanied him. According to Gustavo, Mauro came outside and Gustavo introduced himself and the commissioner. Rubén then explained to Mauro what had been going on with the land and the problem that Angela was causing Gustavo. They then took Mauro out for dinner. Some days later, when the meeting of the IUP was held in La Canoa, the sale of the land came up. Mauro told the ejidatarios that the transfer of land right was totally in order and he told Angela that she had better leave.

According to Gustavo, he and Mauro ended as good friends after he had taken Mauro out for dinner in Autlán. Gustavo claims that he only took Mauro out for dinner in gratitude and definitely does not see this as a form of payment. Gustavo has developed a way of dealing with officials in which, according to him, he 'does not pay' but 'knows how to treat them' and in this way attains his ends.

The Official Settlement of the Conflict: Social Networks and the Law

In the archives of the SRA, I found several documents referring to this land dispute. Angela managed to open the case before the IUP meeting and for that reason the case was registered on the IUP list as an illegal land invasion by Gustavo. After the IUP meeting, which clearly had an unfavourable outcome for Angela, she lodged a complaint at the SRA against Gustavo and Mauro together. She said that they had been conspiring together against her interests. She tried several ways to attain her ends. She used lawyers, went to different offices of the SRA and even wrote a letter to the Mexican president. These are common practices: to pursue the case through different 'entrances' and via different channels and a letter to the Mexican president is always popular (the only thing that happens to these letters is that they are channelled to the offices of the SRA).

In the official documents, Angela never referred to the sale of the land, as she had obviously known about it and had even signed her agreement to it. In this way she herself had infringed the law. Therefore, she tried to recover the land on the basis of other arguments. First, she blamed Gustavo (as he was the one who tilled the land) for invading the land that belonged to her husband. At a later stage she accused Raúl (the officially registered ejidatario) of not living in the ejido. Nevertheless, the resolving departments of the SRA decided in favour of Raúl on the basis of two arguments. First, that, according to the ejido assembly, he had been in peaceful possession of the land for more than twelve years. Second, that Raúl had officially been registered as Mario's heir.

When we look at 'the facts' of this land sale in terms of the law, the situation is clear. According to the law, Gustavo would not only have lost the land he bought, but also the ejido land he already possessed. By entering into the illegal act of buying ejido land and another illegal act of monopolising ejido plots, he would lose all his ejido rights to the land. The seller Mario would also forever lose his rights to ejido lands as well as his wife who had signed her agreement to the transfer. Mario and Gustavo's plots would return to the ejido community and the general assembly could grant the land to others.

Yet, the 'facts' were never revealed in the presentation of the conflict at the SRA. In the documents I found about this case, no comment is ever made about the illegal character of the land transfer between Mario and Raúl. So, the official presentation and resolution of land disputes give a very distorted view of what really happened. People with experience can, to a certain degree, 'read through' the official language and documents and deduce the real version of the events. Every official of the SRA, for example, understands that a voluntary land transfer between non-relatives most probably signifies a sale of land.

However, even if the sale had been denounced, Gustavo would not have had his rights to the land taken away easily. He had the support of the general assembly of the ejido at the local level. However, certain practices had also developed within the SRA, that ejidatarios who had sold their land should not go back on it. Furthermore, the SRA did not easily go against the will of the ejido assembly even though it had a right to do so. This means that certain organising practices had also developed within the SRA itself which went against the Agrarian Law and which gave great power to the local ejido assemblies (even in covering illegal transactions). So, if the assembly said that a certain transaction concerned a voluntary transfer of ejido rights, this was accepted by the SRA. Normally, the SRA did not interfere with decisions taken about individual ejido rights by the assembly, nor did it check information provided by the assembly. In this case, the assembly had declared (supporting Gustavo) that Raúl had been in possession of this land since 1962. Whether this was true or not was not investigated. Angela's statement that Raúl lived in the United States did not make a difference. It was her statement against that of the majority of ejidatarios who had said differently. This enormous influence of the local ejido assembly in land affairs implied that people with much support or control at the local ejido level could barely be 'touched' by the agrarian bureaucracy. By way of conclusion, we can say that a combination of Gustavo's influence at the local level, his use of legal forms and his clever dealings with the bureaucracy guaranteed his illegal transaction.

Sales in the 'New Way'

The new Agrarian Law, which was issued in 1992, allows the sale of ejido plots. Actually, this is an adaptation to reality as land had already become a commodity in most ejidos throughout Mexico. However, before the ejidatarios are allowed to sell the land, the individual plots of the ejido have to be officially measured and registered. Yet, the interesting thing is that the ejidatarios did not wait for their plots to be measured but immediately reacted to this new law by organising the land sales in a 'new way'. They no longer talked about a transfer of right, nor asked the consent of the ejido assembly, nor did they put the buyer as the heir of the seller. Ejidatarios who wanted to sell their plot directly went to a notary or a lawyer to draw the acts of a land sale. One of the first men who wanted to buy an ejido plot in La Canoa after the change of the Agrarian Law, was Ignacio Fábregas. Ignacio and the ejidatario who sold his plot decided to let the lawyer handle the sale, which took place at the office of a notary. To be on the safe side, they invited the ejido commissioner to come as well and sign the document. So, this time neither the ejido assembly, nor the SRA was involved in the transaction. This quick adaptation to a new reality is interesting because, according to the Agrarian Law these new transactions would only be allowed in the future, when the plots had been measured. However, ejidatarios, as well as officials and lawyers, realised that nobody would cancel this new type of sale.

This shows that new legislation will never affect existing practices in a direct way. As F. and K. von Benda-Beckmann point out 'new legislation ... *interferes* with existing property rules and property relationships. Whatever effects the introduction of new property forms may have, they will always be shaped by the historically grown property regimes' (F. and K. von Benda-Beckmann 1998: 2). Most ejidatarios preferred these new rules, as now they no longer needed the consent of the ejido assembly, or the assistance of SRA officials who always asked for money. Since the new law was issued several plots have been sold in La Canoa, but during the period of my research (until mid-1995) no important changes in the ejido land market had occurred.

CONCLUSION: MULTIPLE FORCE FIELDS AND THE ROLE OF THE LAW

We noticed the development of different force fields around the renting out of land by migrants, the selling of plots and the inheritance of land. With respect to ejido land sales, a patterning of organising practices developed which went very much against the 'letter' and the 'spirit' of the Agrarian Law. One element which helped the ejidatarios 'keep the law at a distance' was the fact that the SRA did not keep a register of individual ejido plots and had no means of controlling the use and distribution of plots. Therefore the SRA officials were in a weak position. They were totally dependent on information from ejidatarios, and could only act in cases where someone wanted to start a conflict with another ejidatario.

Although the Agrarian Law was seldom applied it had considerable influence as a 'distant threat'. As far as possible, ejidatarios tried to organise their illegal transactions according to the accepted procedures and in this way hoped to avoid problems in the future. Several organising practices developed as precautionary measures (paying the ejido land tax, coming over from the USA for the IUP meetings, and paying officials and commissioners). The fact that transactions were always carried out 'in the shadow of the law' (F. von Benda-Beckmann 1992) meant that the legal agrarian rules remained a powerful weapon in negotiations and bargaining, even when affairs were settled according to other criteria. This can be called the 'bargaining endowment' which is constituted by state law even when the law is not applied (Galanter 1981). This situation created some room for officials to earn some extra money, but without their having any real effect on what happened to the land.

If an illegal transaction or a conflict case was formally denounced at the SRA and officials became involved, it was not at all clear what would happen. Official documents could easily get 'lost' or procedures be delayed for years. The official bureaucratic world was quite obscure. However, the formal settlement of land conflicts was hardly ever followed to its conclusion. People who felt that they would lose a case, or who feared that it would end in a dirty fight with negative consequences for their personal life, often decided to withdraw from the case in the middle of the process and before a formal decision was taken.

As the SRA has many different offices and a complex organisational structure, ejidatarios often went to many different offices to find officials who were willing to help them. If they were not heard or listened to at one office, they used to go to another to see if they might have better luck there. The notion of 'forum-shopping' for situations in which disputants shop for forums for their problems and forums compete for disputes is applicable to this situation (K. von Benda-Beckmann 1981: 117). The bureaucratic labyrinth of the SRA offers countless entrances. One never knows what the best 'forum' is and where it will finally lead.

Another phenomenon, which we saw in Gustavo's case and which is common in land conflicts, is 'playing the game' at different levels. Local-level relations in the ejido are crucial but we also noticed the necessity of arranging things in Guadalajara and the desire to settle problems at 'the centre' in Mexico City. Often it is not clear whether this is really necessary. For example, for the registration of inheritance papers and assignment of rights, it is sufficient to go to the state capital Guadalajara. From there information is sent to Mexico City. However, people think that the offices in Mexico City are the 'higher' and therefore the more 'powerful' ones. This looking for 'the centre' or the 'highest office' is also a consequence of the obscure workings of the bureaucracy.

What is interesting is that this led to a situation in which procedures and documents acquired meanings which had little relation to their official function. For example, the IUP, a procedure to check on ejido land use, turned into a procedure for the legalisation of illegal transactions and the formalisation of legal actions which had not followed the official procedures. The numbered ejido certificate took on an important symbolic value for the ejidatarios, even though it did not bear a 'real' relation to their plot and their security of land possession rested on the recognition of their fellow ejidatarios. The receipt of ejido tax payment became a 'proof of residence' in the ejido (in the case of migrants), instead of a proof of payment. This phenomenon, in which official documents and procedures acquire different meanings, is what I call the re-enchantment of governmental techniques (cf. Comaroff and Comaroff 1993). It also shows the limitation of perspectives focusing on govern-mentality. Certainly, we find a complex aggregate of institutions and procedures. We find a great deal of official paperwork, many complicated procedures, stamping, taxing and so on. However, this does not lead to a 'strong state' or 'powerful bureaucracy', which exercises control over ejidatarios. On the contrary, we find ejidatarios with great autonomy and freedom in their land transactions and a state-bureaucracy with very little control over local land issues.

In conclusion, we see that the ejidatarios had acquired a considerable degree of autonomy with respect to the parcelled land. In fact, the illegal land transactions were organised and 'legalised' in close cooperation with the agrarian bureaucracy, giving rise to a shadow world of procedures and the re-invention of governmental techniques.[3] The fact that people acquired considerable security in land possession is ironic in the light of the new Agrarian Law, which was introduced with the argument that the measuring and registration of individual ejido plots and the issuing of individual property titles would finally give the ejidatarios legal security. A strong form of legal security had already developed without land titles and without registration by the state.

5 THE 'LOST LAND'
I: THE PRIEST AND THE LAWYER

INTRODUCTION: LAND CONFLICTS AND THE 'IDEA OF THE STATE'

In this chapter and the next I follow the struggle for the 'lost land' of La Canoa, in which the ejidatarios try to recover land that belongs to their ejido but which is in possession of several private landowners. For over 50 years the ejidatarios have tried to recover this land and have demanded that the Ministry of Agrarian Reform (SRA) resolve this conflict, but, without significant results so far.

The land conflict of La Canoa is not a special case. The legal status of a lot of land in Mexico remains ambiguous and land conflicts can linger on for decades without resolution. In fact, this phenomenon attracts little academic attention and many people told me that it was not worth paying much attention to this conflict, as it is improbable that the ejidatarios will ever recover the land. Yet, what fascinated me was that the ejidatarios went on for many years and spent so much energy and money on a case that they themselves on many occasions said that they are doomed to lose. Why do ejidatarios go on fighting for something that is apparently impossible to achieve?

One way to account for this phenomenon would be to argue that such ejidatarios are simple-minded and stubborn figures who have no idea of the workings of the political-bureaucratic system. Yet, this goes against the fact that Mexicans are known to be very cynical about their own political system. Many studies (including large-scale surveys) have argued that the majority of Mexicans think that power is highly concentrated, that they do not expect to receive attention or equal treatment from the bureaucracy and the police, and that they are cynical about their own ability to influence political decisions (Almond and Verba 1980, Camp 1996, Cornelius and Craig 1980, 1991, Foweraker 1994). So how can we explain these continuing struggles in the light of this general distrust of the political system and the bureaucracy? Is it not that the mechanisms that make people go on with their struggle and that

91

forge expectations, dreams and fantasies, are central to power relations and the working of the state?

Imagining the Centre

In Chapter 1 I argued, following Abrams, that 'we should abandon the state as a material object of study whether concrete or abstract while continuing to take the idea of the state extremely seriously' (1988: 75). The ejidatarios themselves never talk about 'the state' and tend to use more decentred notions of power. They talk about *el gobierno* (the government), *los caciques* (local bosses), *los ricos* (the rich people), *los pequeños* (the private landowners), *los funcionarios* (the officials), *el presidente* (the president) and *nosotros, los pobres* (we, the poor people) in their reflections. Yet, on the other hand, the ejidatarios believe in the existence – somewhere – of a centre of control, which can help them settle their conflict over the 'lost land'. In other words, they search for the state in the form of 'a neutral arbiter above the conflicts and interests of society' (Alonso 1994: 381) or in the form of an influential figure (preferably the Mexican president) who is strong enough to make sure that the law is applied. This belief is what I call their 'idea of the state'.

As their dealings with the bureaucracy and politics are so frustrating and unsuccessful and do not seem to get them anywhere, ejidatarios look for intermediaries who are more capable than they are in dealing with the bureaucratic machine. At the same time, brokers present themselves to the ejidatarios as the right person to resolve their problems. Unlike traditional approaches on intermediation, I argue that brokers do not necessarily have a role in effectively connecting communities or peasants with the state, but that they play a central role in the imagining of state power. In the search for the 'right intermediary' and the presentation of themselves as the 'right connection', ejidatarios as well as brokers are implicated in the construction of the 'idea of the strong state'.

Becoming Enrolled in an Agrarian Conflict

What helped me in doing this research was the fact that I could return to La Canoa several times for long periods. In this way it was possible to establish enduring relationships with certain people. I became involved in this struggle through Lupe Medina, the treasurer of the ejido and the second wife of the late don Miguel. Lupe was a religious and independent woman who sometimes felt insecure in the male-dominated ejido world. She liked to talk to me, a woman outsider, about her problems and doubts in her private life and also with respect to the land conflict. As time passed, I became more and more integrated in the group that was fighting for the 'lost land' and also established good relationships with several of the men. Some of them liked talking to me as they wanted me to write down everything about the problems of La Canoa and – what they called – the widespread corruption in Mexico.

Towards the end of the research, my position in this group changed as they noticed that I worked in the SRA archives in Guadalajara and Mexico City and interviewed officials and lawyers about the case. They started seeing me as possibly useful. They asked me to accompany them on missions and visits to the SRA and other offices. When they noticed that I was treated in a different way and sometimes had more access to officials than they had, they gradually tried to position me in the role of broker or adviser and wanted me to talk to the officials. This changed my research to a certain extent. Instead of trying to find out their theories and feelings, it now became much more a form of dialogue in which my own position and theories also became involved. This change of position made it possible to express more clearly doubts about my own theories and theirs and confront them with – what I saw as – contradictions in their views or actions. In this way more 'dialogical' research relations were established (de Vries 1992: 70).

PREDICAMENT OF THE CONFLICT AND OBSCURE ENEMIES

The conflict of the 'lost land' dates from the establishment of the ejido in 1938. Certain lands that officially had to be transferred to La Canoa ended up in the hands of some private landowners. As can be seen on the map in Chapter 2, different tracts of land were involved in the conflict and they all have their own histories and specific legal agrarian aspects.

There were different ways in which people referred to – what I decided to call – the 'lost land'. The ejidatarios talked about 'the land below' as it belonged to the lower part of the ejido. Alternatively, they said 'the land of the *pequeños*' (meaning the private landowners), or more vaguely, 'that land' when they knew that the people present knew what they were talking about. So they used unspecific terms when they referred to this problem. Yet, when they were asked specific questions about this conflict they gave more detailed information and mentioned the names of the different fields (*potreros*) and landowners involved.

Most of the people who illegally possess parts of the 'lost land' live in Autlán. Some of them acquired the land in 1938, while others inherited the land or bought it at a later stage. One of the owners of the land is Ricardo García, who is also an ejidatario of La Canoa and lives in the village. Héctor Romero, a former head of the public security police in

Autlán and cousin of many Romeros in the village, also possesses a part of the 'lost land'. He is not a pleasant person to have as an enemy as the police in general have a very bad reputation in Mexico. Another unpleasant enemy who owns land of La Canoa, is the lawyer Salvador Mendoza. Lawyers are generally distrusted by the ejidatarios (as well as by many other Mexicans) but this is especially true in this case as he is associated with assassinations in the region. José Luna, head of the regional association of horticulture producers is another of the many people who today possess part of the 'lost land'. Most of these people are not really influential anymore within the regional elite. Ricardo García and José Luna both went bankrupt and have huge debts and serious problems. Héctor Romero is considered by other regional powerholders to be a bad politician and has retired as head of the security police. The lawyer Mendoza no longer lives in the region.

Obviously, these *pequeños propietarios* deny that they illegally possess the land and many of them said that they were tired of the continuing accusations of the ejido La Canoa. The ejidatarios realise that the way in which these men oppose the ejidatarios' attempt to get this matter resolved is by bribing the bureaucracy and through their political connections in Guadalajara and Mexico City. Besides money and politics, there is also the threat of violence. Although many people in La Canoa do not personally know their enemies, the stories about them give enough cause for speculation about the bloody revenge that could be expected if La Canoa were successful in their efforts to recover the land. Many people in the village have been murdered for lesser causes. Several ejidatarios say they have been threatened by the *pequeños* in the past.

Although the ejidatarios themselves did not mention General García Barragán as one of their main enemies in this conflict in the past (he died in 1979), I was particularly interested in knowing more about his role in this conflict. Several people told me that the unmarried sisters of the Michel family in Autlán, who are daughters of a famous regional *hacendado* family and who possess part of the 'lost land', gave the General a part of their land in exchange for his support in defending their position against La Canoa.

Although the ejidatarios speculate a lot about who is behind the conflict, they tend to talk in terms of anecdotes and seemingly isolated stories. Histories and analyses of power are highly fragmented. The point is that, although the influence of certain people at regional, state or national level may undoubtedly be present, the actual dynamics of power always remain highly opaque. Who is pulling the strings at different levels, and who influences the officials of the SRA at which moments remains unclear. Even if one could trace that an official had received personal instructions from the General to hinder the investigation of this conflict, this would only have been one anecdote amongst many in an endless struggle that has been going on for over 50 years. [1] However, this does not mean that people are not aware of influences or lack the capacity to see broader structures. On the contrary, we could say that sociological and anthropological analyses sometimes impose a coherence in power games that does not necessarily exist for the people involved. By imposing this artificial order, there is a tendency to neglect one of the most important aspects of power relations; namely, obscurity and opacity. These are central elements in the culture of the state and form part of the world in which people operate and theorise about what is going on.

The Other Enemy: the Ministry of Agrarian Reform

From the very moment the ejido was established, the ejidatarios have tried to acquire all the land the ejido is entitled to. They have repeatedly demanded that the SRA resolve this conflict. In reality, the conflict with the *pequeños propietarios* has turned into a conflict with the SRA about the non-resolution of the conflict. The struggle with the SRA has focused on two elements. First, they have requested that the SRA deliver the definitive map of their ejido. Although it may sound strange that the ejido has no map of its property this is quite common in Mexico. In the agrarian reform procedures were not always strictly followed or finished. Especially under Cárdenas (1934–40) priority was given to handing over the land instead of following of the procedures to the letter. For that reason, many ejidos in Mexico do not possess a definitive map of their lands. So the absence of a map was not necessarily an indication of border troubles or land invasions. However, in the case of La Canoa this map has special importance as it would indicate which lands belong to the ejido and where the *pequeños propietarios* are invading their land. In the second place, the ejidatarios have demanded that the SRA measure their lands according to two other official SRA documents which clearly indicate the borders of their ejido and the total number of hectares they should possess: namely the presidential resolution of the endowment (*Resolución Presidencial de la dotación*) and the act of possession and marking of boundaries (*acta de posesión y deslinde*). So far, their pressure on the SRA has had little result: they never received the map nor was their land ever measured. However, the SRA did not resolve the conflict in favour of the *pequeños propietarios* either. The conflict was simply never resolved. For the ejidatarios this meant that they kept hoping and fighting for what rightfully belonged to them. For the *pequeños propietarios* it meant that all these years they were confronted with accusations from the ejido and formal SRA procedures which they had to counter.

According to the ejidatarios the problem with the SRA is that the officials let themselves be bribed by the private landowners. The ejidatarios themselves are not against bribes, nor do they mind paying for the officials' services, but they feel that they can never pay as much as the *pequeños*. However, apart from possible corruption and bribing of officials, the opaque structure and procedures of the SRA already form an enormous obstacle for the ejidatarios. Without getting into the impressive organisational structure of the SRA we can say that many different delegations and offices within the SRA are involved in the case of the 'lost land' of La Canoa. While the division of the SRA in Guadalajara was relatively easy to handle as it was only one building with different offices, the SRA in Mexico City was a nightmare. In Mexico City the SRA has, since the earthquake of 1985, consisted of many different buildings spread out over the city. Each building is a labyrinth in itself.

Yet visiting the different offices was a necessary evil. It was always stressed that people had to go and put personal pressure on the officials. Letters and documents easily ended up in drawers and might never have been answered if the ejidatarios did not personally present themselves at the offices. The ejidatarios knew from experience that letters were never answered, or only many years after they had been sent or delivered. This left the ejidatarios little choice other than to go to the city. However, all these visits implied an enormous investment on the part of the ejidatarios. The trip from La Canoa to Guadalajara (via Autlán) took them approximately four hours. This means that they had to spend eight hours travelling if they wanted to make the trip in one day. In order to go to Mexico City, they first had to go to Guadalajara and then spend an additional eight hours on the bus to Mexico City: a trip of two days at least. Besides this time spent travelling, it was not easy for the people from the village to go to the metropolis. They were often taken advantage of by cab drivers and other people who immediately recognised *campesinos* (peasants) visiting the big city. In addition, they had to suffer humiliations at the hands of officials and others who often let them wait for hours or even days and treated them with contempt.

Besides the complex organisational structure, the agrarian procedures are complicated and the documents use a language which is often difficult to disentangle. Although I studied the agrarian laws and procedures, and received assistance from both within and outside the SRA, a great part of the documents and procedures remained incomprehensible to me. To a large extent they contained formalities and references to other documents and different delegations in the SRA. So I realised that, for ejidatarios who generally were not very experienced in reading and writing, these documents were impossible to decipher.

STORY-TELLING, MAPS AND MURDERS

There were many stories in the ejido about the 'lost land'. In these stories the late Miguel Romero played a central role. For example, Miguel Romero gave one tract of land that the ejido lost to his brother Javier when Miguel was ejido commissioner. He gave this land as a loan and on the condition that it had to be returned to the ejido afterwards. However, this land was passed on to several other people and parts were sold as private property. This land never returned to the ejido. Although this only concerns a part of the 'lost land', this is the story which was related most often by the ejidatarios. Iginio Núñez, for instance, remembered that when he was a young boy a surveyor from the SRA came to La Canoa and went to the fields with don Miguel. Iginio:

Several boys from the village accompanied them and I was one of them. When they were at the lands, the surveyor asked don Miguel: 'Do you agree that this was all ejido land?' Don Miguel answered: 'Yes.' Then the surveyor asked: 'And did you give all this to your brother?' Then don Miguel turned around and walked back to the village. He did not say a word anymore. From that moment onwards I knew what was going on.

The other tracts of land concerned properties which the ejido should have received but never had in its possession. In these cases it was much less clear what exactly happened and who was involved. However, as don Miguel was one of the founders of the ejido and for a long period was the most influential man in local politics, he was held responsible by many ejidatarios for these problems as well. On the other hand, don Miguel himself made many efforts to recover the lands and to get the definitive ejido map. Several of his sons were also very active in the fight for the 'lost land'.

The definitive map was a common theme in local story-telling. The ejido has many provisional maps and maps of the extension of the ejido, which do not help them any further. They need the definitive map of the endowment. Many speculations circulate about this map. Many ejidatarios say that this map, which clearly indicates the right ejido borders, existed in former times. Several claimed to have seen it. Others said that they never saw it but they knew that it existed. It was said, for example, that don Miguel had documents concerning the ejido, which he kept privately. He told his wife Lupe that, after his death, she should give these documents to the ejido commissioner. It was said that Lupe gave these documents to Ramón Romero and that later they disappeared. However, the only thing Lupe remembered was that one day her husband Miguel sat round the table with two of the sons from his first marriage. They had a map on the table and talked about the land. Lupe thought that perhaps this was the map they always had looked for, but she never saw it again.

There was another story that was often repeated, although in different versions. In this story it was said that many years ago don Miguel himself went to Mexico City to do something about this problem. The ejido had given him money to pay for the hotels, the food and everything, and Don Miguel left for 14 days to get the map. In one of the versions he returned to the ejido and said that he had lost the money. In another version he returned and told them that he had received the document but that he lost it on his way back. This story may refer to the same event or to different ones. But in both stories the conclusion is the same: don Miguel was given ejido money to get the central document and wasted it.

During certain periods, core groups developed in the ejido, which took up the fight, and then, when nothing was achieved, these groups dissolved again. A central figure in these groups was always the ejido commissioner. Without the support of the commissioner it was very difficult to work with the SRA, as it is the commissioner who has to sign all the ejido documents and who is the only legitimate representative of the ejido. Over the years, numerous ejidatarios of La Canoa have actively participated in this struggle. This includes ejidatarios who today do not want to continue with this struggle any longer. In this way, the 'lost land' has become important in shaping a collective memory of struggle even though at a particular point in time only a small number of ejidatarios were working on it. People who actively participated in missions to Guadalajara or Mexico City in former times, still like to recall those times. Stories go round that people only ate beans, or even stopped buying beans, in order to save money for these missions. Others remember how their father sold chickens or a pig in order to finance trips to Mexico City. It was said that the ejidatarios who went on missions sometimes hardly ate or only had water and a potato as they had no money to spend on food.

The period that was best remembered was that when Macario Paz was ejido commissioner (1976–79). He made serious efforts in the struggle for the 'lost land'. Macario himself migrated to the United States, but his wife Teresa still lives in the village. At that time, the ejidatarios received help from a lawyer of the Communist Party and most ejidatarios fighting for the 'lost land' became members of this party. The lawyer never asked them for any money and the ejidatarios could always stay at his home.

Teresa remembered above all the tensions and atmosphere of distrust at the time Macario was commissioner. The men going on mission were often threatened and, for that reason, they always went together to protect each other. During Macario's term as commissioner an SRA surveyor was sent to measure the ejido lands. This surveyor was recalled sympathetically by everybody. The ejidatarios protected him day and night. He was crippled and sometimes they had to carry him to certain parts. He worked well but he never finished the job. The ejidatarios have never seen him again. After some time the lawyer suddenly disappeared and, 20 days later, he was found dead in a ravine with bullet wounds. Then things slowed down. The ejidatarios tried to get help from other places, the CNC and the Liga de Comunidades Agrarias, but didn't achieve much in all those years. Teresa still keeps the little book in which she wrote down who cooperated with how much money during that period.

According to the ejidatarios, a problematic aspect of their struggle is that many people in the ejido are relatives or *compadres* of the private landowners who possess the 'lost land'. Most people are related to the Romeros or Garcías who possess part of these lands. For that reason, it is said, they will not go ahead with the fight. Furthermore, the people know that ejidatarios of La Canoa can also be bribed. For example, Ignacio Romero, who was ejido commissioner from 1985 to 1988 and had achieved a lot in the fight for the 'lost land', was accused of having been bribed by the *pequeños* with a plot of private land. Ignacio said that he bought the land, but several ejidatarios claimed that the land was given to him in exchange for stopping the fight against the *pequeños*. Hence, in their own reflections on this conflict, the case is extremely complicated. The ejidatarios have to fight rich, powerful and dangerous *pequeños propietarios*, corrupt bureaucrats and, last but not least, fellow ejidatarios who are on the side of the *pequeños* or let themselves be threatened or bribed. The ejidatarios knew that the situation was very difficult but the few cases in the coast of Jalisco in which ejidos managed to win land conflicts against private landowners were often mentioned to prove that it was possible to win against the 'rich and powerful'.

RESUMING THE FIGHT AGAINST THE *PEQUEÑOS* IN 1991

President Salinas's discourse on modernisation and his speeches on the eradication of corruption in the SRA had a considerable impact in La Canoa. The change of Article 27 of the Mexican Constitution and the Agrarian Law in 1992, and the accompanying programmes to register all ejido lands, were also well received. Although mixed feelings existed with respect to the plans to privatise ejido land, ejidatarios liked the fact that all the lands would be measured and that the ejido borders would now finally be established. At least, this was what the president had promised. Obviously, in the case of La Canoa the marking of boundaries had a special implication. It meant that a measuring would take place, which they had not been able to obtain in more than 50 years. They hoped that, in this way, the conflict with the *pequeños* would finally be settled in their favour. Especially the speeches by the president himself had a great impact on the ejidatarios. For example, one of the ejidatarios said:

> I think the problem will soon be resolved. President Salinas said that all the problems would be resolved in the last two years of his presidency. I cannot wait to see the changes. Let's see if the government is really going to help us!

Even people who had been very pessimistic about the possibility of ever recovering the 'lost land', now became amazingly optimistic.

A small group of ejidatarios who were motivated by Salinas's messages organised a *planilla* (slate of candidates) for the elections of the executive committee of the ejido in 1991. They had a clear agenda in mind and had organised the *planilla* with the aim of taking up the fight against the *pequeños* if they won the elections. Their *planilla* won by a large majority and so the way was opened for their project. We will follow this group from 1991 to 1994 and see that the strategies and the composition of the group changed several times. Interestingly, the central person in this three-year period became doña Lupe, the widow of the late don Miguel. Women had been active in ejido matters before. For example, Teresa, Macario's wife, had often participated in the meetings and the missions for the 'lost land' in the 1970s. However, this was the first time in the history of the ejido of La Canoa that a woman had such a dominant and public role in ejido matters. I will first present the members of the executive committee and discuss their position with respect to the 'lost land' when they took office in 1991.

Raúl Pradera: Ejido Commissioner Against his Will

Raúl was not very enthusiastic about being a candidate for ejido commissioner in the 1991 elections. He was a shy, not very decisive person and, like the majority of ejidatarios, he preferred not to have any responsibility in the ejido. He was 55 years old and married to Magdalena, a niece of Ricardo García. They had never had children. Raúl only had a small plot of rainfed land and a couple of cows. Iginio and Salvador had insisted strongly on him being the candidate for ejido commissioner and in the end he gave in. Raúl knew that Iginio and Salvador had proposed him with the idea of tackling the question of the 'lost land'. He told them that he was prepared to work for the ejido but only with the support of the other ejidatarios and in a legal way. Like many other ejidatarios, Raúl had mixed feelings about the 'lost land'. He had heard stories about people occupying lands of La Canoa and was willing to work for the ejido to try to get these lands back. The new government discourse of democracy and stories about the final settlement of land conflicts and marking of ejido boundaries also encouraged Raúl. He thought that perhaps this could help them. On the other hand, Raúl thought that it would be very difficult to win against the private landowners who would always go to the SRA in Guadalajara to bribe the officials. Raúl clearly did not have a personal drive to go after the 'lost land': he did not have children. So the unpleasant prospect of having children for whom there is no land available any more and who 'are forced' to go and find a living in the United States did not play a role for him. The fight for the 'lost land' was for him a service to the community. He wanted to do it for them. He saw it as his duty.

Vicente García: Ejido Secretary and Spy

Vicente was one of the younger ejidatarios. He was in his 30s and had four young children. He had a special relation with his uncle Ricardo García who had looked after Vicente after his father was murdered 30 years ago.[2] Vicente inherited his father's land and later bought private property lands. Salvador and Iginio had proposed Vicente García as secretary in the *planilla* as a strategic move to win the elections with García votes. However, everybody around the executive committee seemed to have mixed feelings about Vicente. They knew about his close attachment to his uncle Ricardo, who possessed part of the 'lost land' and was one of the 'enemies' in this fight. In the beginning they thought that perhaps Vicente would really be prepared to work for the 'lost land'. However, the idea that Vicente was a spy for his uncle in time became very strong. The feeling grew that Vicente informed his uncle about what the group was doing and even passed important documents on to him. Actually, Vicente himself felt very uncomfortable with the situation and did not intend to hurt the interests of his uncle.

Lupe Medina: Treasurer and Worrying Mother

The case of doña Lupe was especially interesting as she had been the second wife of the late don Miguel, the cause of all the trouble. Miguel had married Lupe when his first wife had died and most of his children were already married and had left home. Don Miguel was in his 50s then and Lupe was 25. Lupe was born in a village on the coast of Jalisco. At the age of 5 she lost her mother and at the age of 8 she lost her father. A priest then brought her to the Michel family, an important *hacendado* family in Autlán. Two unmarried sisters of the Michel family agreed to look after the young girl. When she grew older, Lupe started working at the market place in Autlán. It was there that she met Miguel, who used to buy his coffee at her stall.

After the wedding Lupe came to live with Miguel in La Canoa. Miguel and Lupe had seven children. Miguel died when he was in his 80s. Lupe always spoke with great affection and admiration about her late husband. Miguel left Lupe 8 hectares of rainfed land near the village, the house, and animals. Lupe had already started a shop years before when Miguel was growing older. For the last couple of years she has also managed the only telephone in the village. She lived off the money she earned from the shop and the telephone, and a small allowance she received after her husband's death. One of her daughters in the United States also sent her money on a regular basis. Juan, her only son in the village who lives with her in the house, together with his wife and young son administered the land.

All of Lupe's children, except Juan, live in the United States, in Los Angeles and Las Vegas. Juan drinks a lot, which makes Lupe despair. Sometimes she called her sons in the States and asked them to come back to the village. She said that her house was big enough for several families. They could also build more rooms outside the house as she owned quite an extensive area around the house. Lupe said that there was enough land and income from the shop for several families to live off. On several occasions she happily told me that one of her sons had decided to come back with his family. But they never came. Lupe worried a lot about her children in the United States and prayed for them often. When they had asked Lupe to be part of the *planilla*, she first refused and told them to look for a better person. However, when they continued insisting she finally accepted, but said that she hoped that the question of 'that land' would never be touched again. Lupe had heard rumours in the ejido that her late husband Miguel had given ejido land away to a brother of his. She said that she never knew about this but she did not deny the possibility either. Yet, despite her hesitations, Lupe was to become the fiercest fighter for the 'lost land'.

THE STRUGGLE BEGINS: *LICENCIADO* SALAZAR

So far, we have seen that the central group in the ejido after the elections of 1991 was very heterogeneous. Of the executive committee (Raúl,

Vicente and Lupe) nobody was really interested in going after the 'lost land'. The people who most actively wanted to fight for the 'lost land' were Iginio, Ignacio, Salvador, Ramón and Roberto. Two ejidatarios of La Canoa living in Autlán also participated. There were several ejido meetings about the missing map and how they should deal with the problem. However, nothing spectacular happened until September 1992 when Lupe had a talk with the parish priest of the church in Autlán.

Doña Lupe was a very religious woman and maintained good relations with the parish priest Father López in Autlán. She kept in regular contact with him in order to organise religious events and pilgrimages to nearby villages. She would not easily bother him with 'more earthly' problems but one day in September 1992, when she felt that their activities to get the ejido map were leading nowhere, she summoned up her courage and decided to talk about it with Father López. She made a phone call and Father López listened to her story. He said that he knew a lawyer in Guadalajara who was very experienced in agrarian problems and who could probably help them. By chance, the lawyer would come to Sayula, a town nearby, next Monday. According to Lupe: 'Everything was arranged, as if ordered by God.' Lupe informed Raúl and it was decided that Lupe would go with Ramón to the meeting in Sayula.

On Monday the delegation from La Canoa went to Sayula and met the lawyer Salazar who arrived with several bodyguards. Father López was present as well and Lupe and Ramón were cordially invited to an abundant meal with meat and fish. Salazar listened to their story and said that he had a lot of experience with agrarian matters and that he could certainly help them. He assured them that La Canoa would get the land back and he promised that he would personally take care of their case. He added that it would 'rain money' in La Canoa as it was a large tract of land that they would recover. At this occasion they gave him 2.5 million pesos (US$830) from the ejido funds as a down payment. In the following months Salazar visited the region a couple of times. He had also taken up other cases Father López had asked him to look at.

Some time later Salazar made clear that he wanted more money from the ejidatarios. Not for himself, as he explained, but to bribe officials in the SRA. He explained to them that he did not approve of these practices but that otherwise nothing would be achieved. The ejidatarios know from experience that nothing can be done without bribes and they were eager to use the money the ejido had earned with the sale of the pasture of the commons to bribe some officials. Anyhow, these bribes were nothing compared to the value of the land they were about to recover! So a delegation from La Canoa went to Guadalajara to visit Salazar at his house and paid him 11.5 million pesos (US$3,800). Lupe and Vicente went as members of the executive committee. Iginio and Ramón accompanied them.

Salazar showed them the letter he had written for the case of La Canoa and which would be sent to President Salinas. The ejidatarios were very pleased with this letter and signed with gratitude. The letter was then sent away. The ejidatarios received a receipt for the 11.5 million pesos they paid Salazar. During this first visit to Salazar's house, the ejidatarios met other members of Salazar's family: his wife and mother. The ejidatarios were impressed by the security measures that were taken. They had to pass several doors, which were immediately locked with keys. Together with the bodyguards they saw in Sayula, they interpreted this as a clear indication of the fact that Salazar was an important man who had made many enemies in his fight for the poor ejidatarios. Salazar said that the matter would be settled in a couple of months.

The Letter to the Mexican President

Village: La Canoa
Municipality: Autlán
State: Jalisco

Subject: complementary execution and marking of boundaries of the endowment and extension grant

Lic. Carlos Salinas de Gortari
President of Mexico

Raúl Pradera, Vicente García, Lupe Medina, respectively chairman, secretary and treasurer of the executive committee of the ejido La Canoa, municipality Autlán, Jalisco appear before you through this letter, representing the ejidatarios belonging to the endowment and first extension of the agrarian community mentioned above, with the aim of asking for your valuable intervention as the highest agrarian authority in our country, with the object of resolving the agrarian problems affecting our ejido, for that reason we take the liberty with all respect, to relate the following history.

On 14 July 1937, our ejido was endowed by Presidential Resolution with 1,843 hectares of pasture lands of which 20 per cent was arable, encumbering the properties of La Canoa and La Herradura, in the municipality of Autlán, Jalisco.

On 11 February 1938, the Presidential order of 14 July 1937 was executed, which endowed our agrarian community with 1,843 hectares for 46 plots, including the school plot, for the use of the petitioners, leaving under reserve the rights of 67 individuals in order that the creation of an agrarian population centre would be promoted, encumbering the estates La Canoa, La Herradura and La Piedra or Ixcuintle.

On 20 May 1942, the Presidential Resolution was pronounced, that granted our ejido 191 hectares of lands of different qualities, of which at the execution of the Presidential order we only received 76 hectares in possession and which are those we till at the moment.

But the point is, SR. PRESIDENT, that with respect to the endowment grant of our ejido, we lack approximately 540 hectares to arrive at the 1,843 hectares that were granted to our ejido, and that at the moment we do not have them all, requesting from this moment a general marking of boundaries and at the same time the carrying out of the complementary execution in our agrarian community, interpreting faithfully the Presidential Resolution dated 14 July 1937.

In the same way we have to clarify SR. LIC. CARLOS SALINAS that with respect to our first extension grant of our Ejido La Canoa, municipality Autlán, Jalisco, we were not given the total amount of 191 hectares of lands of different quality granted to us either, and that we only possess and use 76 hectares, for which reason we request that from this moment, the 115 hectares remaining be turned over to us in order to fulfil the Presidential Resolution dated 20 May 1942.

This means SR. PRESIDENT, that the Presidential Orders that allotted our ejido an endowment grant and a first extension grant were not legally executed, and that in total approximately 655 hectares of which 80 per cent are arable lands and 20 per cent mountainous pasture lands remain to be handed over, for that reason LIC. CARLOS SALINAS, it is urgent for us that as soon as possible you send instructions to THE MINISTER OF AGRARIAN REFORM, LIC. VICTOR CERVERA PACHECO, so that he gives instructions to personnel of the *Dirección General de Tenencia de la Tierra* and that they proceed with the execution of the Presidential Resolutions of the Endowment Grant and First Extension Grant, in the same way we request that the Presidential agreement of land purchase dated 23 October 1950, signed by the President of the Republic LIC. MIGUEL ALEMAN VALDEZ, is carried out so that the lands bought from and paid to SR. ANASTACIO MICHEL can be incorporated into the ejido regime.

What we presented to you here SR. LIC. CARLOS SALINAS DE GORTARI, PRESIDENT OF MEXICO, is the real truth of the problems our agrarian community is facing, and the urgent necessity of the execution of Presidential Resolutions, is because we need the remaining lands, as we have very little arable lands and the lands that remain to be handed over to us are almost entirely lands that can be used for agriculture, which of course would benefit all members of our community by naturally making a fair distribution of the lands that can be used for agriculture among those who deserve to receive them according to the economic contributions made to resolve the present problem, which our ejido suffers, in the same way, we ask you with all respect to order the Ministry of Agrarian Reform, and more concretely, the Secretary of the Department to send personnel and to proceed with the constitution of the Centre of Ejido Population, which is mentioned in our Presidential Resolution dated 14 July 1937, marking of course the best place for the Establishment of the Population Centre, which will be formed by the 67 ejidatarios with rights under reserve, and also by the sons of ejidatarios of the endowment as well as the extension grant of our ejido.

We would like to thank you in advance SR. PRESIDENT CARLOS SALINAS DE GORTARI, as highest agrarian authority in our country, for the favourable solution to the problems we set out to you.

Yours faithfully,
La Canoa, mun. Autlán, Jalisco 8 October 1992

The Executive committee of the ejido La Canoa

Raúl Pradera	Vicente García	Lupe Medina
presidente	secretary	treasurer
(signed by Iginio)		

The ejidatarios were very happy with the letter to the Mexican president. First of all they liked the fact that the Mexican president was addressed and in this way incorporated into their struggle. Second, they liked the number of hectares Salazar had calculated. Not all the members of the group had an idea of the number of La Canoa's missing hectares, but the amount of 540 hectares certainly seemed on the 'right side'. Third, they were pleased by the reference made to the people who had always been active in the fight for the land and that they should be compensated for their efforts when the land was to be recovered. This letter to the president only circulated in the small group and was not presented at the general ejido assembly or to other ejidatarios.

As it was through Lupe that Father López had brought La Canoa into contact with Salazar, she seemed the right person to follow up on this relation. Her central role was emphasised by the fact that she was the only one Salazar wanted to inform and always asked for. Raúl, who would have been the more obvious person, being the commissioner and official representative of the ejido, was glad to have Lupe take over this responsibility. Raúl always felt insecure in relation to lawyers and surveyors and did not feel very capable of handling these matters. So, gradually and without it ever being formally or informally decided, Lupe became 'the person in charge'.

More Expenses and Fantastic Stories at the CNC

When more paperwork needed to be done, the ejidatarios visited Salazar at his office at the CNC (the national peasant confederation, affiliated to the ruling party, the PRI). The number of secretaries working for him impressed them. Salazar described to them how he himself had once been put in prison because he had succeeded in taking land away from large landowners which was then given to ejidatarios. Lupe and the others were very pleased with these stories as this proved to them that he knew how to deal with difficult land problems and had a real fighting spirit.

According to Lupe, Salazar had good connections with President Salinas and had direct access to Los Pinos (the presidential residence). She asserted that Salazar was one of the national leaders of the CNC. When I said to her that if that was true his name should appear in the newspapers and on television, she recognised that this was not the case. However, these logical objections could not temper her enthusiasm. Salazar himself also generated these fantasies about the 'right connection' and influential positions. For example, on the many occasions that Lupe made a telephone call to Salazar's house to ask what was going on and why nothing had happened, Salazar or his wife used to talk about the meetings Salazar had with the state governor or the director of an organisation, and so on.

On several occasions Salazar said that he needed more money and they took money to him in Guadalajara three more times. By the beginning of 1992 they had paid him 23 million pesos (US$7,600): partly from ejido funds and partly from contributions by individual ejidatarios. Salazar explained that the total amount they would have to pay him was 32 million pesos (US$10,600), but that the remaining part could be paid when the ejido received the land. If necessary, they could sell part of this land in order to pay him, he told them. The ejidatarios liked the prospect of selling part of the new land as in this way they could also recover the ejido funds, which they already used for Salazar without the consent of the ejido assembly. The ejidatarios only received receipts for 14 million pesos ($4,600). Naturally, the question of receipts is rather awkward in an 'atmosphere of bribes'. However, the ejidatarios were well aware that in the future they, and especially Lupe, who was ejido treasurer, could be asked to render accounts of the spending of ejido money to the other ejidatarios. They knew that if everything went well, nobody would bother about the spending of this money. However, the question of receipts became increasingly important to them when they did not feel sure about the outcome of their actions.

Every day Lupe became more enthusiastic about the prospect of new land for the ejido and her sons. People who came to her shop sometimes said that it would be better to save the ejido money rather than go on missions and spend it on a lawyer. But Lupe did not let herself be discouraged. Lupe was animated and full of hope. Salazar raised more hopes and expectations by asking the people what kind of project they would like to have for La Canoa, once they received the land. He could arrange an additional project for them. Salazar said that they could think about a chicken farm for the ejido. With respect to the land they would recover, Salazar promised to bring police forces from Mexico City if things got out of hand. He told them again that they should be very careful that the private landowners did not know about the letter they had sent to the Mexican president.

Precise plans were made for the land they were about to recover. Part of the land would be used for a new residential area where houses could be built. The remaining part would be used for 25 plots of about 3 hectares for 'sons of ejidatarios'. They also incorporated plots of 8 hectares for each of the *pequeños propietarios* who would lose their land. This was a generous gesture, but it was also a way of easing their own minds. Lupe in particular sometimes felt bad about taking the land away from the *pequeños*. She hoped that by leaving them 8 hectares each everything could be resolved without serious problems. She very much hoped that everything could be settled harmoniously. However, problems were to be expected not only with 'the enemy', but within the ejido itself as well. The question of the 25 individual plots naturally was a delicate issue. There were a lot more than 25 'sons of ejidatarios' interested in plots of land. So, who was going to take the decision on the distribution of the new plots? Amusingly, Ramón, who was not even a member of the executive committee, decided this. He established the list in consultation with Lupe and Iginio. Raúl, the commissioner, was not even involved. Naturally, the sons of Lupe, Iginio and Ramón were well represented in the list. They put two sons of Ramón who live in Guadalajara on the list, as well as two sons of Iginio and two sons of Lupe who live in the United States. Raúl would also receive one plot. Mónica, the teacher from La Canoa, who lives in Guadalajara and always supported them, was also listed as one of the beneficiaries. In order to justify their decisions to themselves when they talked about it, or to me when I asked about it, they repeated the stories about the sacrifices they and other people had made in the past, for this case. After they had made the decision, the list was sent to the SRA office in Mexico City. It was never discussed at an ejido meeting and never made public.

Meetings in Small Groups and the Forging of a Conspiracy

It was a loose configuration of persons who worked together for the 'lost land', who took decisions and went on missions. In fact, they never all gathered together. Raúl, Iginio, Salvador, Lupe and Ramón visited each other frequently to talk about the issue. However, only two or three of them would meet and deliberate and then talk to one or two of the others. There were no long-standing relations of friendship or close kinship between them either. Naturally, there existed the long-standing relationships of people who have lived together in a small village for a long time and share certain knowledge and memories. But before this executive committee was elected in 1991, these people did not visit each other. In other words, they did not form part of each other's 'socialising circles' (see Chapter 2).

After they started working with Salazar, they no longer discussed the question of the 'lost land' at the ejido meetings. It was Raúl and Lupe (both members of the executive committee) together with Iginio Núñez and Ramón Romero (not members of the executive committee) who decided to use the ejido money for the bribes. Decisions about the missions to Autlán or Guadalajara were also taken within small groups. The ejido assembly was hardly ever informed about their trips or about the spending of money. However, the 'group of the lost land' did not feel completely at ease about their way of operating. They argued that actually the ejido assembly should decide on these trips and should at least be informed about the money that was spent. In December 1992 I asked Lupe if they were taking all these decisions with Salazar without informing the ejido assembly. She responded:

Yes, at the moment we do not talk about this at the ejido meetings. But we will soon have to inform them about the spending of the ejido money. This has to be done with great discretion. For me it is a heavy burden. I am responsible for the ejido money and we have already spent 19 million.

However, on the other hand, there were several good reasons justifying their silence. First of all, talking about their projects at a general ejido assembly would cause a lot of problems as a large number of people would be opposed to spending ejido money on this conflict. So asking for consent at the ejido assembly would probably mean that they would be hampered in their freedom of action. Second, they argued that few ejidatarios attended the meetings. Thus, convening a meeting would be useless anyhow. Third, according to their 'conspiracy' theories a high degree of secrecy was required. Otherwise, the enemy would know what they were doing and all their efforts would have been in vain. Salazar and Father López had also emphasised that they should work as secretly as possible. Father López had even warned Lupe that some people of La Canoa were talking too much and that they had to be more careful.

Father López himself was getting into trouble because of his involvement in the conflict of La Canoa. He was known as a politically involved priest and already had several enemies among the elite in Autlán. Not only did he try to help several ejidos who had problems with private landowners, but he also interfered in other political matters. On several occasions, the bishop had warned López to stay out of politics. The private landowners in Autlán soon learned that López was helping the ejidatarios of La Canoa. López was told by one of the private landowners to stop this interference, adding that López was 'playing with gunpowder'.

MORE DEALINGS WITH SALAZAR AND GROWING DOUBTS

In January 1993, Salazar told Lupe that he had finally obtained the definitive map of the ejido La Canoa. He would come to the ejido to measure the land and see whether the borders of the ejido coincided with the map. He asked Lupe to come to the *plaza* in Autlán. He would meet her there to give her the map of the ejido and the official letter of the land transfer, signed by the Mexican president. He said that La Canoa was the first ejido in Mexico whose problems would now be resolved. Lupe went to Autlán and waited the whole day. Salazar never arrived. Afterwards, Lupe was told that Salazar had had an accident on the way to Autlán and had been busy all day keeping the people who were involved in the accident out of prison. Lupe gradually developed mixed feelings about the *licenciado* and his heroic stories. She told me, for example: 'I do not believe that the president signs this letter. A president does not sign these documents himself.'

Lupe was in constant contact with Salazar and his family. She had his home telephone number and phoned him regularly. Most of the time Salazar was away and his mother or wife talked to Lupe. Some weeks later Lupe said to me that Salazar was lying to her all the time when he said that he was so busy: 'When he wants to come to Autlán, they always call him away for other matters. The other day he planned to come to La Canoa, but then he had to inaugurate a dam ....' Some weeks later Salazar told her that next week the surveyors would come to measure the land and that he himself would visit La Canoa on Saturday. But Lupe was already preparing herself for new disappointments: 'I do not believe that the surveyors will come this week. And Salazar won't come either. Lawyers do not work on Saturday.' Sure enough, the surveyors did not arrive, nor did Salazar.

Several ejidatarios who had been enthusiastic about Salazar in the beginning were losing faith. However, they had no clear ideas about what exactly was going on. For example, when I asked Iginio for his opinion he said that Salazar was not necessarily corrupt but certainly did not give priority to La Canoa. Raúl also said that it was difficult for him to judge Salazar as he only met him on one occasion. During a long period people were not sure about Salazar and were moderate in their opinion about him. The point is that it was very difficult for everybody to judge where the obstacles in their fight were coming from. They always had to base their opinion on scarce and contradictory information, insinuations, rumours and unintelligible documents. When more time passed without anything happening, opinions about Salazar became more negative and he was considered to be a 'corrupt thief' who had robbed La Canoa of a large amount of money.

The actions around the lawyer and the 'lost land' became the territory of a smaller and smaller group. The 'group of the lost land' was reduced to two persons now, Lupe and Ramón. Lupe liked to work with Ramón as he was one of the persons who knew most about the conflict between the ejido and the *pequeños*. Furthermore, he worked with great enthusiasm and did not mind spending time and energy on the case. Lupe also started incorporating Teresa as she did not like to be the only woman when they had to go on missions. As already mentioned, Teresa had had an active role in the struggle for the lost land 20 years before when her husband Macario was commissioner. Teresa was still enthusiastic about the case. As Macario worked and lived in the United States and she did not have small children at home any more, she could easily accompany Lupe. She lived in the house opposite Lupe's, so she often walked in to ask what had happened and how things were going. Teresa also hoped for land for her sons who were working in *el Norte* now.

They were summoned by Salazar to come to Guadalajara several more times. On one occasion Salazar told them to come to Guadalajara in order to accompany the surveyor who would do the measuring work in La Canoa. Lupe went with Ramón and they waited three days at the SRA. Finally, on the third day, they met Serrano, the surveyor responsible for La Canoa, but he did not accompany them to the village. He sent them back home and said that he would let them know when he would arrive in the village. In the next weeks they did not hear anymore from him.

I often sat in Lupe's shop to talk about the case. I asked Lupe what she thought was going on.

M: What do you think is going on? Is Salazar too busy, has he been bribed ... ?
L: I think it is partly that. I think the people at the office work against it because of money, or friendships with the landowners.

On another occasion she told me that she regretted very much having talked about their fight with Rosa Romero. The point is that a daughter of Rosa is married to Pepe Mendoza, son of Salvador Mendoza, owner of part of the land that belongs to La Canoa. According to Lupe things went wrong from the moment she informed Rosa. She presumed that Rosa had talked to her daughter and that they had arranged things in Guadalajara.

Teresa too seemed to have lost her faith in Salazar. Teresa felt that something was going wrong but she still did not define the cause of the evil.

M: But what precisely do you think is going on? Do you think they bribed Salazar or is he just too busy?
T: From what I can see, he is forgetting us.

She does not characterise Salazar as a good guy or a bad guy either. Evil can come from many different directions and can affect all people. This position towards Salazar was characteristic for all the people of the 'group of the lost land'.

However, while Raúl, Teresa, Iginio and Ramón could easily say that they did not believe in Salazar anymore, for Lupe the implications of 'giving up' on him were more severe. As ejido treasurer she was responsible for the money they had spent on him. Furthermore, she was the one who had brought the ejido into contact with Salazar. So, for her the implications were more serious. That was the reason she held on. She wanted to believe in Salazar. She kept phoning him and never broke off the relationship with him as hopes or 'wishful thinking' lingered on. However, her faith in the *licenciado* was eroding seriously. She laughed about – what she now considered to be – the lies Salazar had told her before and which she had believed. The one with the accident and the other one with the exchange of fire on his way to Autlán. But the laughing was painful for her. She was deeply upset by the whole affair and wanted to visit her children in the United States. They had already sent her the money to come over. Two of her children were having their marriages blessed in church and three grandchildren were going to be baptised. For Lupe, these religious events were very important and she longed to go. However, she still hesitated as Salazar had suggested that people would come soon to measure the land. Salazar told Lupe that she had to be around for the marking of boundaries but that everything would be over by 20 May. Then she could leave for the USA. By 20 May nothing had happened.

SHIFTING CONSTELLATIONS AND INDIVIDUAL FRUSTRATIONS

During the year that they worked with Salazar the 'group of the lost land' that had initiated the project before the elections of the executive committee of 1991 completely lost their harmony and team spirit.

Salvador Quits

Salvador, who together with Iginio had been the main organiser of this executive committee and who all this time had participated in discussions and decisions in the small group, quite abruptly left the group. It never became clear to the others quite why. He told them that he was tired of all those years of fighting. However, his decision was also influenced by pressure from his wife and children to abandon the case and by the fact that they had recently discovered that he had a serious illness. He started warning the others of the bloody consequences their activities might have. He said that the *pequeños* would never have their land taken away from them without bloodshed. Although this was something that everybody was convinced of, it was strange to hear this talk coming from Salvador who had always had such a fighting spirit. Salvador did not even want to be put on the list of beneficiaries for the new land. He did not want to have any member of his family on the list. Salvador told them: 'If this goes ahead people will be killed and I do not want my children to be involved in this.' On several occasions Salvador severely criticised his *comadre* Lupe. He said that he would hold her responsible if people got killed.

Iginio's Anger

At this point, Iginio became very critical about everything and everybody. He and Salvador had organised the executive committee of the ejido in order to fight for the 'lost land'. Yet, now he had lost his fighting companion Salvador and was being sidelined by Lupe, who did not invite him to go on the missions anymore. Furthermore, he had lost faith in the *licenciado* whom he now called '*Lupe's licenciado*'. Although at the start he had been convinced about Salazar's good connections, he now said that it was nonsense that Salazar had direct access to the Mexican president. At the same time he became more critical of Father López. He did not accuse him of deceit but he expressed his disapproval of a priest handling agrarian matters: 'Perhaps I should not say so, but I think it is absurd that a priest interferes in agrarian problems.'

Iginio resented the fact that Lupe, when organising private meetings and missions, clearly preferred Ramón to him. Although most people preferred not to go on missions because of the time lost and the tiresome and frustrating interactions with SRA officials, for those interested in the case, missions had their advantages. Information gathered during the missions was often withheld or documents carefully guarded. Participating in the missions was the only way to be on top of what was going on. However, as long as Lupe was the one who controlled their relations with Salazar, Iginio could not do much about it.

Iginio now also started to adopt the accountability discourse of organisation (see Chapter 3). He said that the money they spent on the *licenciado* was money from the community and that therefore they had to render accounts of their activities to the community. They could not work in secrecy. He also argued that it was not right that Ramón had made a list of beneficiaries of the new land as this should be decided by the whole ejido. Hence, now that Iginio could no longer control what was going on, and no longer belonged to the circle of people who made the decisions, he used the accountability discourse to criticise a way of working he had participated in before.

Raúl Tries to Resign

Raúl, the commissioner, had also lost faith in Salazar and agreed with the other ejidatarios that it was wrong to spend ejido money on a hopeless case. Raúl became tired of the whole affair: a lawyer who did not keep his promises, ejidatarios blaming him for badly spending ejido money, and members of the small group who criticised him for being scared. What bothered Raúl most about the whole affair was the lack of unity in the ejido. He was now very much opposed to decisions being made by small groups and also started using the accountability discourse of organisation. Raúl also disagreed with the fact that Ramón had made the list of people who would receive the new ejido plots. When I spoke to Raúl, he said to me that this had to be decided at a meeting of the ejido. Raúl:

Decisions have to be made in public, at the ejido meetings. I would have continued with the case if there had been a majority. But we are not united. ... Something that never happened in the past is not suddenly going to happen now. Furthermore, the people who possess these lands, have influential contacts in the government, or they pay money. ... Even if we recovered the lands, the present owners would not accept it. You can find people who commit a murder for a million pesos. That is what will happen then. What can we do? Everywhere it is the same, it is useless!

Indirect Forms of Accountability

Gradually, the voices in the ejido critical of spending ejido money on the lawyer grew stronger. Now that it had become clear that nothing was going to be achieved, several ejidatarios wanted the ejido money back. Yet, the ejidatarios found it difficult to call Lupe to order directly. She was generally respected and her integrity as treasurer of the ejido was never in doubt. This executive committee was criticised for spending ejido money on a lost case, but it was not suggested that they had appropriated ejido resources for their own use or pleasure. While everybody was talking about the lawyer and the ejido money in informal circles, nobody wanted to take the initiative to ask Lupe formally to render accounts.

However, under pressure from the ejidatarios Raúl decided that the ejidatarios would no longer make payments to Lupe, who was the ejido treasurer. Instead Raúl would collect the money for the tax and the rent for pasture from the commons. Lupe was hurt by this decision. For her this was a motion of no confidence and she became very emotional when Raúl came to tell her this decision. Raúl felt sorry for Lupe. Yet, the next payment for the rent of a part of the pasture was made to Raúl. When Raúl had received most of the money for the pasture, he immediately spent it on the building of water reservoirs in the commons. In this way Raúl made sure that the money could not be spent on intermediaries and nobody in the ejido seemed to object to his decision.

Father López

Then Father López went to the SRA in Mexico City and when he returned he said that things were going well. He said he had had a talk with the Mexican president and he had talked with Salazar. Father López said that the 23 million pesos they had paid Salazar was very little as the people at the different offices asked for enormous bribes. Father López told Lupe not to worry. He also promised her that he would use his personal relations with *Los Pinos* (the presidential residence) to help them further.

Raúl Places His Hope on PROCEDE

By March 1993 the new agrarian institute, the Procuraduría Agraria had opened an office in Autlán and had started its work in the region. Although the young inexperienced officials did not impress the ejidatarios very much (see Chapter 7), the ejidatarios liked the PROCEDE programme which they were talking about. In this programme all ejido lands would be measured, even the individual ejido plots. The ejido did not have to take any initiative as it was a programme organised from above. The ejidatarios would only have to cooperate with the different procedural steps. Raúl was particularly happy with this programme. This meant that everything would be done automatically, without the ejido having to go on endless missions, and without paying lawyers and bribing officials. According to Raúl, the best thing was to wait and see what the government would do with the PROCEDE programme.

CONCLUSION: THE LABYRINTHINE BUREAUCRATIC MACHINE

In this chapter, we saw how the ejidatarios sought the 'right connection' which could give them the necessary access to the 'centre', which would make sure that their problems would be taken care of. The ejidatarios could have decided to invade the 'lost land' but, as far as I know, this was never contemplated. They preferred to enrol the Mexican president in their operations. The Mexican president can be seen as the personification of power in a society where personal relations are central for the organising process. In fact, the ejidatarios create the fetish of the president and give the state a face by writing the president letters and trying to enrol him in their projects. The idea of the state suggests coherence, coordination, and consistent top-down working, from the president to the bottom. According to Abrams the state-idea is a 'message of domination – an ideological artefact attributing unity, morality and independence to the disunited, amoral and dependent workings of the practice of government' (Abrams 1988: 81). Taussig, following Abrams, poses the question of whether it might turn out, then, that 'the fantasies of the marginated concerning the secret of the centre are what is most politically important to the State idea' (Taussig 1992: 132). Is it not the fantasies of the ejidatarios concerning the powerful centre that leads to the fetishising of the state and 'the cultural constitution of the modern State – with a big S?' (1992: 112).

In this context of a decentred bureaucratic machine and the impossibility of getting 'effective access' to the centre, brokers thrive well. In the brokers the ejidatarios hope to find people who, unlike them, know the codes and invisible ways through the labyrinth. The ejidatarios search for brokers everywhere: in different networks of friends and relatives, in peasant organisations, political parties or in the SRA itself. The ejidatarios work with several brokers at the same time in the hope that one or several together may have enough 'political capital' to get the machine working. Yet, by searching for brokers with special access, the ejidatarios contribute to the imagining of state power. They invest in the idea of the state.

In their turn, brokers also invest in the idea of the state by presenting themselves as people who have privileged access and knowledge to make the machine work. An important strategy of brokers is boasting about their relations with influential people. They often claim to have special access to the presidential residence *Los Pinos* or even direct contact with the Mexican president. These stories are a form of impression management which people employ to influence the systems of meaning surrounding them. The fact that everything is played out in the context of a labyrinthine bureaucratic machine means that brokers can never be held responsible for things that go wrong.

Although officials and intermediaries all have their own personal agendas, it would be simplistic to assume that they always deliberately try to deceive the ejidatarios. For example, Father López was a well-known priest in the region. I have no indication that he was a swindler. My impression was that he did not have the slightest idea about agrarian matters but hoped that his contacts were influential enough to help the ejidatarios in their fight for the land. Yet, he also exaggerated his influence and contacts with the Mexican president and often told the ejidatarios about his visits to *Los Pinos*. Engaging in this practice of impression management is part of the culture of the state in which access is a central component. If you want to convince people that you can make a difference for them, you have to impress them with your relations.

Yet, the culture of the state not only consists of practices of impression management but also of practices of interpretation and reading. The ejidatarios were no passive recipients or 'consumers' of fantasies but very much wanted to believe that their brokers were the right connection. The stories and fantasies had to take on enormous proportions as the ejidatarios knew that only a person with 'extraordinary qualities and access' could help them with their problems. In this context, they could even prefer the dubious, influential lawyer to honest but powerless brokers. The lawyer with a great lifestyle, a big house, beautiful secretaries around him, driving around in big cars and with many bodyguards, seemed more able to play a role in this highly opaque politicised bureaucracy and in the fight against the *pequeños propietarios* than people who looked more like the ejidatarios themselves (see Bayart 1993 on the politics of the belly). Hence, the ejidatarios interpreted many events and things in ways that would fit in with their fantasies.

An important pillar of the hope-generating machine is the presidential system in which every new president introduces new programmes and proposes important institutional changes (see Chapter 7). President Salinas who, among other things, promised to bring justice to the Mexican countryside, showed this clearly. This propaganda influenced the ejidatarios of La Canoa to launch another effort to recover the 'lost land'. However, La Canoa was not the only ejido: many ejidos with land problems tried to resolve their problems under the presidency of Salinas (see Torres 1994). Despite bad experiences in the past, the introduction of new programmes with every new president always raises some hopes among the population as sometimes things are indeed changed or achieved (see Grindle 1977). Yet, even in periods when the ejidatario had high expectations, or started to believe the most fantastic stories, doubts were always there. Confidence was never absolute. For the same reason, people never seem to be surprised when things do not work out in the way they had expected or hoped. They are disappointed but never seem to be surprised. Irony played an important role in this process. People could laugh about themselves: about the stories they had believed in and how they had been deceived. But the laughter was always painful. As Beezley et al. point out, 'the use of humour as a cunning commentary on contemporary affairs continues in Mexico ... a kind of "gallows humour" that turns the labyrinthine bureaucracy, the political fraud, and the devalued currency into jokes has become prevalent' (Beezley et al. 1994: xxv). Yet these experiences do not lead to passive resignation. The ejidatarios go on fighting, investing, hoping and believing.

In short, I argue that, in their search for the right intermediary who can make the connection to the centre, the ejidatarios are implicated in the process of the construction of the idea of the state. The power of the state is to a great degree imagined and cultivated through the search for brokers, the reification of maps, the fetishisation of documents and procedures, the incredible stories of the intermediaries and the fantastic beliefs of the ejidatarios. In the next chapter attention is paid to maps and documents as techniques of imagination.

6 THE 'LOST LAND'
II: THE SURVEYORS

INTRODUCTION: THE 'DESIRING MACHINE'

This chapter continues to follow the same conflict of the 'lost land', however the SRA surveyors now play a central role. The unflagging efforts by Lupe and Ramón had not been in vain and the bureaucratic machine of the SRA was set in motion. In a period of 18 months, five different SRA surveyors in succession were ordered to investigate the case of La Canoa. While in Chapter 5 we saw flows of ejidatarios to many different offices in Autlán, Guadalajara and Mexico City, in this chapter we see flows in a different direction: surveyors from Guadalajara and Mexico City visiting the ejido La Canoa.

We saw many characteristics of the bureaucratic machine, which contribute to its hope-generating nature. For example, the fact that agrarian cases are never 'closed' and that the bureaucratic machine can always be set in motion again. Officials or intermediaries never say to the ejidatarios that they should give up but always offer 'new' and 'better' openings and options to get matters finally resolved. In this way, 'legal processes can easily take on a life of their own, in a nightmare of papers, procedures and authorisations' (Harris 1996: 10). But there is more to it. By stressing the importance of official procedures, by employing an unintelligible legal-administrative language, and by claiming that, by following the official steps it is possible to recover the 'lost land', officials and surveyors contribute to the 'idea of the state'. They provide the techniques of imagination and give the ejidatarios new ideas for their struggle. The stress on the importance of formal procedures suggests that logic exists in the operation of the bureaucratic machine. Yet, in reality, the working of the bureaucracy is fragmented and dispersed and there is no 'hidden reality of politics, a backstage institutionalism of political power behind the on-stage agencies of government' (Abrams 1988: 63). The hope-generating bureaucratic machine does not work according to functionalist principles but is, instead, made up of thousands of uncoordinated actions without a centre of control. We could even argue that what gives the machine coherence are the enjoyments and pleasures, fears and expectations it produces. It becomes a 'desiring-machine' (see Deleuze and Guattari 1988).[1]

Lower officials normally have little insight into what exactly is going on within the bureaucracy. Furthermore, they have little influence on political decisions in relation to land conflicts. Officials are under pressure from different sides and develop their own styles of operation in a complex politicised bureaucratic world (cf. Arce 1993, de Vries 1997). As they seem unable to resolve La Canoa's problems, ejidatarios and officials together theorise, speculate and gossip about what is happening behind their back and about who is the man, or which is the SRA department, that is working against the ejido La Canoa. In this process it is normal, for ejidatarios as well as officials, to handle contradictory information. They work with different options at the same time and will not easily discard a new possibility. Never discarding any option (even the most extreme ones) and never being completely sure about the position of anybody is an important aspect of attitudes produced by the 'desiring-machine'.

As I argued in Chapter 1, notions of governmentality as a complex aggregate of institutions and procedures and modern forms of discipline and ruling through which power is exercised over people (Foucault, Corrigan and Sayer, Rose and Miller) are of limited value for the Mexican case. These works stress the standardisation of procedures through which people become impersonal clients of the institutions. Yet here we do not find standard governmental techniques, but an endless diversity of agencies and administrative procedures. New plans of action and openings to the system can be invented all the time. We do not find the impersonal treatment of the clients of the system. On the contrary, officials as well as ejidatarios will always try to 'personalise' relationships, as this is considered to be the only form of meaningful and useful interaction. On the other hand, governmental techniques such as stamps, maps, official (unintelligible) terminology, and the use of formal titles of officials play an important role as the everyday routines and rituals of the bureaucratic machine. However, as Comaroff and Comaroff argue, this routinisation and ritualisation of practices 'always require[s] careful and situated reading' (1993: xxiii).

THE SRA SURVEYOR SERRANO ARRIVING IN THE VILLAGE

The Presumed Delivery of the Definitive Ejido Map

In September 1993, Davíd, one of the officials of the SRA office in Autlán, personally visited the ejido commissioner Raúl at his house to inform him enthusiastically that finally, after 50 years of waiting, the map of the ejido La Canoa had arrived. He said that a delegation of officials from Autlán and Guadalajara would come and deliver the map to La Canoa and he suggested that the ejido should at least prepare an abundant meal for them to celebrate this special event. Raúl and the other ejidatarios did not seem to believe that the 'real' map would be delivered but a meeting was convened anyway.

At the meeting a delegation of five SRA officials arrived: the three officials from the Autlán office and two from the Guadalajara office. Some 18 ejidatarios attended the meeting. Davíd solemnly declared that they had come to deliver the map that was requested by Commissioner Macario Paz in 1976. Then he pulled out several maps. Ramón was the first person to look at them. He passed them to Ignacio Romero and Iginio Núñez. They immediately said that these were the same maps they had already received on many occasions. These were the project map and the definitive map of the extension. Not the desired definitive map of the endowment.[2] Then a discussion started about the problems of the 'lost land'. Davíd and the other officials declared at length that they had every intention of helping La Canoa, and that the ejidatarios should come and see them at their office next week. After the meeting, the officials and several ejidatarios had a meal and abundant drinks at Iginio's house. Lupe and Ramón did not go.

What is interesting about this event is that nobody seemed surprised or annoyed about the course of things. This event also shows how ejidatarios try to maintain good relationships with officials even if they do not trust them. As it is never clear what role each official plays in the obstruction or execution of the procedures or what his or her role may be in the future, the ejidatarios are very careful not to spoil relationships. This is also related to the general awe and caution with which those in authority are treated. Even though nobody in the ejido had expected that the real map would be delivered, they still considered it necessary to 'treat the officials well'. During the meal, ejidatarios and officials ate and drank together in a pleasant atmosphere. There was much laughter and enjoyment. This is characteristic of the relation between ejidatarios and officials: even if not much has been achieved, one at least tries to foster the relationship.

Serrano Shows Up

In Chapter 5 we saw that Serrano, a surveyor from the SRA office in Guadalajara, received orders to go to La Canoa and do the measuring work in the ejido. Several times he gave the ejidatarios a date but he never showed up. On 25 November 1993, Serrano again said that he would arrive that day in La Canoa. Lupe and Ramón were waiting in the shop for his phone call from Autlán where they would meet him. Ramón expressed his feeling as: 'between hope and disbelief'. Ramón was in a negative mood. He talked about the infamous television newsreader (Zabludowski) who always acted as a spokesman of the PRI. As he put it: 'I do not believe in the Mexican president nor in politics anymore, I have been through so many things.' Lupe and Ramón recalled everything that had happened to them in the last two years and laughed at all the promises they had believed in. While the three of us were waiting in the shop, Lupe decided to call Serrano's office again. The secretary told her that Serrano had left with his suitcases for La Canoa. However, even with this information we did not really expect him to arrive. Yet this time Serrano did arrive.

He visited La Canoa in the evening. He was a man in his 40s and was pleasant in his dealings with the ejidatarios. He was surprised to meet Raúl, the ejido commissioner of La Canoa. During his visits to Guadalajara Ramón had pretended to be the commissioner of La Canoa. Serrano was annoyed by this fact but Ramón did not mind. Ramón knew that pretending to be the commissioner was the only way to be taken seriously and he had achieved his goal. Upon his arrival in La Canoa, an ejido meeting was convened for twelve o'clock the next day. Serrano stayed in a hotel in Autlán. Lupe was tired and nervous; she took several aspirins. Rumours soon spread throughout the village. Nobody else had been aware that a surveyor had been sent to do the measuring work in the ejido. Hopes were raised and more ejidatarios expressed their enthusiasm about this development. Even Iginio, who was so critical about Lupe and Ramón's operations, thought that this would be their last chance to get things arranged.

The next morning, the atmosphere was exceptionally harmonious. Lupe was happy as she felt that the ejido was united again. She was pleased that other members of the executive committee were participating again. There was a general feeling of unity and generosity that was very rare in the ejido. When Serrano arrived, everybody entered the ejido building and the meeting started. Ramón was very nervous. Some 20 ejidatarios attended the meeting. Serrano read his work order and said that they had given him ten days for the job. He said: 'It is my duty to work in the interest of the ejido. This ejido has many problems and complications. We want to clarify that. If there are no legal or technical impediments, we will elaborate the definitive map.' Serrano explained that he would start the measuring next Wednesday and that all the neighbours of the ejido had to be formally informed by then that land of

La Canoa would be measured and their common borders marked. The ejidatarios also had to organise teams to carry the measuring instruments around in the fields and clear some paths if necessary.

Serrano opened a provisional map of the ejido and Ramón, Iginio, Raúl and Vicente went to have a look. Some other ejidatarios were also having a look. Other ejidatarios left the meeting and went outside. The men at the map were all talking at the same time. They often disagreed about the neighbours of the different plots who had to be notified, and it was clear that few ejidatarios had a view of the total situation. After the meeting Serrano went to Raúl and asked him for the payment of his hotel night in Autlán and the expenses of his trip from Guadalajara to Autlán. Raúl said that he did not have any money at the moment but promised that they would pay him these expenses on Tuesday. I asked Raúl why they were going to pay Serrano. Raúl said: 'That is usual and it is important to treat these men well, so that he will do a good job. Otherwise he might not finish the work.' Iginio agreed with Raúl and repeated this point. However, they all hoped that Serrano would stay in the village next week as the costs of a hotel in Autlán were high.

Waiting for Serrano

On Tuesday several ejidatarios went to the town hall for the meeting with Serrano and the neighbours of La Canoa. One by one the *pequeños propietarios* entered the town hall. Finally, there were some six of them; much less than the total number of neighbours who had been invited to come. It was a tense atmosphere of confrontation of the ejidatarios and the *pequeños propietarios*; both parties in the conflict were waiting together for the SRA surveyor who would resolve their conflict. Lupe was very nervous. Raúl was terribly nervous as well and started to apologise to the *pequeños propietarios*. After they had been waiting some time, Lupe went to a restaurant to call the SRA in Guadalajara and ask what had happened with Serrano. They told her that Serrano had not been to the office since last Thursday. They continued waiting in the town hall. After an hour a clerk asked for Raúl Pradera. He gave him the message that Serrano had just called to tell him that his car had broken down. Everybody reacted with disbelief. One of the *pequeños propietarios* said: 'His car broken down, nonsense! Why doesn't he come by bus then?!' Raúl seemed relieved that a confrontation with the *pequeños propietarios* was avoided. Raúl and the other men from La Canoa shook hands with the *pequeños propietarios* and they all left the building. Serrano never came to Autlán or La Canoa again.

Lifting Part of the Veil

Some weeks later Ramón and Lupe got hold of Serrano on the telephone. He told them that if the ejido was prepared to pay for it, he would do the measuring as a private project in the Christmas holidays. Then they did not hear from him again. Shortly afterwards, I made an appointment with Juan Fernández, head of the department of development and local organisation of the SRA office in Guadalajara. I established contact with him through friends who were active with peasant organisations and whom he used to help with advice on agrarian matters. After a more general talk, I presented Fernández with the case of Serrano in La Canoa. It appeared that Fernández knew Serrano well and had been his boss at another department of the SRA. To my surprise, Fernández summoned Serrano to his office before I had even finished talking. I will present part of the conversation that followed after Fernández had called for Serrano.

M: What is the sense of calling for Serrano now? He will only give the official version of what happened.
F: From the answers he gives I can deduce what has happened.
Serrano entered the room displaying great deference to Fernández.
F: What were you going to do in La Canoa?
S: The demarcation of a land area that supposedly was bought for the ejido by the SRA and that seems not to have been completely handed over to the ejido.
After a discussion on the technical side of the job in which Fernández disagreed with Serrano about the implications of his work in La Canoa, Serrano became uncomfortable.
F: Why was the work stopped?
S: Orders from the delegate [head of the SRA office in Guadalajara], he told me to stop.
Fernández gave me a significant look and Serrano left.
M: So the delegate himself stopped the work?
F: He said so, not me ...

So, apparently Pelayo, head of the SRA in Guadalajara, had personally interfered to stop the measuring work. I told the people in La Canoa about my findings in Guadalajara. As usual, they listened with great interest and were not surprised.

A NEW BROKER: THE GATEKEEPER IN MEXICO CITY

All this time Lupe and Ramón continued paying visits to the SRA offices in Mexico City to keep applying pressure for the measuring work to be done. Sometimes they were summoned to come to the offices in Mexico City to sign papers or to bring some documents. During one of those visits to the SRA buildings they met a man, Antonio Macías, who offered his assistance. There are always many 'gatekeepers' at the offices of the SRA; men who worked at the SRA or the peasant unions before and know their way around the bureaucracy. As most of the ejidatarios feel lost in the SRA, these gatekeepers offer their assistance. This assistance is normally paid for in meals or money. These men can be useful to the ejidatarios as they lead them around and bring them to the right places. However, there are also people who only try to take advantage of the insecurity of the ejidatarios.

Ramón and Lupe explained to me that at first they had been a little bit afraid, as they did not know Antonio, but when they showed him their papers he took them to the various offices. He helped them a great deal and Lupe and Ramón were impressed that he seemed to know all the people at the different desks. Lupe stressed that he had been so nice and did not want to charge them anything. But they gave him 100,000 pesos (US$33) which made him very happy. Antonio said that he would help them with everything and said that he did not agree with the insolent way in which the officials treat ejidatarios.

During this visit to Mexico City, Lupe and Ramón stayed with two sons of don Miguel's first marriage, stepsons of Lupe. The wife of one of them accompanied them to the offices of the SRA. She noticed that Lupe and Ramón were going around with Antonio and warned them that this boy would only 'relieve them of their money'. Yet, Raúl and Lupe interpreted the fact that the people at the various offices appeared to know him and treated him well as meaning that he was an important person who might be of great use to them.

According to Lupe, Antonio was head of the *Liga de Comunidades Agrarias* (a peasant organisation affiliated to the ruling PRI). According to a friend of mine, who did some research, Antonio Macías did indeed work for this organisation, but was only one of the assistants of the head of the Liga de Comunidades Agrarias. Ramón told me that Antonio was their last hope. Yet I was amazed that, after two years of deceit, Ramón could believe in a person he had just met and be so enthusiastic about him. So, I asked Ramón: 'Don Ramón, how can you believe in Antonio when you just met him and do not know him?' Ramón replied: 'It is not a question of belief but of hope. I hope that this will work out well. I do not believe in anything anymore. But hope is the last thing one gives up.'

After this visit to Mexico City, Antonio regularly phoned them (expensive reverse-charge calls) to ask how things were going. One day, Antonio offered to come to Guadalajara to 'undo the knot' at the SRA office. According to him, the SRA office in Guadalajara was obstructing the procedures for measuring the land in La Canoa. Antonio wanted his airplane ticket and his expenses for the day paid for. Lupe did not want to go to Guadalajara as she refused to spend more of her own money on the matter. So Ramón would go on his own to receive Antonio. Lupe and Ramón convened a meeting with the supporters of the fight for the 'lost land' in order to collect the money. Some twelve people arrived at this private meeting but they did not collect the required amount of money and Ramón would have to pay part of the expenses out of his own pocket. In Guadalajara, Antonio and Ramón went to the SRA office and Antonio asked for the work order, which Serrano had received for the work in La Canoa. He made copies of it and gave one to Ramón. Ramón gave him 650,000 pesos (US$217) but Antonio said that that was not enough. He told Ramón that he not only needed money for the airplane but that he also had to maintain his family and his parents. So he asked Ramón for more money. Ramón also had to pay for his breakfast and the cab to the airport. Then he left for Mexico City again.

On the basis of this visit Ramón's faith in Antonio decreased. The only thing Antonio did was to get Serrano's work order. However, Ramón was above all disappointed because he noticed that Antonio was not the important man Ramón had assumed him to be. At the Guadalajara office nobody knew Antonio and they paid little attention to him. They asked him for an identity document, which he could not give. According to Ramón, he only had a little piece of paper, which did not impress anyone in the Guadalajara office. Ramírez, the surveyors' boss, did not even want to receive him. All of this made Ramón conclude that Antonio was not an important person and could therefore never be of much help.

When Antonio later phoned them and said that he wanted to come to Guadalajara again, Ramón told him that he should only come with orders from Mexico City. Yet, Lupe and Ramón remained in contact with him. When they were working with the different surveyors, they also kept in touch with Antonio as they might perhaps need him in the future. At the beginning of December 1993 Antonio phoned them and told them to participate in a demonstration in Mexico City for Colosio, the PRI candidate in the presidential elections of 1994, but they did not go. Sometimes Lupe became annoyed with Antonio as his frequent reverse-charge phone calls from Mexico City were very expensive.

Like Salazar and Serrano, Antonio made many promises and told them many things that appeared not to be true. For example, in December Antonio phoned Lupe to tell her that Serrano would come again to the village on 20 December. Lupe told me: 'Antonio always pretends to be an important person.' Serrano did not arrive.

However, in the beginning of January 1994 Lupe was very enthusiastic again after a phone call from Antonio. He called on Friday to tell her that he had gone to Guadalajara with the *oficialía mayor* (high official) of the SRA in Mexico City. According to Antonio, the *oficialía mayor* had been very angry with Pelayo, the head of the SRA in Guadalajara, and had asked him what was going on in Guadalajara. He gave Pelayo orders to start the work next week. Antonio told Lupe that the surveyor would come on Monday and that he himself would visit La Canoa next Tuesday or Wednesday. However, he urged them to send him 700,000 pesos immediately, as he did not have money to travel next week. He needed the money before Monday. Lupe believed Antonio but had her doubts as well. Together with Ramón she decided to collect the money Antonio had asked for but not to send it right away. When I was at Lupe's house on Monday, Antonio phoned from Mexico City. Lupe asked me to listen with her on the other telephone. The conversation between Lupe and Antonio went as follows.

A: The work order will now be sent to Guadalajara by fax and then everything will start.

L: You remember that you told me on Friday that they would come today?

A: Yes.

L: I called Guadalajara and there they say that they know nothing about it. You know, people here lose confidence by these small things. For that reason I could not collect the 700,000 pesos. The people do not want to contribute anymore.

A: Don't worry, you know that the high official committed himself to La Canoa's case on Friday. I will call you tomorrow after they sent the fax.
[Antonio phoned from his home and we could hear a baby crying in the background.]

L: What is the name of this official and what is his telephone number?

A: His name is Raúl Pineda. I don't have his telephone number at hand but I will give it to you tomorrow. Then you can check for yourself that everything is all right. But tomorrow I will phone you after the fax is sent. If you allow me to reverse charges again. Otherwise, I will let them call you directly from the SRA office.

L: Tomorrow we are not here.

A: You are not?

L: No, we are going to Guadalajara to talk to the head of the SRA, Pelayo.

A: But that is not necessary any more, everything is arranged.

L: Yes, but we have an appointment for tomorrow.

A: I don't think it a good idea that you go to Guadalajara. Naturally, you have to decide yourselves, but it is a pity to make a trip if it isn't necessary. It is a pity because of the money you will spend on it. They are already working on the case here. But you have to decide for yourselves. I will call you when you are with Pelayo then. The fax will probably arrive at Pelayo's office at 12.00.

L: We have an appointment with Pelayo at 11.00.

A: Then I will call you there. You will see that everything is fine.

L: The point is that the people here have lost faith after all the experiences we have had. I haven't lost faith, but the other people have.

A: They will arrive this week. But it will not necessarily be the same surveyor that comes.

Then the phone call ended. Lupe did not feel very confident about the distrustful way in which she had addressed Antonio. She liked the person of the *high official* in Antonio's stories: that sounded like an important person. On the other hand, she did not trust Antonio's stories and promises any more.

Several things surprised me in this phone call. First of all, it was clear that Lupe had become much more skilful in her dealing with brokers. She confronted Antonio with the contradictions in his own stories, but she did not directly say that she did not believe him any more. She said that the others in the ejido had become distrustful, not she. Second, Antonio directly reacted to the changing attitude of Lupe. He was respectful and did not talk about money any more. We can see here that actions labelled as 'corruption' are made up of complex practices, with strong performative aspects (Gupta 1995: 379). It is a play one can be good or bad at. It is not a vulgar way of wheedling money out of other people. When Antonio felt that he was losing ground, he changed his attitude and did not raise the issue of the money any more. Another reaction could have been to become angry at this incredulity on the part of the ejidatarios and say that they are ungrateful for everything he had done for them. Actually, that is a much more common reaction of officials or brokers when they are confronted with criticism or distrust from ejidatarios. However, Antonio chose another way out. Nothing happened that week and Antonio did not call for quite some time. According to Lupe, he certainly felt exposed.

However, some time later Lupe herself decided to call Antonio again when they did not achieve anything through the other channels. When Antonio offered to come to Guadalajara again, she responded that it would be better for him to try to get a mission organised from Mexico City. They would then pay him afterwards when they received the land. Antonio never showed up again.

THE PRIEST VISITING THE HEAD OF THE SRA IN GUADALAJARA

Lupe and Father López

Lupe had lost faith in the lawyer Salazar. When she phoned Salazar, he never answered any more; he was never at home, nor at his office. After a while Salazar moved to another house and also changed his telephone number. Salazar was unreachable. During a visit Lupe and I paid to Father López, he said that he was very sad that Salazar had behaved in such a miserable way with La Canoa and had only been interested in money. He explained that his faith in Salazar was based on the fact that Salazar was the *compadre* of the former priest. Salazar had caused Father López several other problems. Besides La Canoa, Salazar also had been dealing with other ejidos for Father López. Father López had tried to find out where Salazar had moved to and had discovered his new telephone number which he passed on to Lupe. Now he was trying to find out Salazar's new address, so that he could pay him a 'surprise visit'.

Father López said that Héctor Romero, the former head of the security policy and one of the *pequeños propietarios* who possessed a part of the 'lost land', had visited him twice now to tell him to abandon the case of La Canoa. Héctor had added that he was the godfather of the Mayor of Autlán and that Father López should be very careful. Another *pequeño propietario* had also told him to stop and did not greet him any more when he came to Mass on Sunday. However, Father López said that he was not afraid and that from now on he would spend more time on La Canoa. Some weeks later I met Father López in the street and he told me that the bishop had told him to stop interfering in agrarian conflicts. Father López did not agree with the bishop, he said. He wanted to take advantage of the time that Salinas was still in power. Then he could still use his influential contacts. He explained to me that he had been to school with one of the guards of President Salinas and in this way he was able to arrange certain things. He also knew the Governor of Jalisco from a party where they had had a chat together and this was also a contact he could use.

The Priest Meets the Head of the SRA

At the beginning of 1994, Father López used his contacts in Mexico City to make an appointment with the head of the SRA in Guadalajara, Pelayo. Pelayo had the reputation of being very corrupt and, as we saw before, it was said that Pelayo himself had ordered the suspension of the measuring work in La Canoa. For Lupe and Ramón the prospect of meeting Pelayo was very exciting because they knew that he was very influential and they hoped that through Father López and his powerful contacts, Pelayo could be pressed to work in the interest of La Canoa. So the appointment with Pelayo was a special occasion and everybody was nervous. Lupe, Ramón, Father López and I went to the appointment. Lupe tried to persuade Raúl to come as well but he did not want to go. He only gave his written authorisation as commissioner. I had made an extensive file with copies of all the relevant official documents. Lupe and Ramón had not slept well the night before. Lupe told us that she had had nightmares in which her son took her from La Canoa to the bus station in Autlán and while they drove on and on, they never arrived at the bus station.

At the SRA Father López presented us to an ejidatario of Tuxcacuesco. It became clear that Father López's visit to the head of the SRA was not only to defend the case of La Canoa, but also those of the ejidos Tuxcacuesco and Apulco and of the *comunidad indígena* of Autlán, which all have serious land conflicts with private landowners. Apparently, Father López was becoming a broker in agrarian conflicts. At eleven o'clock Father López was called for the appointment with Pelayo. The five of us entered the room. Father López shook hands with Pelayo.

Father López started to explain the reason for his visit. In contrast to the usual attitude of ejidatarios, the priest was self-confident and gave lengthy explanations. He carefully stressed the point that he was the friend of one of President Salinas's personal secretaries. Pelayo was a little irritated by all this talking but remained respectful. López noticed Pelayo's impatience but went on with his roundabout descriptions. He talked about the lawyer who had asked 20 million pesos from the ejidatarios of La Canoa and then disappeared. When López talked about the problems of La Canoa, Pelayo asked for more precise information. I will present part of the dialogue that followed.

Pelayo: What kind of problems are you talking about?
López looked at Lupe to answer the question.
Lupe (insecure): Eh, we have a '*rezago*', a problem ...
Pelayo (irritated): But does it concern an agrarian action [*acción agraria*] that was never finished or internal agrarian rights? What is the problem about?

Ramón took over and started with much enthusiasm a very unclear story about land that was taken away from the ejido. Pelayo phoned Ramírez and told him to come immediately to the office.

Pelayo (irritated) to Lupe and Ramón: And who are you, are you members of the executive committee of the ejido?
Ramón: No, I am not.
Pelayo to Lupe: And you?
Lupe: I am the treasurer of the ejido.
Pelayo: And the ejido commissioner, he didn't want to come?
Lupe: Eh, no eh, a relative of his is ill and he couldn't come, but he (pointing to Ramón) is the secretary of the ejido.
Ramón: I am the substitute of the secretary [he said substitute at a very low voice so that only the word secretary was well heard].
Pelayo: And don't you have any documents with you?

Ramón came to me to get the documents I had with me and I gave him the ones I thought were most relevant. Ramírez, the head of the surveyors, arrived now. He was very friendly to us and Pelayo gave him the documents and asked Ramírez: 'What is this all about?!' Ramírez read the documents and said to Pelayo: 'This is what we were discussing lately.' They started discussing the matter between the two of them in legal terms, which were unintelligible to us. Pelayo read the work order of Serrano and asked the visitors: 'And this work has never been done?'

Ramón (vehemently): No, he only came for one day, then he invited all the neighbours of the ejido to a meeting and never came back, then you apparently recalled the order, then on the telephone he offered to do the measuring work during his Christmas holiday but then we would have to pay for it ourselves!
Pelayo to Ramírez: This work has never been finished?
Ramírez: No, I wanted to talk to Serrano about it but then the holidays came ...
Pelayo to Ramírez: What kind of work is this of these surveyors! Issue immediately another work order for another surveyor!
Pelayo to us: We will immediately write a new work order.
Lupe: Does that mean that they will measure all the ejido land and not only the 126 hectares; they are invading us on all sides.
Pelayo: This commission only concerns informative work, which will be sent to Mexico on the basis of which they will elaborate the definitive ejido map. Where lies La Canoa, near Autlán?
Father López started explaining to him in great detail how to get to the village.
Pelayo: Perhaps we will come and visit you one day.
Ramón and *Lupe* (happy): That would be fantastic!

It was decided that next week a surveyor would come to the village to finish the work. Practical issues were now discussed. When the discussion on La Canoa was finished they continued with the case of Tuxcacuesco. The same dynamic repeated itself. Pelayo asked for very technical and formal procedures and neither the ejidatario from Tuxcacuesco nor Father López could give any answers to these questions. Again many new work orders were immediately issued. When everything was discussed, Father López gave a final speech in which he explained that he, as a priest, preferred not to interfere in these matters, but in these cases thought it was necessary to intervene. Pelayo and Ramírez listened without any expression on their faces. Father López extensively and patiently thanked Pelayo and Ramírez and again dropped the names of the people at the SRA in Mexico City and the office of Salinas who had arranged this meeting for him. We all shook hands and said goodbye.

Father López, Lupe and Ramón were very pleased with the results of this meeting. Most of all they liked the fact that so many decisions seemed to have been taken and that a new surveyor had been ordered to go to La Canoa. However, Lupe was bothered by the fact that Pelayo had said that the work only concerned information-gathering. Ramón was full of enthusiasm, although he said that he was not so hopeful as when

Serrano had arrived. However, he thought that the priest's involvement
had made a big difference.

The conversation shows several characteristic elements of the
interaction between ejidatarios and functionaries. First the usual
questions in formal legal terminology, the question of documents, and
the asking for the ejido commissioner. Then, when reference is made to
irregularities on the part of the SRA office, the functionaries do not react
at all. Although this time Ramón was very direct in his insinuation of
Pelayo's involvement in the withdrawal of the work order, the ejidatarios
do not easily call functionaries to account for irregularities. In his turn,
Pelayo blames everything on Serrano, he is indignant at the way in
which the surveyors work and reacts with a flurry of action. He
immediately issues new work orders and appoints new surveyors. In this
way, he suggests that the problem is of a technical-administrative nature
and will soon be resolved. He raises hope by suggesting that he will visit
them soon.

THE SECOND SURVEYOR: CASTAÑEDA

Two weeks after our visit to Pelayo, the next SRA surveyor from the
Guadalajara office arrived: Castañeda. The executive committee of La
Canoa and the neighbours of the ejido were summoned to a meeting at
the town hall in Autlán, but this time quite a different situation
developed. This time there was an attractive young woman among the
pequeños propietarios whom nobody from La Canoa knew. After
Castañeda had read out his work order, the girl went towards him with
some documents, which he silently read, in great detail. The other
pequeños propietarios grew impatient and wanted to leave. Iginio asked
the young lady who she was. It became clear that she was the daughter
of one of the families that illegally possess part of the 'lost land'. After
reading the documents the girl had given him, Castañeda asked the
ejidatarios a lot of silly questions about the situation of the land he had
to investigate and it looked as if he had not prepared for the job. He looked
for a long time at the maps and then very slowly folded the maps one
after the other. Everybody was watching him in astonishment and the
ejidatarios of La Canoa started to get bad feelings about this surveyor.
Castañeda proposed to take a look at the fields. While we left the building
Castañeda stayed on the staircase talking with the girl and a man who
joined them. The people of La Canoa noticed this and their distrust of him
grew. The surveyor was apparently establishing good relationships with
the 'enemy'. The girl left to get her truck and said that Castañeda could

come with her. Ramón, immediately joined the girl and Castañeda in her truck. The others all followed in other cars.

In the field the atmosphere was very negative. Everybody realised that things were going badly. Castañeda was only reading documents and walking around with the girl in the sugarcane fields. Castañeda and the girl separated themselves from the ejidatarios and they talked in a confidential way as if they had known each other for a long time. They started eating some of the sugarcane in the field. The 15 ejidatarios from La Canoa stood in small groups commenting that the situation looked unfavourable. After some 15 minutes, Castañeda said: 'Let's go and draw up a report.' Although everybody from La Canoa agreed that the surveyor was not doing his job, nobody asked him a question. Castañeda said that he would draw up the report at the office of Albamex in Autlán (the company and home address of the girl's father). So now a situation was created in which the ejidatarios were going to draw up a report at 'the house of the enemy'. At the office of Albamex it was decided that Castañeda would finish his report on his own and that he would present it later in the afternoon in La Canoa. The ejidatarios left the surveyor and returned to La Canoa.

A Meeting with Castañeda in La Canoa

The ejidatarios realised that this time they had been openly taken in by the SRA surveyor and only some 15 ejidatarios showed up at the meeting with Castañeda in the afternoon. They wanted to question Castañeda's work, but they did not know how to do this well. The meeting with Castañeda started in the following way.

Ignacio: The Indians took it in their own hands [referring to the rebellion in Chiapas, which broke out at the beginning of 1994], we are not much Indian.
Ramón: It would be good to be Indian, to be taken into account!

Castañeda was chewing gum, had a very uninterested expression on his face and did not react. The others started complaining about all these surveyors who always come to the ejido and never finish their work.

Ramón to Castañeda: How did you see the field, what land are we lacking?
Castañeda: That is something that I have to calculate now.

The ejidatarios gave Castañeda some documents to show that the land of the Pabellón, where they had been in the afternoon, had been bought by the SRA for the ejido.

Ignacio: Here it says that the SRA paid for the land.

Castañeda: I have searched for documents to prove that but I haven't found anything.

Ignacio started a detailed explanation but Castañeda showed no interest and was looking at other papers.

Ignacio: We did not expect you to do only the work you did today.

Ramón started reading out another document that proved their point, but Castañeda did not react and continued reading his own material.

Ignacio: In that case we take up arms, just like in Chiapas!

The ejidatarios started making jokes among themselves and Castañeda continued reading.

Ramón: El Pabellón is already known in the whole of Mexico; in all the different offices, even in Los Pinos [the presidential residence]!

Castañeda now started reading out the report he had written about his activities. The report gave a description of the land area. Quarrels arose among the ejidatarios about many details in the report. Castañeda took advantage of the division among the ejidatarios and accused Iginio of giving him false information.

Castañeda: And afterwards they will think that I deliberately made these changes. So everybody should know that you gave me this information!
Ramón: The report says nothing about the land that is lacking.
Castañeda: That is a calculation that I now have to make.

Doubts were rising among the ejidatarios as to whether they should sign this report or not. Everybody felt that Castañeda was deceiving them. Several people went outside and were deliberating about whether they should sign his report or not. One of the ejidatarios noticed that the work order talked about work till 28 January, while today it was only 24 January. The general conclusion was that Castañeda's work was very suspect and that they had better not sign agreeing with the report. All entered the ejido building again. When Castañeda finished reading his report, Iginio was the first to bravely show the dissatisfaction of the ejidatarios with his work.

Iginio: I do not agree, nothing has been measured!
Castañeda (angry): And haven't we been to the fields then?! This cannot be measured.

After this angry outburst of Castañeda, the ejidatarios became insecure and changed their attitude. They started criticising Iginio. They said that the work order only talked about a *localización topográfica*. Iginio himself also felt insecure now.

Castañeda: I do what they order me to do.
Vicente García to all ejidatarios: Are we going to sign this or not?
Ignacio Romero: I say yes.
Alberto Alcázar: The fear of signing is natural after what has happened, but this report does not oblige us to anything.
Ramón: I think it is correct.
Vicente: Some say it is all right, others say it is not.
Alberto to Castañeda: Why does it say five days on the work order?
Castañeda: The other days are for the calculation in Guadalajara.

Now there were no means left for the ejidatarios to judge or question the surveyor. No one made any further critical remarks and everyone signed the report. When he was packing his things together Castañeda accused the ejidatarios of having caused Serrano serious trouble by accusing him of corruption. As Castañeda put it: 'Rumours circulate in Guadalajara that Serrano asked 100 million to do the job and this caused him serious problems with Pelayo.' Ramón and Lupe responded that Serrano had offered to do the job in his holidays but that he had not mentioned a sum of money.

Afterwards it became clear that Castañeda had misled the ejidatarios in several ways. First, the work order of *localización topográfica* of the field El Pabellón implied that he should have stayed several days to measure the land. Second, Castañeda had received a second order for more measuring work in the ejido, which he never showed the ejidatarios.

This meeting is illustrative of several aspects of the relation between ejidatarios and officials. First, although there is a strong atmosphere of dissatisfaction on the part of the ejidatarios, they preferred not to directly express their disapproval. At the start of the meeting this discontent was indirectly expressed by several references to the armed struggle in Chiapas. They do not feel related to the Indian population, but they had great sympathy for the problems these groups had with the Mexican state and private landowners. Other indirect remarks by the ejidatarios also made it clear that they were dissatisfied with Castañeda's work. Actually this was one of the few occasions in which the ejidatarios openly, and in front of the official himself, questioned his integrity. The ejidatarios dislike direct confrontations with officials. In this case, obscure agrarian terminology was a central weapon of the official. He could easily eliminate the opposition by lying about agrarian procedures and the meaning of certain administrative terms. When the official pretended to be offended by the distrustful attitude of the ejidatarios, the ejidatarios quickly lost their confidence and signed the report. It is also significant here that the ejidatarios do not want to break off relations with the SRA. Even though they distrust officials, they do not want to spoil the relationship. They want to continue the relation with the bureaucratic machine. Signing documents is one of the acts through which this relation is maintained and they invest in the idea of the state.

Castañeda, in his turn, did not try to establish a friendly atmosphere. All the time he remained cool and distant. He lied about the procedures and acted offended when they openly criticised him. From the start of the meeting, he tried to create dissension among the ejidatarios and took advantage of quarrels among them. His hand was also strengthened by the fact that only a small group of ejidatarios came to the meeting.

DISTRUST, CONSPIRACY AND DEALING WITH CONTRADICTORY INFORMATION

As they were working through different channels and nothing seemed to work out well, mutual distrust as well as mutual accusations continued among the ejidatarios. I maintained contact with the different people separately and they could express themselves in very negative terms about each other. For example, Ramón expressed negative views of Raúl and Iginio.

R: Raúl is a fool and Iginio a shameless devil. Iginio works with the 'other party'.
M: But isn't Iginio also working to recover the land?
R: Yes, but through other channels. But he also works for the others; he probably received money!

In their turn, Raúl and Iginio accused Lupe and Ramón of operating on their own in the hope that they could keep the 'lost land'. Iginio: 'They hope to divide the land between the two of them.' People blamed each other for everything that went wrong and insinuated that others had their own private agendas against the interests of the ejido.

One phenomenon that bothered the ejidatarios fighting for the 'lost land' was the fact that the private landowners always managed to know what they were doing. According to the ejidatarios, the *pequeños* always seemed to know about their missions and made sure to bribe the officials before they arrived at the office. Roberto Sánchez said:

When we went on a mission to the SRA in Guadalajara we saw the *pequeños* in the bus coming back from Guadalajara. We always had secret meetings for this case but there was always a traitor. He informed the *pequeños* and they went to Guadalajara before we arrived. When we arrived at the SRA offices, the officials were already bought.

Others told similar stories. Lupe, for example, said that on their last trip to the SRA she saw Ricardo García at the bus station in Guadalajara. She assumed that he had been to the SRA to counter their actions. Teresa recalled that on one occasion in the past she and Macario had been waiting in a restaurant for somebody who would help them. When they looked through the window they saw the person they were waiting for, talking to 'the other party'. In Teresa's words: 'Sometimes you do not know whom you can trust and whom not. Not even of your own family. Sometimes it is better to work with outsiders.' To stress this point she gave another example of a relative of Lupe who worked at the SRA and promised to help them with everything. Afterwards it became clear to them that she was working for the *pequeños*. So, according to Teresa not even relatives were to be trusted.

In this way the ejidatarios were always speculating about the role of everybody else and an important component in their strategies was secrecy. Failures were often blamed on information reaching the 'enemy'. Information leakages were a main danger as the private landowners could directly impair anything La Canoa had accomplished. This caution about passing on information also concerned the ejido documents. Even within the loose configuration of people that was working on the 'lost land', they were very reluctant to pass important documents to each other. However, plenty of other reasons, besides traitors who passed information to 'the enemy', could always be found to explain why things went wrong. For example, somebody could argue that they had not reacted in time to certain letters, or that the commissioner had signed the wrong document. A common critique was also that they had not paid the surveyor enough, or had not treated him 'well enough'.

In their conspiracy theories the ejidatarios also speculated about the 'location of evil'. Some ejidatarios considered the SRA office in Guadalajara to be the main problem and thought that, as long as everything was arranged through Mexico City, it would be all right. They hoped that their superiors in Mexico City would overrule the officials in Guadalajara. Some also commented that the documents and the maps in Guadalajara were falsified and that the 'true documents' were still in Mexico City. On other occasions it was said that the 'real documents' were in Guadalajara but that the officials refused to give them.

The continuous stream of contradictory messages they received from different sides fomented all these speculations. All the people they worked with said something different to them, and all the time they received information they should act upon. Many times they were told to come immediately to Guadalajara and Mexico City to arrange some documents. On one occasion, for example, an official of the Guadalajara office told Iginio that La Canoa should hurry with their case as he had heard that a lawyer in Autlán was 'legalising' the illegal land titles of the *pequeños propietarios* for 1 million pesos per hectare. This was a disquieting message. However, fortunately it was followed by a much more hopeful message. Suddenly, one day, the happy news was spread in La Canoa that the Mexican President Salinas had said on television that La Canoa would be the next ejido to be measured. Several ejidatarios, Lupe, Iginio, Ignacio Alcázar and others passed me this rumour. Some said that Salinas had made his declaration on television and others said it was on the radio, but all were equally hopeful and enthusiastic after this fantastic news.

As I had been doing some research of my own, I gradually discussed with the ejidatarios the information I had found in the SRA and the conclusions I myself was arriving at. I felt that this might lead to difficult conversations as my ideas sometimes went against their views. However, it was obvious that the idea that there could only be 'one valid theory' was my problem and not theirs. They had no difficulty with different theories. They always listened carefully when they received new information. They were looking for all types of data and were interested in all findings. But they did not necessarily arrive at conclusions about the truth or reliability of information. Nor did they try to arrive at coherent and absolute theories. They could live with contradictory information and opposite versions at the same time. For the same reason, they never seemed to be surprised by information that was in apparent contradiction with their own versions and beliefs.

ABOUT MAPS AND OTHER 'HARD DATA'

As I myself became fascinated by this highly complex conflict and tried to come to grips with it, I studied many documents and maps. I also tried to arrive at a clear analysis of the situation and talked everything over with the ejidatarios. Yet, after researching for some time I came to the conclusion that my use of maps, documents and figures was different from that of the ejidatarios. First, I discovered that there was great uncertainty about the size of the 'lost land'; figures for the numbers of hectares that were involved differed. Most ejidatarios said that they did not know how much land was involved. Others gave different figures. For example, Salvador said that it concerned approximately 100 hectares, whereas Iginio told me that it was 200, almost 300 hectares. Manuel Pradera said that he heard people say that it concerned more than 100 hectares and three or four different land areas. Vicente García told me that, besides the fact that they did not know how much land they lacked, nobody actually knew how much land La Canoa had in its possession. Once, when I mentioned the 540 hectares that were missing, according to the letter that Salazar had written to the Mexican president,

Raúl exclaimed: 'So many hectares?!' Some time later, I worked one afternoon with Ramón and Raúl to make a summary of the problems of La Canoa for Father López, who had asked for a clear and understandable explanation of the problems of the ejido. This analysis was above all based on Ramón's information. On the basis of what he told me about the different fields and problems I arrived at a figure of approximately 260 missing hectares. The greatest part concerned rainfed land, but an important part was irrigated land.

Yet, after Salazar had sent the letter to the Mexican president, which said that they were lacking 540 hectares, the ejidatarios started using this figure. For example, Lupe, who had never before mentioned the number of hectares involved, started talking about the 540 hectares the ejido was missing. Iginio, who had before talked about 200 or 300 hectares now also talked about the 540 hectares they were missing. In other matters I also noticed that people who had studied the documents sometimes gave exactly the same information as I had found in the archives. Thus, they seemed to use figures they had found in the documents.

In this context I also developed mixed feelings about the role of the ejido map in their struggle for the 'lost land'. As we saw, the ejido map is the central object for the ejidatarios in their struggle. By recovering this map, they hope to win the conflict. So, I showed the ejidatarios several maps of La Canoa and asked them to explain to me the problems of the different fields and the problems with the existing maps. However, when I showed Lupe the map of the extension of the ejido on which the endowment lands were also indicated, and asked her to indicate the location of the lands that were 'lost', she responded that she was not capable of doing so. She said that she could not do anything with the map and instead started explaining the situation to me in 'physical terms' referring to certain points in the lands: a bridge, a house, certain fields, etc. So, she did not know how to link the land she knew so well in practical terms with the lines on the paper. Teresa could not do so either. However, when I showed the map to Teresa she recognised the names of certain fields on the map and, like Lupe, she explained the physical position of these lands and their histories. Men who had not been actively involved in the struggle also could not 'read' maps. For example, when I showed the commissioner Raúl maps of the ejido and asked him if he could tell me where the 'lost lands' were situated he said that he could not do anything with a map.

As many people apparently could not 'read maps', I developed the feeling that the map they were chasing after perhaps stood for something else. The men of 'the group of the lost land' who for many years had studied documents, maps and the Agrarian Law, certainly had no problems in indicating the different parts of 'lost land' on the map, but all their stories differed. Some gave more technical details to distinguish the 'real map' from the 'useless maps'. For example, according to Iginio the name of this 'real map' was the 'combined map' (*plano conjunto*) and it clearly indicated the correct ejido borders. Iginio said that in order to distinguish between good maps and bad maps it was important that the maps were signed by the right surveyor.

Naturally, the fact that people do not agree on the data concerning the 'lost land', can be explained by the difference between the lifeworld of the ejidatarios and the official legal-bureaucratic world. Furthermore, many different fields are concerned in the 'lost land' which all have different histories and are involved in conflicts with distinct legal and adminis-trative aspects. As we saw, the establishment of the ejido has been unclear from the beginning; procedures have not been followed, lands have never been measured, and documents gave contradictory information about borders and areas. This explains why local story-telling about the 'lost land' is to a certain degree shaped and changed by the interactions and experiences with the agrarian bureaucracy.

Yet, the most interesting phenomenon is the way documents, events and maps are read and interpreted in the light of a labyrinthine bureau-cratic machine. Their focus on the map should be seen as the embodiment of the conflict in an administrative artefact: a re-enchantment of a governmental technique. Their concentration on the map makes it possible for the ejidatarios to establish a relationship with the bureaucracy; it is a recognised administrative document they can ask for. In this way, the map has become a fetish. Besides making it possible to engage the bureaucracy, the fetishised map also plays an important role in the local mobilising of people; it is a material object upon which a collective sentiment is fixed (see Durkheim 1965 [1912] on fetishes). Although the ejidatarios disagree amongst themselves about the details of the conflict, the fetishised map can raise feelings of collective interests and makes people join forces when necessary.

This also explains why the ejidatarios have no problems in dealing with contradictory information and can easily switch positions. For example, after researching for some time, I told them individually that, according to the official data, a definitive ejido map of La Canoa was never made when the ejido was established. This meant that there was no map that got 'lost' and that there was no map hidden somewhere in an office. I thought that this was a sensitive theme and that the people who were closest to the fight for the 'lost land' would not be pleased with me talking about the possibility that the map had never existed.

However, they did not mind hearing 'another theory'. For example, Iginio and Ramón listened to my findings with interest, but without drawing any conclusions. Others even seemed to like my theory about a map that never existed. When I said to Lupe that I believed that the definitive ejido map had never existed, she said that she agreed with me and that everybody had always falsely accused her husband of giving the land to his brother and getting rid of the map. She said: 'I never knew anything about that. The map that I saw here on the table perhaps was not the definitive map. Maybe it was only a big map of the surroundings ... of the state of Jalisco!' Raúl also liked 'my theory' that the map was never made. He said that this information was new but convinced him that they could never influence the state of affairs and should not spend any more money on the case. Raúl felt that 'my theory' strengthened his position. Again this shows that the map is an artefact, an embodiment of the fantasies constructed about the 'lost land'. It is the embodiment of a struggle which people want to play out in different ways. At the same time, it is very probable that the ejidatarios who today are tired of the struggle and say that the map was probably never made, tomorrow will again go after 'the map that once got lost' when they try to recover the land.

After they had lost contact with Salazar, Lupe and Ramón easily distanced themselves from the data Salazar had given them that they had believed in before. For example, on one occasion, I carefully tried to say to Lupe that after a thorough study of their case it could appear that they really lacked much less than 560 hectares. But Lupe was not hurt by my remark. She said that she had never known the number of hectares they were fighting for anyway. When I suggested that Salazar had perhaps written this letter to please them, Lupe reacted: 'Not to please us but to deceive us!' When I talked to Ramón about the fact that the letter to the Mexican president and the list of beneficiaries for the 'lost land' that they had established had, according to other people, not been done properly, Ramón reacted: 'The lawyer only did that to get money from us, he brainwashed us ...'

The conclusion to be drawn from this is that, in their struggle for the 'lost land', the ejidatarios are always theorising, speculating and 'reading' messages. The point is not that the ejidatarios 'believe' everything officials or brokers tell them. Rather, they deal with many points of entry to the bureaucratic machine, work with many brokers at the same time, receive numerous often contradictory messages, and it is not clear precisely what is happening. In this labyrinth they try to construct a certain logic which helps them to decide how to go on. But they never hold on to their own theories strongly. They quickly change ideas and never seem surprised about anything. One day they can say of one of the ejidatarios that he is probably 'bought' by the *pequeños*, and the next day they can work with him again. They have the same attitude towards brokers. They can have lost faith in a broker or official because of a bad experience or an apparent lie, but can work with him again shortly afterwards.

THE THIRD SURVEYOR TO ARRIVE AT THE EJIDO: MORALES

The next time Raúl and Ramón visited the SRA in Guadalajara to demand the continuation of the measuring work, they found the building almost empty. They were told that everybody had gone to the funeral of one of the surveyors: Serrano. Serrano had supposedly died of a liver disease. For the ejidatarios, however, Serrano was added to the long list of SRA surveyors who had 'vanished' after they had started a measuring job in La Canoa.

After Castañeda a third surveyor was assigned to La Canoa, but the man refused to go to the ejido. By now La Canoa had the reputation among the surveyors of being a difficult ejido and nobody wanted to go there. Then another surveyor was appointed who suddenly was called away for another job. Finally, a fifth surveyor, Morales, was given the task. He was the third surveyor in this period to arrive at the ejido. Morales arrived in La Canoa on 15 March 1994. Lupe happened to be away then as she had left for the USA to visit her children. Her son Juan decided not to tell her anything about the arrival of Morales.

Morales was in his 30s and had a pleasant, open attitude towards the ejidatarios. He knew many details about the land problems of La Canoa and had apparently done a thorough study of the case before coming to the ejido. He was the only surveyor who brought the instruments for the measuring. The ejidatarios were delighted with this surveyor and had a lot of confidence in him from the start. At his first meeting in La Canoa Morales told the ejidatarios that they should say at the SRA office: 'If the measuring work is not done well, we will do the same as the people in Chiapas ...' Morales had a populist style of operating. He was very capable in his dealings with the ejidatarios and the other parties. At the meetings he gave answers to the many unrelated questions people always ask about agrarian procedures and made many jokes. He said that he was a great admirer of Emiliano Zapata, the revolutionary fighter who demanded land reform in the beginning of the twentieth century. He stressed that the work had to be done quickly before Salinas left the presidency as then the SRA programmes would probably be changed again.

At the meeting at the town hall in Autlán in which the neighbours of La Canoa were informed again about the measuring work, the same girl arrived who had been walking with Castañeda. This time she arrived with a man who told Morales that he was a friend of the girl's family who owned lands that adjoined the lands of La Canoa. He said that they were prepared to help Morales with everything he needed. Morales said that the owner of the land himself should come or that otherwise they should come with a letter authorised by him. The man was displeased by Morales' answer and he and the girl left without saying anything. After this event, the ejidatarios were even more pleased with 'their surveyor'. Although I understood that the ejidatarios liked this surveyor much better than all the others, again I was surprised to see them so hopeful and enthusiastic. I asked Teresa how it was possible that people seemed to believe without reservation every time, when they had been deceived so many times. Teresa said: 'That is because we are exhausted and want this so very much to happen. You can compare this with the situation that you are very tired and very thirsty; then you buy a glass of water at any price.'

There was only one drawback with Morales. It soon became clear that he was an alcoholic. Although drinking by men was never considered to be a problem in the village, in the case of Morales people soon noticed that this was a serious case. He did not eat, drank enormous quantities and had trembling hands. However, the ejidatarios did not think that this was necessarily a problem for the measuring of the land. During the day Morales could function fine. It was only in the evening that he started drinking and passed out.

Morales stayed several days in a hotel in Autlán. The ejidatarios had several informal gatherings with him. He very much enjoyed talking about agrarian matters and explaining his views and theories. To my surprise, even Raúl, who I had never seen drinking before, was drinking during these meetings. The ejidatarios expressed their feelings, doubts, and presented their 'conspiracy theories' about who was sabotaging them. Morales gave his own views on the matter and said: 'I am conscious of the fact that there are many interests in this zone that work in the favour of the private landowners. General García Barragán has had great influence here.' According to Morales, Serrano's work was not cancelled because of political pressures or because Pelayo, the head of the SRA, had been bribed by the *pequeños* but because the rumour was spread that Serrano had asked 100 million pesos to finish the job. He said that Serrano died of cirrhosis and had not left a report. About Castañeda, Morales said that he was corrupt: he never finished the job, did not leave a report, and it was rumoured that he was walking around 'in love'. According to Morales, his boss Ramírez was honest otherwise he would not have sent him to do this job. Ramírez had only told Morales that it was a very difficult case but had not given him 'special instructions'. Morales gave the ejidatarios many copies of important documents he had found in Guadalajara and told them not to tell in Guadalajara that he had given those to them. When I took a photograph of him with the ejidatarios, he did not want the documents to appear on the photo and put them away.

So, Morales claimed that the problems with the different surveyors so far had little to do with bribes or political influence. On the other hand, he did not deny the possibility that people might try to stop him. He explained that he was aware of the influence of the late General Barragán and his allies in this region and suggested that they might try to influence the measuring work. He acknowledged that it was possible that *pequeños propietarios* were now talking to his boss to try to recall his work order. He therefore suggested that the work should be done very quickly and promised the ejidatarios that he would immediately inform them if his work order was recalled. He stressed the necessity of putting pressure on the offices. Morales was only sent to do the measuring of one land area, El Pabellón, and he said that as soon as he was finished they should demand that the SRA measure the next part. Morales advised that: 'If necessary you should go with large groups from La Canoa to the office and with the women as well.' He gave the example of an ejido who arrived with a group of screaming women and explained that that is something they are very afraid of. He explained that the situation in Chiapas also worked in their favour as well as the fact that Salinas's term was coming to its end. According to Morales, Salinas wanted to finish most of the projects he had started. He suggested that, if necessary, the ejidatarios should look for publicity in the newspapers and through other channels. So Morales was giving the ejidatarios practical advice to deal with the SRA in a more political way. However, he also blamed the ejidatarios themselves for not knowing their own borders well and for quarrelling among themselves.

On another occasion when I was alone with Morales we talked for a long time about the problems of La Canoa and their dealings with the SRA. I explained to him why we thought that Pelayo and Ramírez were involved and had cancelled the measuring. Morales listened carefully and said that it could be that they were indeed involved. He said that personally he did not like Pelayo and explained that when he had to arrange difficult matters he called his friends at the offices in Mexico City to ask them about the best ways to 'play the game'. Besides contacts at the SRA, he also had good friends in other government offices (*gobernación*) who could sometimes help him. According to him, La Canoa was not such a difficult case. Morales said: 'People are much too scared. They always talk about killings and murders but in reality this does not happen so often.' He said that he was against the uprisings in Chiapas but that he used Chiapas if this helped him to pressure the SRA and search for fair solutions to land problems. Morales said that he loved his work at the SRA and that according to him there was no other job in which you experience so much. He hoped for a career through PRI networks and supported Colosio as PRI candidate for the presidency. He aspired to the position of Ramírez or even Pelayo with the change of president in 1994. Unfortunately for Morales, Colosio would later be killed and Zedillo would become president. This meant that other PRI networks became influential.

Measuring the Field

The measuring of El Pabellón would take place on Saturday. At seven o'clock in the morning everybody was waiting at the ejido house in the village but Morales did not arrive. Then they decided to go to El Pabellón but they did not find him there either. Then they went to Autlán, where they found him at the hotel, which he was just about to leave. He had been drinking the night before. At a quarter past eight the work in the field started. There were 30 men, which was a high number as only approximately 30 ejidatarios possess lands in El Pabellón and not so many people were needed to carry the instruments. Teresa and I were the only women. Some men were paid to help with the measuring work by the ejidatarios who possessed plots in El Pabellón. Others who did not possess land in El Pabellón participated to see what would happen. Some were accused of only coming out of curiosity and others of participating out of interest in the land that might be recovered.

Morales decided to measure the land that the ejidatarios actually possess. In that way he could later calculate how much they lacked. Ramón did not agree with this procedure as he preferred to measure the land that belonged to the ejido according to the 'act of possession and marking of boundaries of the endowment of 1938' (*acta de posesión y deslinde*). Ramón did not agree with the point where they started the measuring operation either and the whole day he stood aside of the rest. For the measuring procedure sticks were put in the ground following the present borders of the ejido and a laser instrument which stood at the next stop determined the distance to the stick. When this was done, the next part of the border was measured. Morales wrote everything down in great detail. He also noted the names of all the neighbouring owners of the lands.

It became clear that the ejidatarios who knew most about the problems with the 'lost land', did not agree about which lands formally belonged to La Canoa. According to Ramón, they were missing lands on all sides, but according to Iginio and others they were only missing on the northern side of El Pabellón. As Morales only measured the land the ejido has in actual possession these disagreements about the right borders did not cause problems with the measuring work. Despite the disagreements and some quarrelling, it was a pleasant day in which we walked, talked, ate and laughed a lot.

In the afternoon the measuring was finished and money was collected to buy beer and soft drinks. After the bottles were finished the group broke up. Morales decided to stay in the village and continued drinking with Iginio. In the morning he was invited to a party at another house. From there they took him to the football game in La Canoa and afterwards Morales left for Guadalajara.

Morales' style of operation obviously differed from that of the other surveyors the ejidatarios had been dealing with so far. Morales was ambitious, enthusiastic and enjoyed being in the field with the ejidatarios. The fact that he slept in Iginio's house and stayed part of the Sunday in the village illustrates his different style. However, we can also see similarities in the way he deals with politics in the SRA. Like many officials, Morales did not deny the fact that political pressures influence agrarian conflicts and that the efforts to measure the ejido lands of La Canoa could be sabotaged from above. Again we find an official who will not deny the possibility that others, or he himself, may become involved in the political game. It is also apparent that he has no insight into what precisely is going on and who are pulling the strings. Although Morales appreciated Ramírez, he listened to critical theories about him and he did not deny the possibility that Ramírez might be playing a dubious role in this affair. Although, on the one hand, he acknowledged the political pressures that probably work against the ejido, on the other hand, he used the formalist bureaucratic discourse, which says that the case is not difficult at all providing one follows the formal procedures. Yet, Morales puts more stress on the importance of other forms of pressure. He suggested the ejidatarios put pressure on the SRA by going there in large groups with screaming women and looking for publicity.

The Struggle Comes to an Unhappy Ending

At the end of March, Morales told the ejidatarios that he had finished the job and that they should come to Guadalajara to demand the continuation of the measuring work. Morales did not say anything about the number of hectares he had calculated. They received a provisional map which Morales had produced of El Pabellón but nothing was said about the number of hectares that were lacking, nor about the people who were invading ejido lands. Many visits to the SRA followed. Morales was also drawing up the total map of the ejido but without coming to the ejido and measuring any of the other land. The group of the 'lost land' realised that the map that was going to be produced would not include the 'lost land'. However, everybody was tired of these years of struggling and they seem to come to terms with the idea that they would never recover the 'lost land'. La Canoa was now confronted with new problems with the neighbouring ejido La Piedra that had invaded a large part of the commons of La Canoa. For that reason, many ejidatarios felt the urgent need to have a definitive map, even if it contained errors, to fight possible future conflicts. They agreed that Morales had done a good job and was not to blame for their problems. The ejido paid Morales 10 million pesos (US$3,300) to finish the map.

In May 1994 I left the region to go and settle in the neighbouring state of Michoacán. Up to the end of 1995 I paid several visits to La Canoa. At the beginning of 1995 Father López had been replaced and sent to another region. Before he left the region he had told Lupe that the ejido should be happy with the land they possessed and that they would get into serious trouble if they continued this fight. President Salinas's administration had ended at the end of 1994 and numerous scandals about murders, drug trafficking and stealing by his administration had followed his leaving office. Lupe laughed about the hopes they had had when Salinas came to power and talked about helping the ejidatarios.

Lupe about Salinas: He brought the campesinos down, we failed [*nos hundió a los campesinos, no pudimos*]. Salinas also stole from Mexico; I saw that on television in the United States; there they say everything, here they don't.
M: Would you try it again?
Lupe: I have no faith any more, it is impossible to beat the rich [*Ya no tengo fe, contra el rico no se puede*]. In Chiapas the rich people possess everything.

She made an additional remark about Serrano's death.

Lupe: That was a suspicious death ... he did not return to the village; he got cirrhosis, they say he worked well ... perhaps they startled him.

Lupe was never called to account for the money she had spent on Salazar. No questions were asked about it at the ejido meeting in which the ejido accounts were presented. Raúl had asked the other ejidatarios not to cause her any trouble as she had spent the money with good intentions and she herself had suffered a lot. Lupe was very grateful for this: 'They are good people, they do not blame me for anything. I can breathe quietly now.'

Ramón had also become resigned to the idea that most of the 'lost land' would not be recovered in the near future, but he concentrated on the struggle for the land that was lacking in one small part of the 'lost land', El Pabellón. He had found more documents at the SRA and thought that they would have a chance. Ramón had contacted the man who in former times had helped them at the Communist Party and this man had recommended two lawyers affiliated to the PRD (Partido de la Revolución Democrática) opposition party. Ramón continued working with two older men and with two young ejidatarios who had never been involved in the struggle for the 'lost land' before. So, a new configuration of people was formed and the struggle for the 'lost land' continued. A never-ending story ...

CONCLUSION: MODERN MYTHS AND THE CULTURE OF THE STATE

Considering the history of agrarian reform and land conflicts in Mexico it is improbable that the ejido La Canoa will recover the 'lost land' in the foreseeable future. Many academics and officials with whom I discussed this desperate struggle for agrarian justice and these repeating stories of hope and deceit told me that, although this was a common phenomenon in Mexico, not all ejidatarios let themselves be treated in this way. They used to say that the ejidatarios in La Canoa had to become more alert, and had to read documents more carefully in order to deal with officials on equal terms. Naturally, it is true that ejidatarios with more nerve will be treated with more care and will less easily be deceived than others are. For example, during the time of the research Lupe became much more clever in her dealings with brokers and officials. However, their increasing skills in dealing with the bureaucracy would not fundamentally change the force field around this land conflict (in the next two chapters I return to this discussion).

In the interface situations between officials and ejidatarios we can distinguish, what by others would be called, 'rituals of rule and resistance' (Beezley et al. 1994). Rituals in terms of symbolic practices which form part of 'more embracing "discourses" and "technologies" that establish or contest regimes of rule' (Comaroff and Comaroff 1993:

xvi). These rituals form part of the culture of the state. Elements in these rituals are first of all the establishing of a position of authority by the officials. There may be a certain severity in the way officials address ejidatarios, while ejidatarios behave very politely using the titles of the officials, not taking too much of their time, apologising for their problems, thanking the officials extensively when they leave again, and offering presents and meals. When a more workable relationship has been established between ejidatarios and officials, the rituals can become much more festive. Ejidatarios and officials both celebrate their deals together in a pleasant atmosphere.

The officials can use more specific techniques to deal with the ejidatarios. First, they have access to unintelligible legal terminology and procedures which they can easily use as a weapon to eliminate the opposition of the ejidatarios. Second, they can deliberately engage in the practice of fantasising, theorising and boasting about their contacts. It is obvious that the interface situations do not follow a fixed script as they have a performative dimension (Gupta 1995) which manifests itself in the different 'operation styles' of the officials (de Vries 1997: 97). Some officials like Pelayo (head of the SRA Guadalajara) and Castañeda have an authoritarian style of operation, while Serrano and especially Morales use a much more populist style of operation with the ejidatarios. In Morales' case this style of operation formed part of his political project within the PRI and the SRA.

Ejidatarios also have different styles and can improve their skills in dealing with officials. For example, during the time of the research Lupe became much more clever in her dealings with brokers and officials. Ramón had already had many years of experience in the fight for the 'lost land' and had a much less submissive attitude towards officials than most ejidatarios. In general, ejidatarios are very careful with authority relations but sometimes openly contest the position of officials. The ejidatarios can be extremely hopeful and cooperative with the surveyors when they come to do the measuring of the land. However, at the same time they are suspicious and look for signals to know whether the man is to be trusted or not. In all these situations trust is very important but can never be absolute. During the same meeting with government officials, one can find elements of enthusiastic cooperation and agreement, but also distrust and cynical jokes by the ejidatarios. The ejidatarios know that officials may be under pressure from different sides. They recognise that they have not necessarily been bribed but can also be threatened or just taken off the case by their superiors. However, the ejidatarios want to maintain their relation with the bureaucratic machine, as that is the only way in which their problem can be solved.

So, while in other situations we sometimes find strong forms of distantiation or resistance to the 'state machine', in this case they need the 'state machine' to operate on their behalf.

In the struggle for the 'lost land' imaginings play a central role in trying to gain control over a messy labyrinthine machine. The ejidatarios construct theories which help them to find a certain order or logic and in this way makes it possible to decide how to proceed. By attributing logic to the uncoordinated actions of the bureaucratic machine, ejidatarios as well as officials become implicated in processes of fetishisation and reification. Maps, presidential resolutions and agrarian documents can all become 'sacred objects', fetishes. The definitive ejido map, on which the ejidatarios focused their struggle, is the embodiment of the conflict in an administrative artefact. This becomes especially clear when we realise that most ejidatarios cannot read maps in an administrative way. Yet, their imaginings around the map help the ejidatarios to deal with the bureaucratic machine. The map is the source of much local storytelling, speculation and fantasies, a kind of myth. But it is a 'modern' form of mythology; a mythology which developed in relation to a 'modern' administration (cf. Comaroff and Comaroff 1993).

Finally, this case clearly shows the spatial dimension of the working of the state machine. In the struggle for the 'lost land', 'flows' of people, documents and telephone calls go in different directions. Ejidatarios travel to government offices in Autlán, Guadalajara and Mexico City. In their turn, SRA surveyors and brokers travel back and forth between Mexico City, Guadalajara and La Canoa and often 'disappear' on their way. Documents concerning the 'lost land' are scattered over many offices in different cities. Letters and documents move from one place to another, sometimes taking years to arrive, or 'disappearing from the face of the earth'. Important documents may be found in plastic bags in the private houses of ejidatarios, or at one of the numerous desks of officials of the SRA. Many phone calls are made to offices and private houses in different cities. This continuous movement of ejidatarios, brokers and surveyors between the ejido and offices in different cities shows the constitution of the state through a complex set of spatially intersecting representations and practices (Gupta 1995: 337). These manifold activities and travels characterise the decentred nature of the bureaucratic machine and at the same time point to the 'spatial matrix materialised in the operation of the state system' (Alonso 1994: 384). Another important 'spatial element' of the operation of the bureaucratic machine are the encounters in different 'locales' such as offices, private houses, restaurants and other places in which all kinds of transactions are negotiated and celebrated by meals, breakfasts, drinking sessions and parties. These encounters show that the 'symbolic and material organisation of social space' are central elements in the construction of the idea of the state (Alonso 1994: 381).

All these flows and situated actions contribute to the construction and imagination of places with specific significance (Gupta and Ferguson 1997a). We find theories and imaginations about what happens in the different places, reflections about the localisation of evil, the localisation of the fetishised map, or of centres of power. At certain moments, the ejidatarios located evil in the SRA office of Guadalajara, and at other moments in one of the agencies in Mexico City. The bureaucratic machine itself contributes to these spatial constructions and imaginings. Ejidatarios are summoned to come to different places in the bureaucracy and the officials participate in the theorising about which offices they should avoid and which places the obstacles come from. In this way, the bureaucratic machine contributes to the imaginings of 'evil places'.

7 INSIDE THE 'HOPE-GENERATING MACHINE'

INTRODUCTION: THE WORLD OF THE OFFICIALS

It is remarkable that few studies have been made of the working of state bureaucracies, while discussions on the power of the state abound. For example, in Mexico, despite its central role in agrarian matters, the agrarian bureaucracy has been a largely neglected subject in the academic literature. The bureaucracy is generally depicted as a highly corrupt political instrument, which has only contributed to the continuing exploitation of the peasantry. Despite a few good studies (Grindle 1977, Hardy 1984) there has been far too much loose theorising about the internal functioning of Mexican government institutions and the lifeworld of the officials (see Binford 1985 and Heyman 1999 for a similar critique).

The aim of this chapter is to show how officials deal with the political dimension of their job, and the role that the discourse of corruption plays in the bureaucracy. To that end, the focus shifts from the lifeworld of the ejidatarios to the lifeworld of the officials. Attention is paid to the ways in which officials constantly problematise ongoing issues and how they themselves deal with the contradictions created by the 'hope-generating machine'. Interestingly, within the bureaucracy there is much more discussion about corruption and how to fight this phenomenon than among ejidatarios. This concern with the subject is related to government discourses that stress the fight against corruption in government agencies.

A case study is presented of the introduction of the new agrarian institute, the Procuraduría Agraria (PA), in the region of Autlán, which was preceded by a widespread anti-corruption campaign. A new style of state intervention was propagated, in contrast to the so-called corrupt approach of the SRA. In this chapter it is shown how this raised high expectations among young officials of the new institute. However, this 'new bureaucratic style' and the enthusiasm with which young officials implemented the new programmes could not possibly change the historically developed relations between ejidatarios and officials. Furthermore, I argue that the very discourse of corruption can be instrumental in the reproduction of an authoritarian regime.

Before presenting the introduction of the PA in the region of Autlán, a short overview is provided of the academic discussion about corruption in Mexico. This is followed by a discussion of the ways in which officials deal with politics inside the bureaucracy.

THE INTERRELATION BETWEEN POLITICS AND THE BUREAUCRACY

Much has been written on the pervasiveness of corruption in the Mexican bureaucracy. In general, corruption is blamed on the close connection between party politics and the bureaucracy. Since its establishment in 1929 the PRI has been the official party, a position it could sustain by manipulation of the electoral system and intimidation of opposition parties. Prior to 1988 the dominant position of the PRI was under little threat and the party won all presidential elections. In the 1990s opposition parties, such as the PRD and the PAN (Partido Acción Nacional) grew stronger and gradually the PRI lost control over the electoral process. In 1997 for the first time in history, the PRI lost the presidential elections and a PAN president came to power. However, in spite of this historic change, party politics and the bureaucratic system remain closely connected (Gledhill 1997).

An important characteristic of the Mexican political system is the centralisation of power in the office of the presidency. 'The president, operating with relatively few restraints on his authority, completely dominates the legislative and judicial branches' (Cornelius and Craig 1991: 24–5). We saw in the previous chapters that the ejidatarios in La Canoa wrote the Mexican President Salinas a personal letter about their problems, and the rumour was spread that Salinas himself had talked about La Canoa in the media. Several intermediaries also claimed to have special access to the president. These stories, in which the president himself becomes enrolled in a local struggle, are very common in Mexico. Many authors consider this kind of imagery around the Mexican president to be the result of the importance of personal relations in political power. As Lomnitz-Adler puts it, 'because people know that personal links are the prime force of access to political favour [...] it is no wonder that in Mexico the president of the republic makes public appearances like a kind of deus ex machina who heals by mere contact' (1992: 308).

With every change of president almost all high- and middle-level personnel in all government bureaucracies are replaced. This does not mean that the people who are removed from their posts remain unemployed. Many find a job at another government institution. So an enormous shift of personnel occurs. The frequent turnover of high- and middle-level personnel also means that officials are often placed in charge of organisations and programmes they know little about. These processes have been well demonstrated by Grindle (1977) in her study of CONASUPO, Mexico's staple commodities marketing agency, under the presidency of Echeverría (1970–76). In spite of the great changes that have taken place since, I find Grindle's analysis of the workings of the Mexican bureaucracy still highly applicable. She argues that, because all bureaucratic positions which become available depend upon personal connections, future employment possibilities depend upon the cultivation of personal and political ties to individuals who might be influential in the future (Grindle 1977: 49). However, the networks through which individuals are tied into extended coalitions and alliance structures within the government are not stable or durable. The individual's future generally does not depend upon relations with a single influential person but on the ability to call upon a wide range of contacts and alliances (1977: 51).

On the other hand, Grindle also draws attention to the fact that the bureaucracy is accessible to the wider population. She shows that bureaucratic positions are widely spread throughout the population. Most members of the middle class have held a political or governmental office at one time of their lives, or else have had a relative or *compadre* involved (1977: 46). All this makes it clear that the bureaucracy cannot be seen as an apparatus separate from the rest of society. It is directly linked to high and low politics and everyone, from lower social groups to members of the opposition, in one way or another may be or become part of the bureaucratic machine.

Yet this does not mean that job performance does not play a role and that everything within the bureaucracy is organised according to political considerations. Within the bureaucracy, there is frequently great pressure to achieve performance goals. Hence, there exists a tense coexistence of the two principles for success in the bureaucracy: good job performance and the cultivation of personal/political relationships.

Although Grindle provides one of the best analyses of the bureaucracy in Mexico, her work still falls within the tradition of literature that defines the Mexican political system as a corporate and authoritarian regime, dominated by a party-bureaucratic apparatus and pervaded by extensive clientelist relationships among the population and the political elite (Camp 1996, Cornelius and Craig 1991). In this literature, corruption is defined as a negative attribute, which is the result of the too-close relationship between party politics and bureaucratic practices. In this line of thought, the 'solution' to the 'problem of corruption' is defined in terms of the eradication of politics from the bureaucracy by the introduction of more democratic procedures and forms of transparency and accountability. This discourse against governmental mismanagement and corruption is very strongly expressed by the Mexican state itself. However, in my view, by analysing 'corruption' as a dysfunctional side effect of the bureaucracy, we ignore the role corruption plays in maintaining regimes of power (Hansen 1998). As will be shown, formal campaigns against corruption often only hide and enforce existing relations of power.

GETTING ACCESS TO THE BUREAUCRATIC LIFEWORLD

The fact that politics and bureaucratic practices are intricately related can immediately be felt in any study within Mexican institutions. First of all, there is always much politicking going on and officials will be careful about providing sensitive information. However, the high mobility of personnel in the institution also makes it possible to meet people who are about to leave office and who are prepared to talk more freely about what they know and think. So, in this sense, the politicised character of the bureaucracy can be both an advantage and a drawback for research.

A common strategy in conducting research within an institution is to use 'contacts' in order to get access to certain people. In this way networks within the bureaucracy can spread out in many different directions. Officials tried to help me through their personal friends within the institution and never in formal ways. When I asked them, for example, where I could get certain information they never answered in terms of the departments I should go to. They always thought about whom they knew at certain offices who could help me.

Although these contacts used to help, a strong atmosphere of suspicion and conspiracy reigned in the different offices of the SRA. Even when it was possible to establish valuable relations with certain officials, there always was much discretion and caution. This atmosphere in the SRA coincided very well with the public image of the SRA as a highly politicised institute. Many SRA officials, and especially the ones in higher positions, clearly did not like people sneaking around in the institution. Officials in the SRA worked in different networks and there was considerable distrust within the ministry itself. Within the SRA there were officials with different personal projects and not only was there distrust towards 'outsiders' but also among themselves. This made it important to strike up strategic alliances. For example, Laura, a young lawyer who detested the corruption at the SRA, was happy to provide me with information. She hoped that I could help the ejidatarios of La Canoa.

Searching for agrarian documents was a labyrinthine endeavour. The description of the SRA archives given by Zaragoza and Macías still seemed very accurate:

> The archives of the agrarian files probably constitute one of the most archaic forms for keeping documents. There is no registration or control of current files. ... There is nowhere where one can get information about the processes that are going on with respect to a file in the different offices and departments of the SRA. (Zaragoza and Macías 1980: 586, own translation)

There was not one central archive of the SRA in Mexico City in which they had all the documents of the ejido and an overview of the official state of affair of the different procedures. Many departments had some bits and pieces of information on La Canoa. Officials themselves sometimes had great difficulty in locating specific files for their own work. SRA officials were allowed to take files out of the archive, which implied that files of an ejido could be spread out over many offices in Mexico City and could stay there for many years. Documents could easily 'get lost' after some years on a desk. As Laura rightly put it when I asked her if it would be difficult to get access to the SRA archives: 'You will get access to certain archives. But the problem is to find out why papers are lacking, why maps have not been made and in whose interests that has been ...'

For the research in the agrarian bureaucracy I had to adapt my 'language'. When I explained the problems of the ejido La Canoa in 'normal terms' officials did not take me seriously. They often became annoyed – in the same way as they did with the ejidatarios – that I could not express myself in official agrarian terminology. Hence, I undertook an extensive study of agrarian legal procedures in order to understand the legal side of the problems of La Canoa and in order to have a 'meaningful' conversation with officials.

Yet, even when I explained the problems of La Canoa in formal terms, the many irregularities did not interest the officials. The fact that the map of the ejido La Canoa was never made and that surveyors never finished their measuring work, were considered to be normal phenomena. The fact that not all land had been handed over to the ejido was also very usual according to the officials and could be related to many different factors. Hence, all these 'abnormalities' were not exceptional and did not deserve special explanations.

For example, during one of my talks with Laura she looked through the documents in her desk to explain to me what was going on in La

Canoa. After having read the documents, she said that the ejidatarios of La Canoa had sent a letter to the SRA in 1977 in which they asked for the map of the ejido and the measurement of the ejido lands. As the SRA did not react, the ejido started a lawsuit against the SRA (an *amparo*) which they won. The judge ordered the SRA to pay several fines and to answer the letter. In 1993 the SRA finally answered and said that they could not comply with La Canoa's request as neither a provisional, nor a definitive map of the endowment of La Canoa existed.

L: That is the way in which matters are settled: purely formally.
M: Isn't it strange that a letter from 1977 was only answered in 1993?
L: That is quite normal, there are much worse cases.

However, in the many talks I had with SRA officials, they often studied the technicalities of the documents of La Canoa and in this way I discovered two administrative flaws that amazed them. Namely, the fact that the presidential resolution of the endowment of the ejido was never published in the *Gazette of the State* and, second, that an extension of the ejido had been executed without the endowment having been completely finished (without publication in the *Gazette of the State* and without a definitive map). To me this did not seem very interesting. After the many irregularities I had found, these seemed only insignificant details. However, for the officials this was very different. Their attitude completely changed when they found out about these two matters. All officials I met were extremely surprised when they found out that the extension of the ejido was carried out without the endowment having been finished. They were amazed and said that this was impossible, adding that they had never heard of such a case before.

Several elements are interesting in this context. First of all, it is clear that in this SRA world full of irregularities, some irregularities are 'normal' and others are 'abnormal'. It was 'normal' that presidential resolutions under the presidency of Cárdenas (1934–40) were executed before the presidential resolution was formulated. It was 'normal' that the SRA took ten or twenty years to answer a letter. It was 'normal' that no definitive map of the ejido was made after the execution of the presidential resolution. It was 'normal' for ejidos to request the measuring of their land from the SRA and never get a response. It was 'normal' that surveyors arrived to do a measuring job and suddenly disappeared. These were all common practices in the SRA that did not surprise any official. Yet, the fact that the presidential resolution of an endowment was never published in the *Gazette of the State* was certainly 'not normal'. The fact that an extension followed an endowment that had never been completely finished was 'not normal' either. These irregularities were highly exceptional. Although to me these two elements did not seem especially interesting, I had finally found the way to get the attention of officials and talk to them on their own terms. This information always triggered their professional interest and made it possible to have a dialogue.

Another interesting point is that, while these were the most important irregularities for the officials, the ejidatarios of La Canoa were not even aware of these 'highly uncommon and special details' of their ejido. When I discussed these points with the ejidatarios, it appeared that nobody in the group of the 'lost land' knew about them, nor were they very interested.

OFFICIALS DEALING WITH A POLITICISED BUREAUCRACY

In the previous chapters we have seen that officials reacted to La Canoa's problems with the 'lost land' in a number of standard ways. Even after they had recognised that political influences probably interfered with the measuring of the land in La Canoa, and after they had drawn the conclusion that the ejidatarios in La Canoa would probably never recover the land, they could give a long explanation of the procedures to be followed. In addition, they gave long lists of recommendations to make the struggle of the ejidatarios of La Canoa possible: they had to draw up formal contracts with all the professionals they were working with; they should carefully study all the work orders before signing their agreement with the work of the surveyors, and so on. In sum, the ejidatarios should go on focusing on the procedures and putting pressure on the SRA. This contradiction of stressing the importance of procedures while acknow-ledging that the real basis of these conflicts is distinct becomes clear in the following example.

An External Agrarian Lawyer's Assessment of the Case

I will present part of a conversation I had with Manuel, an agrarian lawyer in Mexico City who had worked for many years in the SRA and was finishing a book on agrarian law in Mexico. Manuel worked for the agricultural office of the PRI in the Mexican Congress and I had already had several conversations with him about land rights in Mexico. The day that Serrano did not arrive at the town hall (see Chapter 6) I decided to call Manuel and ask his opinion about the situation of La Canoa. I explained to him the events surrounding Serrano, the surveyor who had not turned up.

Manuel: And didn't they phone him at the SRA to ask what had happened?
M: The surveyor himself phoned the town hall to say that his car had broken down and that he would be there in four days.

Manuel: But he has to come now, because they gave him these days to do this measuring job, he cannot wait four days. What kind of land is it?

M: Irrigated land.

Manuel: Then it is very probable that the case has been stopped by the private landowners, especially as it concerns irrigated land, and the SRA itself is probably heavily involved in the matter. Do the people of La Canoa have a copy of the work order of the surveyor? That is very important; it is important that they keep on putting pressure on.

M: I don't know whether they have a copy of the work order, but anyway what is the sense of putting pressure on when they have been fighting for this case for more than 50 years and these officials have always been bribed!

Manuel: What kind of Kafkaesque ideas are these? Let them come to Mexico City.

M: They have been there recently but they told them that the case is sabotaged in the office in Guadalajara.

Manuel: And does the office in Mexico City have no authority over the office in Guadalajara?! They have to keep on putting pressure on. And they have to come to Mexico City to 'buy functionaries'.

M: They have recently paid a large amount of money to a private lawyer in Guadalajara who was going to help them and then disappeared.

Manuel: They shouldn't pay private lawyers but functionaries of the SRA!

The interesting element of this conversation is the fact that Manuel accused me of Kafkaesque ideas when I talked about the impossibility of the case proceeding any further, whereas he himself made clear that this is a political case which has probably been stopped from above. Another interesting element is that, although he said that it is a political case, he kept stressing the importance of formal documents and of following the official procedures. This contradictory attitude is typical of officials. They will immediately admit the political side of land conflicts but afterwards will continue to stress that the legal and administrative procedures have to be followed. Although Manuel has nothing to do with the case and has no personal interest in it whatsoever, he also suggests that the ejidatarios should do things differently: that they should go to Mexico City and buy officials instead of paying a lawyer in order to speed up the bureaucratic process. This also is a general phenomenon. Lawyers, officials and others always know the 'right way' to get these things resolved and can always tell you why things are going wrong. In this way, the officials also live in a world of contradiction which they themselves help to reproduce by suggesting new ways of handling (un-resolvable) conflicts and by offering new openings and raising hopes again. Actually, this is the same kind of dynamic we have already seen among ejidatarios: 'knowing how things work', but at the same time 'hoping and believing' in the rationality of formal procedures. In this way, both ejidatarios and officials actively engage in the cultural representation of the state.

In their own daily work, this reification of procedures by officials is even more understandable as they have to deal with myriad procedures and bureaucratic steps. They only operate in a very small part of the whole administrative process, and normally do not have an overview of the whole problematic of specific ejidos. They tend to concentrate on technicalities and numbers of files. They know that within the SRA many activities concern a legalisation of illegal transactions (see Chapter 4) and they know that serious land conflicts are negotiated at other levels. They themselves may become involved in a small part of these negotiations but most of their time is dedicated to a small technical part of the administrative-bureaucratic process. Even if a surveyor receives orders from above to change a map in favour of certain private landholders, he can still dedicate a great deal of time and skill to producing a technically well elaborated map.

Besides the 'big land conflicts', like the 'lost land', the SRA plays a role in many other matters. These include, for example, internal ejido conflicts over plots, the selling and legalising of land sales. In the different chapters, we saw that the awkward agrarian rules and procedures gave ample room for manipulation by officials. However, not all officials take advantage of the many opportunities offered by these situations. Officials could reflect extensively about different colleagues and what was acceptable behaviour and what was not. For example, Rigoberto of the SRA office in Autlán expressed very negative views of his colleague, Davíd, who during all these years had greatly enriched himself by asking for money for every service and never said no when people asked him to arrange illegal matters. Although Rigoberto himself also accepted money in exchange for favours, in his view, Davíd was 'over-demanding'. Actually, many people in the region, officials as well as ejidatarios shared this view. Many officials do not deny that they themselves also receive money (Federico: 'We all like money') but they make a distinction between reasonable forms of exchange and abusing one's power. In their comments they tend to make elaborate distinctions between different forms of favours. However, there were no absolute standards for corruption.

Even when I spoke to officials for the first time, they often started talking about corruption. Officials felt the need to define their own position towards the phenomenon of corruption even when I had not touched this theme. Some enjoyed talking about their games in the 'corrupt' atmosphere. On many occasions, fun and joking accompanied discussions about the phenomenon even in public meetings. Corruption was a 'hot issue' within the bureaucracy. Naturally, this is an indication of the political importance of the phenomenon that is also reflected in the attention given to it in the media. However, I argue that the 'talk of corruption' by officials is more than an attempt to conform to a politically powerful discourse. By reflecting on corruption, officials also problematise the wider workings of the agrarian bureaucracy, the ongoing changes in the Mexican political economy and their own role in this process.

A NEW INSTITUTE AND OFFICIALS FIGHTING CORRUPTION

I will now discuss the way in which the change of Article 27 of the Mexican Constitution, which formed the basis of land rights in Mexico, was presented in 1992. The public debate around the reform of Article 27 clearly shows the political importance of the discourse against corruption. Together with the change of Article 27, the Agrarian Law was changed. The changes in the law were rather drastic and caused many emotional debates.[1] The most important elements of the new Agrarian Law in comparison with the old federal Agrarian Reform Law are the following. First, the Mexican agrarian reform has come to its end; land will no longer be expropriated in order to establish or enlarge ejidos. Second, the ejido form of land tenure will continue to exist, but in a 'modern' form. In this new form, ejidatarios will be allowed to sell, buy, rent or lease their land, activities that were all forbidden under the old Agrarian Reform Law. Third, the law opens the possibility for ejidatarios to work in association with private enterprises (stockholding companies) and individual investors. Furthermore, a new programme was introduced, PROCEDE, aimed at measuring all the individual ejido plots. Hence, for the first time in history, ejidatarios would now have their individual plots registered and receive individual land titles.[2] Once the land was registered, ejidatarios could decide to change from the ejido regime to private land ownership. In the government propaganda accompanying the changes it was claimed that all these transformations would bring more legal security in land tenure for ejidatarios. Furthermore, ejidatarios would now be able to mortgage their land, obtain credit at commercial banks and become 'dynamic entrepreneurs'. According to the official propaganda all these improvements would finally lead to an increase in agricultural productivity. It is no coincidence that this argument carried weight at a time when Mexico was negotiating the free trade agreement (NAFTA) with Canada and the United States.

The most important institutional change that accompanied the reform of the Agrarian Law was the creation of the Procuraduría Agraria (PA) (Attorney General's Office for Agrarian Affairs) in March 1992. In government publications the widespread corruption in the SRA was presented as the main source of agrarian problems in the country and the cause of the continuing exploitation of the ejidatarios. It was declared that drastic changes were required and a new agrarian institute, the PA, was established which would bring justice to the Mexican countryside. This public blaming of corruption in a certain institute as the cause of the problems, and presenting the solution in terms of new programmes is not new. The same happened, for example, with CONASUPO under the presidency of Echeverría (Grindle 1977). The new PA would now deal with agrarian problems and would direct the different programmes, such as PROCEDE, that would make the transfer from the ejido regime to private land ownership possible. However, the SRA still had to settle the huge number of unresolved agrarian conflicts, the famous *rezago agrario* (agrarian arrears) which included cases such as the 'lost land'.

However, as we will see, the fascinating part of this story is not so much the legal and institutional transformations but the fact that large parts of the population, not least in intellectual circles and in large sectors of the bureaucracy, let themselves become inspired by this governmental discourse of democracy, the cleaning up of the institutions and new ways of governing.

First Reception of the Changes in the Region of Autlán

Shortly before the new Agrarian Law was to be issued, government officials from different institutions in the region were mobilised to inform the ejidatarios about the coming changes. After taking a short course on the new law in Guadalajara, the officials were sent to the ejidos. In La Canoa a meeting was held on 8 December 1991.[3] This meeting deserves some attention as it shows how the officials had totally adopted the Salinas discourse of radical change and democratisation. It also gives an idea of the usual reaction of ejidatarios to new government programmes. Two officials made the presentation in La Canoa, and 22 of the 97 ejidatarios attended the meeting.

One of the officials talked extensively about past government corruption and failures and declared that all this was about to change. He referred repeatedly to the theme of social transformation. The image of the president played a central role in his narrative, with Salinas cast as the great initiator and mover of the new transformations. The official stressed that he had been sent by representatives of the president himself. Official: 'The president has become aware of the situation in rural areas. He is conscious of the low living standards and therefore has decided to take these initiatives. He wants communities to have a better life.'

It was a discourse of modernisation and liberalisation: the rural areas are poor but the government will invest heavily to improve the situation. Agricultural enterprises should be big and modern, and farmers should work together and with agro-industrial enterprises. There was a strong emphasis on joining plots together and working in associations. He made much reference to responsibilities, rights and obligations. The functionary made it clear that paternalism would come to an end and that farmers would have to take responsibility for themselves: if they take out bank loans, they should repay them; if they want services from the SARH (Secretaría de Agricultura y Recursos Hidráulicos), they will have to pay for them, etc. The functionary made the point that the ejidatarios themselves are responsible for determining the future of the land.

The ejidatarios toned the functionary's message down by relating it directly to concrete situations they are involved and interested in, such as the case of the 'lost land'. If the official gave an example from a distant ejido, the ejidatarios responded with examples from neighbouring ejidos. They also tried to elicit information with direct bearing on particular personal situations, such as their debts with BANRURAL. They showed minimal interest in the official's calls to work together and form associations. Most ejidatarios did not participate in the discussions, preferring to 'wait and see'. Those who did participate expressed their dissatisfaction and frustration with the bureaucracy. For example, the following dialogue.

Iginio Núñez: But can we still receive land that has never been handed over?
Official: Yes.
Iginio: We've got to support these changes!
Another ejidatario: And now the surveyors are willing to do the surveying, right?
Official: Yes. I know about the problems you've had with the surveyors, who never came, who didn't take the measurements properly, etc. But from now on it will be different.
Another ejidatario: But they never come to measure the land.

As will be clear, all these remarks were related to the struggle for the 'lost land'.

In the following part of the dialogue they referred to the problems with BANRURAL.

Salvador Lagos: BANRURAL has treated many of us very badly. For example, we wanted to plant in May but we didn't get our loans from BANRURAL. We only got the money much later. In the meantime, the people at the bank were speculating and making money on our loan money!
Iginio Núñez: The government is going to invest a lot of money in agriculture. In years past, the government money never reached us.

Official: If you're talking about people who used to monopolise the money, we want to put a stop to that.

So the functionary enthusiastically used the official discourse to present the changes to the ejidatarios, but could not conceal the effects of past experiences. Elements of radical change, modernisation, blaming the corruption of the SRA and an end to paternalism were central in his speech but did not convince the ejidatarios. In this meeting the ejidatarios assumed their usual sceptical attitude. Their distrust towards new government programmes was apparent, as well as their lack of faith in government officials.

OFFICIALS AND AMBIGUOUS INSTITUTIONAL ENVIRONMENTS

The establishment of the new Procuraduría Agraria was fascinating from an institutional and political point of view. The head of the new institute was Arturo Warman, a recognised academic who had published excellent works on the way in which ejidatarios and landless peasants in Mexico had been exploited by the Mexican state.[4] According to some people the appointment of Warman was a clear case of the famous co-option of critical outsiders by the Mexican state. However, many other people considered it to be an indication that the government really was prepared to do things differently. Warman repeated the government rhetoric about doing justice to the Mexican countryside. He expressed this goal in *Espacios*, a magazine published by the PA.

Our goal is to resolve issues. ... It is also to treat the peasants with respect. We must play a key role in creating a new agrarian culture that rejects paternalism and puts peasants in charge of their own lives. (Warman in *Espacios* no. 1 March–April 1993, p. 3, own translation)

The PA tried to develop a 'modern' institutional identity that would contrast with the SRA. PA functionaries should establish friendly and egalitarian relationships with the 'new rural producers'. Its new ideology and energetic institutional identity extended to all PA offices, from Mexico City to Guadalajara to Autlán. Many young PA officials started their work with great enthusiasm and expectations. To underscore the contrast between themselves and the SRA, some of the new PA functionaries even refused offers of soft drinks when they visited the ejidos, emphasising that it is strictly forbidden for them to accept anything from the ejidatarios. The young professionals from the PA were very proud of their different style. Federico, one of the new PA officials, for example, said:

The ejidatarios are often amazed to see how young we are. It is a different image. Sometimes they think we work in the same way as the people before. They prepare meals for us and offer us money. Or they bring homemade cheeses to the office. We can't accept these things, but we have to refuse them tactfully. ... This causes trouble with the SRA. ... They want to make money out of everything.

The fact that Warman was the head of the new institute was a source of inspiration for many young officials.

At the higher levels within the PA, officials were well aware of the political aspects of land questions and the many problems the implementers would find in the field. I had several interviews with officials working at Arturo Warman's office in Mexico City, who developed the new programmes of the PA. They were bright, enthusiastic people who enjoyed having critical discussions about the agrarian problems in Mexico. Yet, in the same way as many other critical officials I had talked with, they also seemed to see the 'solution' to the exploitation of the ejidatarios in terms of education and organisation. They used a strong discourse of raising consciousness among ejidatarios and making them 'take control of their own lives'. They hoped to counter the influence of local and regional powerholders by educating the ejidatarios.

An Enthusiastic Head of the Regional PA Office

The Autlán office opened its doors in March 1993. It was one of five offices of the PA in Jalisco and covered 20 municipalities encompassing 244 ejidos. The staff of the Autlán office included six agrarian specialists and lawyers (*visitadores*) and 16 assistants. The specialists were professionals with varied academic backgrounds: for example, a biologist, agricultural surveyors and lawyers. Their work consisted primarily of resolving disputes over land in the ejidos and initiating the PROCEDE programme. Like other PA offices, the Autlán office started with young people recently graduated from the university and with little or no experience with agrarian issues in Mexico. After having completed intensive courses on the old Agrarian Reform Law and the new Agrarian Law and six months of fieldwork, these staff came to the PA office in order to prepare for the survey of ejido land (PROCEDE) and settle land conflicts.

When I first met José Luís, the head of the Autlán office, in April 1993, I found an enthusiastic, informally dressed, ambitious young man in his 20s. He appeared to be a social worker rather than the lawyer I had expected. José Luís explained to me that before entering the PA, he worked in a hospital. When he saw the announcements for the PA he decided to attend the training course. He asked for leave of absence from his job to do the course. The course went very well, so José Luís decided to leave his job at the hospital and go and work with the PA. I asked José Luís what he hoped to achieve in his work for the PA.

José Luís:

What I intend to do in this job is to bring progress to rural Mexico, so that the campesinos won't be deceived anymore. If I can make a contribution, that's it. If one of the 244 ejidos under my responsibility makes headway because of my involvement, I'll be satisfied.

Another example that José Luís stressed of the new approach was that they were going to listen to the ejidatarios and treat them as adult people. Ejidatarios could receive free legal assistance at the PA and if ejidatarios arrived with lawyers, the lawyers would be ignored.

José Luís:

When ejidatarios visit the office with a lawyer, the lawyer often starts talking. We tell them to let the ejidatarios speak for themselves. Then the lawyers often react by saying that the ejidatario is not able to talk about it very well. We then say that the ejidatarios are very able to talk about it and if not we will find another form of understanding each other. We ask the lawyer to keep quiet or to wait outside. After the talk we tell the ejidatarios that they can get a free lawyer at our office.

Naturally, this sounded like a very sympathetic aim. But after the many conversations I overheard between officials and ejidatarios I did not see quite how officials and ejidatarios would find 'new ways of talking to each other'. This was another clear example of the new approach adopted by the PA. José Luís talked in caring terms about the exploited ejidatarios. He had taken photos of ejidatarios and meetings of ejidatarios, which he had put in the entrance hall of the PA building and he enjoyed explaining the pictures to me.

In the talks I had with José Luís it became apparent that he knew most of the articles of the old and new Agrarian Law verbatim and became angry with himself if he made a mistake. Yet it was difficult for him to distance himself from the books and talk about real-life agrarian issues. He had fully adopted the discourse and ideology of the new institution and tended to answer my questions and doubts in terms of articles of the law. I explained this by the fact that he had never had any experience with rural people and agrarian problems and seemed to be 'brainwashed' by the PA courses. Yet he was the head of a regional office responsible for 244 ejidos!

Antonio: Living the Tension between Reality and a New Institutional Project

Antonio was one of the assistants who, in contrast to the university-educated *visitadores*, came from a rural village. Instead of being proud of using a different institutional style he saw the problems of suddenly changing common practices to which people had become accustomed:

People are often offended when we do not want to stay for a meal. They say: we are poor, but you can eat here; the food isn't poisoned. But we hardly ever accept. Sometimes it is a pity, especially in the more isolated villages. There people are used to being hospitable and they automatically serve you a plate of food. They do not want anything else from you. But others start talking business.

He was one of the few PA officials who, from the start, were sceptical about the possibility of recovering lands. After a talk between Ramón Romero and Antonio in which Ramón had told him about the 'lost land' and that he expected that they would soon recover these lands, Antonio talked to me when we left the village.

A: That man thinks that they will recover the land, but that will never happen.
M: But if these lands officially belong to the ejido?
A: The private landowners are politically very strong. No land will be taken away from them any more.

This went against the optimistic legalistic PA discourse that maintained that in the end all conflicts would be legally settled. However, although Antonio was one of the few PA officials who expressed himself in a more realistic way about the possibilities for change, on other occasions he also used the strongly legalistic discourse of the new institution in his relations with ejidatarios. An example is the following dialogue with Ramón Romero.

R: Two people here in the ejido recently sold their plots.
A: The law does not yet allow that. First the land has to be measured; then when the new certificates are issued, ejidatarios can sell their land.
R: You say that because that's what is written down, but the reality is different! We are very cunning in finding other ways to get things done. These people got their papers, went to a notary, and completed the sale.
A: But these land sales can be annulled.
R: Maybe according to the books. But it's not registered as a sale; they say that the rights were ceded to the new buyer.
A: In that case nothing can be done about it.
R: We are very clever. That's how we used to sell our land.
A: But do you think it's okay to let people tinker with the rules?
R: Maybe not. Davíd at the SRA office has bent the rules a lot. That office is terrible; it's a snake pit.
A: Why do you go back to these people when you know they are corrupt and that we provide free services?
R: Why do you think? Because Davíd knows the law so well and he knows how to get around it, whereas you just say that we can't sell the land.

This exchange sheds light on the double attitude of the ejidatarios towards the corrupt practices at the SRA. On the one hand, they detest corruption when it hinders their efforts to get fair treatment in their conflict with the *pequeños proprietarios*. On the other hand, they themselves use the services of 'corrupt' officials, when necessary, to arrange matters outside the law. So far, the young functionaries of the PA had not been able to convince the ejidatarios that their new institutional style was of practical use.

On the other hand, this dialogue is also interesting with respect to Antonio's position. Antonio himself comes from an ejido and knows from experience that Ramón is right. However, he now has a job in which programmes are presented in a legalistic way. Ejidatarios like Ramón, who seriously doubt the feasibility of the new project, make Antonio's work difficult from the very start. Actually, Antonio was very displeased after this conversation, as his authority had been seriously questioned. This shows well the difficult position of officials who have to introduce supposedly legal, modern, democratic programmes into situations which are characterised by negotiations between ejidatarios and officials. Afterwards, Antonio expressed his frustration with the ejidatarios of La Canoa. He visited the ejido on several occasions and said to me that he was irritated by the fact that people did not come to the meetings, showed so little interest in their own affairs and did not know the rules.

Encountering a Difficult Reality

Despite their enthusiasm, the young PA staff in Autlán soon encountered severe problems. Most of the specialists had never lived in rural areas or worked with farmers or ejidatarios. Since they came with good intentions, determined to change established practices in the agrarian sector, they were surprised by the ejidatarios' mistrust. While the staff were eager to start the work that lay ahead, the ejidatarios often showed little interest in cooperating. Rubén, one of the lawyers of the PA office in Autlán, was from Guadalajara. He was the first of his group (of politically active lawyers) to move to the agrarian sector. According to Rubén: 'Our work in the ejidos isn't easy. The people are very distrustful. The point is that policies have changed 180 degrees and people still have to get used to that.' Others complained about the fact that the ejidatarios are such closed people and not prepared to settle their conflicts harmoniously. So, while they started their work with the image of the good farmer who had been exploited for so many years, they now started repeating the same old stereotypes.

The PA staff also became frustrated by the fact that they were presented as the initiators of change but in practice had little influence. They discovered early on that they lacked authority. For example, when they couldn't get the disputing parties to reach an agreement, they had to send the case to the new agrarian tribunals, even when it was very clear who was in the right. Moreover, the situations before them were much more complex than they had been told. The very legalistic and transformationist discourse of the PA was not much help in conflicts with long histories and in which multiple interests were involved. In these highly political conflicts over lands, in which the SRA is often directly involved, the PA officials felt that they could do nothing, exacerbating their feelings of powerlessness.

So, they had to deal with distrustful ejidatarios in complex and conflictual situations in which they lacked authority. Last but not least, the workload was enormous, with six officials responsible for 244 ejidos. Moreover, there was great emphasis on extensive registration of all activities in the PA. The officials had to fill in many forms and were working constantly to have their reports ready before deadlines. I often found them working until late in the evening. Besides their daily work, they also had to continue with courses and examinations on agrarian matters.

By the time of my later visits to the Autlán office, the atmosphere was changing. Although they were still friendly, the functionaries were always worried and tense. José Luís had changed from an enthusiastic, relaxed person into a harried boss. He tended to answer my questions more and more in terms of the standard PA discourses, articles in the Agrarian Law, and by giving me PA booklets. After six months of being head of the PA office in Autlán, José Luís was sent back to the PA office in Guadalajara where he had to work as a *visitador*. This was a demotion. Some time later I happened to meet him there. He was very friendly and relaxed and said that he was happy with the new situation. In his new position he could learn many things. José Luís was not the only person to be moved from his position. Many of the PA officials in Autlán disappeared after a while. Some of them had been fired, while others were sent to other offices. There was much reshuffling of personnel at the PA at all levels. In October 1994, the *visitador* who had been responsible for La Canoa was also moved to the PA office in Guadalajara. Several secretaries of the Autlán office also left the institute.

The PA and the SRA Growing Closer

José Luís was replaced by Guillermo, a much older agricultural engineer, with years of experience in the SRA! I asked Guillermo how he had arrived at the PA:

I never thought of applying for a job at the PA since they wanted young people and nobody from the SRA. However, I had previously worked on a project with Arturo Warman [now head of the PA] and his people, and they wanted me in the new institute. I had to take the course with all these young people who had just finished university, and I came out among the top five of 215. ... They offered me my choice of state, and I decided to come back home, to Jalisco.

Guillermo also had a social motivation for the job:

There is still much inequality in Mexico and very bad government. I will only be happy when the poor in Mexico, including the peasants, have a dignified life. The stories that everything is changing and the people are having a better life now are nonsense. I once started a book about my experiences, but you do not earn anything with books.

It is interesting that Guillermo was asked by former colleagues at the SRA to 'come over' to the new institute. Here we see again that with new projects and programmes, political changes are made in the bureaucracy and the new heads try to take people with them with whom they have worked before. It is also an indication of the fact that, in the end, the break with the practices of the SRA would not be that drastic. Gradually, more and more officials from the SRA entered the PA. The higher positions in particular were filled with people from the SRA. The fact that certain 'cliques' in the SRA moved to the PA reinforced inter-institutional networks between the two organisations and caused more frustration among the young PA officials.

In October 1994 I had a talk with Cristina, a young lawyer and one of the *visitadores* of the PA office in Autlán, who had then been working there for one year. When I remarked that I had noticed that many SRA officials had entered the PA, she said:

They told us that they wanted new people, but the reality is different. The high PA functionaries come from the SRA. SRA people take the best positions; they are more experienced. There have been many frictions and problems between the PA and the SRA. A fight. They tell us that we have to temper the situation, but that is difficult, they hinder you in your work. The SRA offices in Autlán and La Huerta are the most difficult ones. There are things we cannot do. The new head of the PA in Jalisco comes from customs; these are all political appointments; they sometimes put people in charge who have no idea at all about these matters.

Defining a new institution that was clearly differentiated from the SRA had been a theme present in all the offices of the PA. However, the relationship between the PA and the SRA became a different one. In fact, from the very start, the two institutions were not separate at all; they were closely related, both in their formal organisational structure (the

PA falls officially under the SRA)[5] and in their interpersonal networks. The PA and the SRA also overlapped in their tasks. Although responsibilities and tasks were supposedly different and separate, in practice they often converged (for example, both agencies advised and assisted in many ejido affairs). This led to a complicated relationship between two parallel, competing and overlapping institutions.

Forms of competition between the local offices of the two institutions in Autlán developed. The SRA officials refused to allow the PA to see ejidos' files and the PA tried to cancel illegal land sales, which Davíd of the SRA had organised. In March 1994, Guillermo, head of the PA office in Autlán, expressed frustration over his lack of authority vis-à-vis the SRA. Guillermo: 'I even received orders from above to avoid conflict with the SRA since "in the end we are one and the same organisation".' These tensions between functionaries reflect the ongoing power struggles within and between the two institutes at higher levels. However, this was not primarily a conflict between two institutions. It would be better described in terms of a clash between different institutional projects related to political struggles that cross-cut institutional borders.

The institutional experiences of the ejidatarios of La Canoa with the PA have not been very different from their earlier experiences with the SRA and other government institutions. In the beginning the atmosphere in the PA was certainly very distinct from the atmosphere at the SRA. There was a more open, cordial and relaxed ambience. But soon the same practices, which they had condemned so much in the SRA, entered the PA. Appointments were made with ejidatarios but the officials never showed up. Many promises were made to the ejidatarios, which were not kept. Ejidatarios who came from far away had to wait for hours in the building to speak to an official. So the image of the waiting ejidatarios was reproduced as well. Officials refrained from interfering in politically sensitive matters and did not interfere in many cases, even if they were explicitly asked to do so. In many cases they could not really do anything. Together with the other problems, the atmosphere in the offices also changed and became much more like that of the SRA. According to most ejidatarios in La Canoa, the officials of the PA will end up just like those of the SRA.

The idea was also growing among the officials that, in the end, things might work out in a different way and that the PA might develop characteristics similar to other institutions. Several enthusiastic young officials at all levels left the institute disappointed. At the top, Arturo Warman was replaced under the new President Zedillo (1994–2000). The atmosphere of optimism and radical change had disappeared. A third head of the PA office in Autlán was appointed. I spoke to him in July 1995 and to another head in August 2000. Instead of using a legalist, modernist discourse claiming that everything would soon be different and that lands would soon be measured and conflicts settled, they said that they found many problems everywhere. Whereas the PA had started with the declaration that all lands would be measured within a short period, these men both said that PROCEDE would take at least ten more years. Distance was taken from the rhetoric of the former president of the republic, Salinas, and from the former head of the PA, Warman.

Some Reflections on a New Law and a New Institute

Looking back on this period, it is clear that Salinas's discourse on democracy and his promise to eradicate corruption was extremely successful in raising hopes regarding the possibility of bringing about fundamental changes in society. The disappointment when he left the presidency in an atmosphere of economic crisis, political murders and drug trafficking in which he apparently played a central role, was all the more severe. As we saw in the previous chapters, his projects for the agrarian sector made some ejidatarios believe that they would finally recover lands that belonged to their ejidos. However, many officials also thought that, with the support of this president, they could fundamentally change the agrarian situation. They hoped that justice would finally be done. All were in the end deceived.

PA officials as well as ejidatarios realised after some time that nothing had changed and that they had to readjust their aims. A new agrarian law and the establishment of a new institution obviously did not change the political character of many land conflicts in Mexico, nor the established practices in the relationship between ejidatarios and the state bureaucracies. The old practices and stereotypes about sceptical, closed ejidatarios and unreliable, dishonest officials soon re-emerged, seemingly stronger than before. It was obvious that the political conjuncture had not changed in favour of the ejidatarios or landless peasants. On the contrary, despite an official government discourse in which the ejidatarios would finally receive what rightfully belonged to them, the Salinas regime supported the large private landowners.

CONCLUSION: OFFICIALS IN A WORLD OF CONTRADICTION

In order to understand the working of the state machine, we need a sophisticated analysis of the bureaucracy and the lifeworld of the officials. The image of the 'corrupt and unscrupulous official who only tries to exploit the poor peasants' is a stereotype that does little to increase our understanding of this dynamic. Officials develop certain professional standards for their work, while at the same time they are part of a politicised bureaucracy in which they have to ensure their own position. The state bureaucracy is a complex constellation of people, projects, social networks and more or less organised groups, which seem to be in continuous movement. Like ejidatarios, officials may sometimes feel more like 'a victim' of the bureaucratic machine with little room for manoeuvre, than 'an implementer' of the state programmes. The majority of officials try to do their job, while at the same time they enjoy the favours of being part of the state bureaucracy and certain political networks. Most officials do not deny that they themselves ask favours or sometimes operate on political/personal instead of professional/bureaucratic grounds.

Undoubtedly, there is considerable pleasure in 'playing the game'. As Gupta demonstrates well, the practice of bribing is not simply an economic transaction but a cultural practice that requires a great degree of performative competence (Gupta 1995: 379). It is obvious that people develop different standards and degrees to which they agree with favouritism, or follow formal standards. For that reason, 'there are always divergent and conflicting assessments of whether a particular course of action is "corrupt"' (Gupta 1995: 388). However, ejidatarios, as well as officials, are confronted with contradictory demands in their daily lives. Yet the difference between ejidatarios and officials is that, in the world of the official, party politics and political lobbying are much stronger and dominate a much greater part of one's life than in the daily lives of most ejidatarios.

On the one hand, the discourse of corruption forms part of the 'culture of the state' and 'analysing the discourse of corruption draws attention to the powerful cultural practices by which the state is symbolically represented to its employees and to citizens of the nation' (Gupta 1995: 385). In government propaganda in Mexico the fight against corruption is presented as a central facet of a successful modernisation of society and the lack of effectiveness of the government apparatus is often blamed on corrupt elements within the system. Furthermore, accusations of corruption have become a powerful weapon in the political power game. In this context the discourse of corruption deflects attention from more fundamental types of criticism of the regime and has conservative effects. By blaming 'corrupt elements' for things that go wrong, the 'idea of the state' as 'a neutral arbiter above the conflicts and interests of society' remains intact. Within these theories no radical changes of society are necessary. Once the 'rotten' parts have been removed from the system, 'the state' can do its work. Agencies are closed, programmes cancelled, and new initiatives are presented with great enthusiasm and optimism. The hope-generating machine continues its work.

Among officials there is much specific talk about different types and degrees of corruption. By reflecting on the subject, officials not only subject themselves to a dominant discourse but also problematise their role as officials and the working of the bureaucracy. This leads to several contradictions in committed officials' theorising. On the one hand, the discourse of corruption defines different categories of people, such as the innocent and credulous ejidatarios and the 'corrupt' official. Functionaries often talked about ejidatarios as victims of the corrupt bureaucracy. On the other hand, officials also blamed the ejidatarios for being distrustful, not willing to change and for doing nothing to improve their own situation.

In their strategies to fight corruption officials tend to stress the importance of knowing the rules and following formal procedures. Yet, by stressing the importance of formal procedures in the fight against corruption, it is suggested that there is a 'logic' in the operation of the machine, which one can learn. Yet, the more political a conflict has become, and the higher up socially those whose interests are at stake, the less the bureaucracy follows formal logics. In previous chapters I argued that by stressing the importance of the official rules and procedures officials contribute to the 'idea of the state'. Officials are not naive and know better than anybody else that many matters are not arranged according to official rules but according to other criteria. However, by recognising this reality they put their own legitimacy as officials in jeopardy.

In the same way as the ejidatarios, these officials are not innocent about their society, but they are entrapped in a world of contradictions. While the ejidatarios may distance themselves from the bureaucratic machine and react cynically, for the officials the bureaucracy is their world of work. The reproduction of the state mythology by government officials is important as it leads to a 'daily, routinised reassurance' of the importance of their work (Blom and Stepputat 2001: 17). Officials have to believe in the new projects and programmes and in the potential of the bureaucratic system in order to be able to do their work. They themselves are part of it. This leads to the image of the optimistic official and the sceptical peasant, an image one often comes across when officials come to introduce new government projects.

Like the ejidatarios, the officials may be deceived once they start believing the fantasies created by the hope-generating machine. This happened with the change of Article 27 of the Mexican Constitution and the establishment of the Procuraduría Agraria. Officials who worked with enormous enthusiasm and believed that they could change established bureaucratic practices were, in the end, as deceived as the ejidatarios. This shows that officials who start taking the messages too seriously may also fall prey to the 'fantasies of the machine'. Situations soon returned to 'normal' and the old stereotypes of the lazy ejidatarios and the unreliable officials were reinforced in the interactions between ejidatarios and officials. It is argued that this characteristic of generating hope is an important element of the culture of the state. Although many people react cynically to all these promises, at the same time they start believing in some of them. This is not a form of false consciousness but it is a form of fantasising; and sometimes part of the fantasies may come true as many things happen and change in society. However, for the officials, the new programmes and promises are more than fantasy; they are their daily work environment. Although upon reflection they may recognise the impossibility of the programmes and the contradictions in their own theories, believing is the only way to survive and make headway in the bureaucratic machine.

8 DEVELOPMENT DISCOURSES AND PARTICIPATORY APPROACHES

INTRODUCTION: A TOP-DOWN IMPOSITION OF PARTICIPATION

Much development literature gives a central role to local organisation for improving the situation of the poor. In these works participatory approaches and grassroots initiatives have become very popular. However, these approaches tend to ignore the ways in which forms of organising and external interventions are always already embedded within wider fields of power. This explains why many so-called 'participatory bottom-up' projects often turn into top-down impositions bearing little relation to the organising priorities of the 'target groups'.

This chapter discusses in detail the implementation of one of the programmes that was introduced with the new Agrarian Law in Mexico, the programme of the Internal Ejido Rules (*Reglamento Interno*). This programme aimed to improve the organisation of the ejido at the local level. A 'bottom-up participatory' approach was used in order to stimulate ejidos to formulate their own internal regulation. The implementation of this programme is followed in detail in the period between 1993 and 1994. This study makes clear what may happen when 'local organising capacities' are made central to government programmes 'imposed from above'. It shows how the implementation of the programme was influenced by the contradictory and strained relationship between ejidatarios and the Mexican state.

First a short overview is presented of the role of organisation and participation in the development debate. Then, an analysis is presented of the implementation of the programme of the Internal Ejido Rules (IER). Finally, some remarks are made about the implications of this study for the debate about local organisation and development.

ORGANISATION AND PARTICIPATION IN THE DEVELOPMENT DEBATE

The image of the rural poor as 'victims' of exploitation who lack organisational capacities is pervasive in much development literature. The same applies to the high expectation that new collective forms of organisation can improve the situation of the poor. Literature such as this depicts poor villagers and peasants as 'traditional', 'unmotivated' or 'apathetic' or, conversely, as 'victims' of the pervasive and 'corrupt' bureaucratic machine. At best they are viewed as 'opportunistic' and highly 'self-interested' people, unable to align themselves with a wider socio-political project. The pursuit of this line of thought arrives at the argument that development workers can 'empower the poor' by helping them to develop better forms of organisation (Curtis 1991, Uphoff 1992). In these works 'the stress is on the deficiencies of traditional institutions which people, treated as passive objects, are incapable of changing' (Hobart 1993: 12). Today local communities and local organisations are also given a special role in natural resource management. Many approaches to sustainable development formulate solutions in terms of returning responsibility for the management of natural resources to local communities (Berkes 1995). This emphasis on organisation is accompanied by a stress on education and consciousness-raising in order to make the poor understand their own problems and encourage them to work on possible solutions (World Bank 1996).

Although these works are based on a real concern for the position of the poor, they can be criticised for their unrealistic views of the relation between ways of organising and power. First, these approaches tend to ignore the multi-dimensional differentiations among the poor or rural people themselves based on economic differences, gender, age and ethnic identities. As Leach et al. argue, 'it is striking the degree to which simplistic notions of community are being reinvented in the context of practical efforts towards community-based sustainable development' (1997: 11). It is obvious that any form of community is characterised by differentiation, struggles and forms of domination. Second, these approaches are not able to deal with power relations in the wider force field in which peasants are situated. An important reason for this is that they do not sufficiently take into account existing forms of organising and how these are related to power and the state. For example, they do not pay attention to forms of organising which are not based on collective projects but are of a more fragmented, non-formal nature. Although they claim to work from a 'bottom-up view', they do not try to understand why, in many situations, people prefer to work in individual networks instead of collective projects, or why we can find villagers working in continuously changing constellations instead of in more enduring groups. However, as shown in this book, historically developed patterning in organising practices often implies loose constellations of social networks, within trans-local social fields. More formalised

collective actions may imply political dangers and risks, and intervention itself may have a dividing effect on people. For that reason, people
often have good reasons for adopting a wait-and-see attitude instead of
making a 'personal cost-benefit calculation' which shows whether 'the
benefits of the project outweigh the costs' (Curtis 1991: 30). The point is
that people may choose different kinds of involvement and appropriation, which change over time and which cannot be captured by a model
based on so-called 'rational decision-making'. The general point of
critique is that these works ignore existing fields of power and the
capacity of the poor villagers to analyse their own situation and deploy
forms of organising which fit best in these contexts. By ignoring this
capacity of the local people and by ignoring the logics behind existing
organising strategies, these development projects may even 'disempower'
the poor.

Even among progressive bureaucrats, the figure of the 'distrustful,
closed and distant' ejidatario deeply informed their thinking. Officials had
elaborate ideas about the problems in Mexican agricultural development.
Most blamed the Mexican government for its bad policies in agriculture
and animal husbandry. Many also argued that the USA intended to
destroy Mexican agriculture in order to avoid competition with Mexican
products on the markets, which were opening up under NAFTA (the
North American Free Trade Agreement). On the other hand, in the case
of the ejidos, officials also used to blame the ejidatarios themselves for
their difficult situation. Ejidatarios were depicted as lazy, uneducated and
lacking initiative. Officials always commented upon the widespread interpersonal distrust in the ejidos, and the existence of factions, which
impeded the development of local projects to the benefit of all people. So,
besides being distrustful and lazy, ejidatarios were also characterised as
conflictive and uncooperative. Together with bad government policy and
the USA as enemy this seemed to be the worst scenario for development
and progress.

These stereotypes were reinforced by experiences officials had with
ejidatarios in their daily work. The point is that ejidatarios often do not
show much interest in new government programmes and do not attend
meetings or walk out in the middle of them. They also tend to make
cynical comments about the officials' speeches and show little faith in
the governmental discourse used by them. Obviously, this attitude of
'passivity' and ejidatarios' distrust of officials and new government
programmes has developed on the basis of many bad experiences in the
past. When I confronted officials with this explanation, they would
immediately recognise the point. Yet, they still felt that ejidatarios had
to change their attitude for their own benefit. Many officials who wanted

to work on behalf of the ejidatarios had become frustrated by these experiences. This has led to the contradictory situation in which, on the one hand, the ejidatarios are considered to be 'the victims of a corrupt system' and, on the other hand, they are considered to be responsible for this situation due to their 'apathy'.

Officials saw this 'lack of initiative and education' on the part of the ejidatarios not only as an enormous hindrance to development but also as an obstacle in the fight against corruption. During my research I spoke to many officials and people working for other organisations who tried to fight corruption in general and in the agrarian bureaucracy in particular. Their ideas about the solution were very consistent: education and organisation. These were the means through which the ejidatarios could defend themselves against a corrupt government bureaucracy. This leads to the paradoxical situation of officials trying to improve the situation of the ejidatarios by helping them to organise themselves against the 'corrupt state'.

The stress on new forms of organisation in development debates is accompanied by a stress on education and consciousness-raising. During the research I found this emphasis also strongly present among officials and other people trying to work for the benefit of the ejidatarios. They said that the ejidatarios should develop their knowledge of official rules in order to fight a corrupt bureaucracy. On the one hand, it is certainly true that ejidatarios with more nerve, more knowledge of the rules and better capacities in 'playing the game' with officials, will be treated with more caution and will be less easily deceived than others. On the other hand, 'empowering people' is not only about improving one's qualities in 'games'. For example, learning about the official rules and procedures did not change the existing power relations around the conflict of the 'lost land'. We could even assert that we engage with a dangerous ideological fallacy when we argue that education can make a crucial difference. There is a danger in this belief of getting lost in a world of voluntaristic fantasies in which we ignore the political dimension of many developmental problems.

THE IER PROGRAMME IN A NEW INSTITUTIONAL ENVIRONMENT

In Chapter 7 it was discussed how, in 1992, together with the radical change of the Mexican ejido system, a new style of government inter-vention was introduced. The PA introduced a new style of intervention in which officials should no longer treat peasants in the usual paternal-istic way but instead as capable individuals. According to the official PA propaganda the ejidatarios had to become 'independent' and 'self-reliant', after more than a half-century of state tutelage. One of the programmes that was introduced with this change, was the programme of the Internal Ejido Rules (IER). The possibility of formulating these rules already existed under the old Agrarian Reform Law, but was given new prominence. In the IER each ejido could specify rules concerning the internal administration of the ejido at the local level. So the IER was presented as the perfect way for the ejidos to show their self-determination. It was propagated that consciousness-raising and local organisation were central to progress in the ejidos and that each ejido should formulate its IER according to its particular local situation and the aspirations of the ejidatarios.

Although such a project sounds sympathetic, it becomes much less appealing when we take into account that ejido organising practices have developed in a way that bears little relation to the official rules. As we saw, in La Canoa the ejido assembly only plays a limited role in the management of ejido affairs and no centre of decision-making exists. Taking this into consideration, the project of formulating internal rules becomes much less appealing. One might ask, what could be the use of formulating more rules?

Before I describe in detail how the implementation of the IER programme evolved in La Canoa and the region of Autlán, let me mention my own role in the process. By the time the IER programme started I had already been working in La Canoa for a long time and the ejido commissioner and several other ejidatarios relied more and more on my information and advice. This has to be seen in the light of many bad experiences they have had with government programmes and officials in the past. So several ejidatarios tried to put me in a sort of broker's role. This role had two sides. First, they liked me doing the information-seeking with officials at different institutions. Second, they hoped that my presence in meetings and negotiations with officials would prevent them asking bribes from the ejidatarios. So, on several occasions I felt like a 'buffer' between the ejidatarios and officials.

Although at the start of the IER programme in the region of Autlán several institutions participated, it was decided at higher bureaucratic levels that the SRA should take over and gradually the other institutions withdrew from further activities. Many ejidos were disappointed that they had to work with the SRA again. On the basis of past experiences, they were convinced that the SRA officials would ask the ejido for money in exchange for assistance with the IER.

In June 1993 a meeting was held in La Canoa about the IER. Manuel, the head of the SRA office in Autlán came to the meeting. He never used to visit the ejidos but he was under great pressure from the Guadalajara office to get ejidos to finish their IERs. Manuel explained that a small committee had to be formed in La Canoa, which could elaborate the IER. He said that he would personally give assistance to this committee. He stressed the importance of the IER for getting loans in the future. After various questions, a discussion started about who should be on the IER committee. Two young men were proposed, sons of ejidatarios who had received secondary education. Then I was proposed as a member of the committee. Finally, it was decided to have some older experienced ejidatarios as well. So two older men also became part of the committee. The five of us signed the papers of the IER committee. The meeting came to an end and it was decided that the IER committee would meet with Manuel the next day at his office.

At the meeting with the head of the SRA at his office the next day, Manuel made it clear that he did not have much time to work with the ejidatarios. He said that he had written down ten points to start the work. He read out the points which were formulated in a very legalist terminology and which the people from La Canoa clearly did not understand. The ten points he had written down came directly from the agrarian law and had nothing to do with the situation in La Canoa.

Some days after the meeting it became clear that the two older ejidatarios on the committee did not see the point of the IER and that they would not come to the meetings anymore. The whole project of the IER seemed a ridiculous endeavour. Framing this document was too big a challenge for the ejidatarios. The rules had to be based on the new agrarian law, as the law restricts what themes can be addressed. Therefore, the ejidatarios first had to know the law in detail in order to know where variation was possible. On the basis of that study, they could then formulate their own Internal Ejido Rules. Since many ejidatarios can barely read, this task of studying the agrarian law was all but impossible. However, more importantly, the new agrarian law appeared to be open to various interpretations and, again, education did not seem to be the only issue here. This became clear when a university-educated Mexican friend who was working in another region helped an ejido to formulate its IER. This IER was then rejected by the RAN (National Agrarian Registry) for including local rules which went against the agrarian law. In this way, it seemed that the new laws were used to stifle local creativity and only strengthened the practice of legal reification.

Some entrepreneurial types soon grasped that the new programme offered interesting possibilities and they went to the ejidos to offer their services in developing the IER, in exchange for substantial payment. For example, the SRA office in Autlán offered its services to several neighbouring ejidos, for 20 million pesos (US$7,000). They had also told some ejidatarios that La Canoa would have to pay 20 million pesos for assistance with the IER if the committee did not succeed in doing the job on its own. In other ejidos people from outside the region arrived to offer their assistance with the IER and charged large sums of money. However, some officials of the SARH (the former Ministry of Agriculture and Hydraulic Resources) office in El Grullo became aware of this and managed to convince the ejidatarios not to work with these people. A drawback for these entrepreneurial types was that in many ejidos the ejidatarios didn't see the value of developing the IER. So, these types threatened the ejidatarios that without an IER they wouldn't get credit from the banks anymore. Although this threat seemed to work in some cases, in most ejidos the people were not impressed, and the price for assistance with the IERs dropped (in the Autlán region, the price fell from 20 million pesos (US$7,000) to between 3 million and 5 million pesos (US$1,000–1,700)). Officials of the PA office in Autlán were very well aware of what was going on. However, there had been many tensions between the PA and the SRA and the PA office was operating very carefully and trying to avoid conflict with the SRA office in Autlán. So, there was little support for the ejidatarios from that side.

When the two older ejidatarios on the IER committee of La Canoa withdrew from further activities, I was left on the committee with two young men who were not even ejidatarios. So there seemed little reason to continue with the job. Furthermore, most ejidatarios did not show any interest in the project and I myself did not believe in the usefulness of more rules. However, the ejido commissioner Raúl urged us to go on. He was afraid that otherwise the officials of the SRA office in Autlán would take over and charge the ejido a large sum of money. So we continued the work and I was amazed by the zeal and enthusiasm of the two young men, who clearly hoped to become ejidatarios in the future. The work on the IER led to many interesting discussions in a small group of ejidatarios. Yet, the majority of ejidatarios showed no interest in this project of new ejido rules.

At the request of the ejido commissioner Raúl, I had gathered together some IERs of other ejidos and on the basis of the Agrarian Law and these examples we formulated a framework in which the local rules could easily be integrated. After several discussions in small groups we elaborated a provisional IER in which the local ideas were 'translated' into a formalist legal terminology. The idea was that this provisional IER would be discussed at the ejido assembly, which would take the final decisions about the different rules. When we visited Raúl to discuss this provisional document, Raúl did not react very much. After asking several times what he thought about it, he said that several things were unclear to him. On further questioning it became apparent that he had not understood anything of the formal language. As it seemed ridiculous to have an IER that not even the ejido commissioner was able to understand, we talked about the possibility of writing a short IER in normal language for use in the ejido and a formal legalist IER in order to deal with institutions. The commissioner was very enthusiastic about that idea.

In conversations with officials at the headquarters of the PA in Mexico City in August 1993, I learned that they were well aware of what was going on in the field with respect to the IER programme. Two young lawyers working for Arturo Warman realised that not only was the IER programme failing to promote the new ideology of an independent ejidatario, it was creating new opportunities for people who wanted to exploit ejidatarios. Their boss Fabiola, who was an anthropologist and part of the head team of the PA, had just returned from a meeting with Warman and said:

I just received orders to work further on an instruction booklet for the IER. We wanted to distance ourselves from former practices in which the SRA dictated everything. We wanted the ejidatarios to do it themselves. It now appears that it did not work that way. The regional assistance offices of the SRA jumped in and now ask for money from the ejidatarios: they sell IERs. For that reason we decided to make an instruction booklet after all.

So, the central office of the PA had finally decided to publish a booklet in which the project of the IER was explained and in which a sample of IERs was presented which the ejidatarios could copy, filling in sections where there was room for variation. Hence, the IER project had turned into an arena of conflict between different institutions of the agrarian bureaucracy (the SRA, the RAN, the PA), and in which some ejidos were the 'victims'. When I returned to La Canoa, I informed them about this latest development and they decided to wait for the new PA booklet before continuing with the IER.

One day when I was working in the local ejido archive of La Canoa, I was amazed when I suddenly found an IER of the ejido that had been elaborated two years before. I showed it to the ejido commissioner who was also surprised and said that he had never known of its existence. He asked me to read it and explain what it said to him. I talked about it with other ejidatarios but only some seemed to remember that, a couple of years ago, some people had talked about an IER, but it was never heard of again and was never presented at a general assembly. The IER had been elaborated by an official of the SRA office in Autlán and was very extensive and well done. Many of the rules that the ejidatarios wanted to include in the new IER, such as fines for people who did not attend the meetings, were already in this IER. After having found this IER, I became even more convinced that the formulation of more new rules was a useless endeavour.

The PA booklet about the IER appeared in December 1993, almost a year after the IER project had begun in the Autlán region. As the PA published the booklet, most ejidatarios never learned of its existence; the IER projects in Autlán were in the hands of the SRA. We had some more meetings in La Canoa and, using the booklet, we made a provisional IER. At the SRA office in Guadalajara we heard that specialised assistants were soon going to be sent to the region to give free help with the IERs. The ejidatarios decided to wait for the assistance of this specialised SRA official from Guadalajara to do the final work.

However, by now Manuel, the head of the SRA office in Autlán, had become very angry with our 'laziness'. He was under great pressure from the Guadalajara office to get more ejidos in the region to finish their IERs. Autlán was the regional assistance office of Jalisco that had the fewest IERs finished. So, on several occasions Manuel talked to Raúl and to me and asked us why we did not work harder. We gave evasive answers, as we did not want to mention the forthcoming assistance. However, Manuel had to report about the progress of the IERs to his superiors and he suggested Raúl write a letter saying that La Canoa did not want an IER. In that way it was no longer Manuel's responsibility. However, that was something that had to be avoided. We tried to keep Manuel on a string and avoided him as far as possible.

However, in March 1994 Manuel arrived at a meeting in the ejido together with an SRA official from Guadalajara. The young official presented himself and explained that he had been sent with the special task of helping ejidos with the IERs. He would be the person responsible for the IER in the region of Autlán. As I was finishing my fieldwork period in the region I could not participate in the meetings with this official. But the ejidatarios later told me that they had several good meetings with him and that he finally finished the IER. Afterwards, when I returned to La Canoa it was obvious that, despite new rules, nothing had changed in the management of the ejido. Most ejidatarios did not know the new rules, nor even the fact that new rules had been formulated.

INTERVENTION AND RITUALS OF RESISTANCE

In the same way that we cannot assume the existence of a hegemonic state project, we cannot assume the existence of a popular project of resistance to the state either. In the foregoing chapters interactions between ejidatarios and officials were described in many different settings. On the basis of this material I conclude that, in the Mexican context, the basic problem with the notion of resistance is that people often do not have clear images of the 'opposing class' or the categories they are fighting against. They may talk in broad terms about *los ricos, los pequeños* or the 'corrupt officials', but in concrete situations it is very hard to determine whether somebody should be resisted or cooperated with.

Ejidatarios often do not know whether they should support or oppose a state official or whether they should support or resist a new government programme. They have ample experience with projects and programmes that they perceive to be highly corrupt. Hence, the apparent distrust, lack of interest, and the wait-and-see attitude that officials complain about manifest a sensible scepticism with regard to the hopes and expectations raised by the bureaucracy. It is in the process itself that attitudes and positions develop and they often remain ambivalent. A government official should be received with some suspicion but can in the end prove to be a 'good guy'. Alternatively, he could prove to be a man with good intentions but who is manipulated by his chiefs.

So, when ejidatarios do not show much initiative or do not participate in new government programmes, it is not that they deliberately refrain from every form of action that is initiated by the government, or that they manifest a form of resistance against interference from outside. The distant and distrustful attitude can best be described as a form of 'keeping a distance'. This 'keeping a distance' is not part of a larger project, and their attitudes can change according to how the situation develops. In this way we find complex attitudes which combine elements of resistance and compliance at the same time. In addition, any initiative or programme can develop and be appropriated in unpredictable ways (Arce 1993, de Vries 1997, Long 1988).

When the ejidatarios really felt that they were being deceived, they could make this clear to the officials. In many meetings they made objections to and cynical remarks about the propaganda talk of officials. Their wait-and-see attitude, cynical jokes, moments of enthusiasm, but also their silently leaning against the wall and leaving in the middle of the meeting can be analysed in terms of a ritual or a style that they have developed on the basis of many experiences. It is not 'lack of interest', 'lack of initiative' or 'lack of education', but styles and rituals in which practices of dominance and resistance interact in complex ways; rituals of rules and resistance (Beezley et al. 1994) that form part of the culture of the state.

This brings us to another point, namely that when officials present new government programmes they think in terms of incorporated ejidatarios. In fact, ejidatarios are always already incorporated in official structures, but not in standard ways. For example, the big entrepreneurs among the ejidatarios have been quite skilled in establishing useful contacts with some bureaucrats and influential politicians in the region, who can give them the information, and ways in, that they need. Hence, these big entrepreneurs are often not enthusiastic about attending the meetings convened by officials who come to introduce new programmes, as they have their own contacts. At the same time, ejidatarios live in a world that develops, to a large degree, outside the grip of the state bureaucracy. For example, the fact that ejidatarios do not show much interest in more 'modern' and 'advanced' forms of production, may be very frustrating for the SARH officials, and confirm their opinion that ejidatarios are backward. However, when we take into account that many ejidatarios are migrants and that they may combine their ejido plot with several other sources of income, they should perhaps be seen as very 'modern'. They are at least quite able to find their ways in modern transnational settings. While officials may fantasise about raising production in ejidos by joining several ejido plots together, the ejidatarios generally prefer to combine their ejido plot with migration to Los Angeles. This 'independent' and 'distant' attitude of the ejidatarios frustrates the work of many officials: it makes the ejidatarios 'uncontrollable'.

Staying out of the Grip of the State Machine

It is obvious that there are many ways in which people organise activities in their daily life, for example, the skills ejidatarios from the village have developed in organising the crossing of the well-guarded US border and maintaining themselves in illegal circumstances in *el Norte.* For these matters no organisations are set up, but networks are mobilised which provide crucial information, financial support and practical help. The ways in which ejidatarios have also managed to circumvent the law with respect to land transfers is another clear indication that there is absolutely no lack of organising skills and inventiveness. On the contrary, people have been very inventive and skilful in organising different personal matters and in defending their own interests in their daily life.

As was shown in the ethnography, the most effective organising strategy is often the use of personal political networks and not necessarily forms of collective action (Cornelius and Craig 1991). Many authors try to explain the difficulty of collective organising among Mexican peasants (Foley 1990) and talk about 'the apparently contradictory quality of peasant politics wherein the major political manifestations are individual "apathy" and collective revolt' (Lomnitz-Adler 1992: 125). However, what is called apathy is generally a form of 'taking a safe distance' from formal collective organisation and the state bureaucracy. Organising through informal personal networks is often the most 'rational' way to operate.

The above-mentioned forms of organising remain to a large degree outside the control of the state bureaucracy. According to Appadurai, large residual spaces exist where the techniques of nationhood, directed towards spatial and social standardisation, are likely to be either weak or contested (Appadurai 1997: 190). This points to a weakness in governmentality and indicates that there is considerable room for 'exit' from the official system and for avoiding state regulation (Hirschman 1970, Reno 1995). Thus, much organising remains outside the control of the state, and this can have important advantages for the people concerned.

Although in development debates so-called informal or corrupt practices are considered to be detrimental to the poor, they can also provide them with a certain freedom and liberty in their actions. This is well illustrated by the way in which migrant villagers in La Canoa argue that there is much more freedom in Mexico than in the USA, since in Mexico rules can always be bent or 'bought', whereas in the USA rules are applied much more strictly. Ejidatarios feel this strict application of rules as a restriction on their personal freedom. In this study, it became clear that there were advantages, especially for ejidatarios, in remaining at a distance from the law and outside an effective controlling state machine. With respect to the individual ejido plots and the common lands, the ejidatarios and landless villagers acquired a high degree of autonomy. Despite a strong 'presence of the state' in the field of individual ejido plots, there was little 'control by the state', and the effects of intervention were minimal.

The idea that by avoiding full incorporation into a bureaucratic organisation, ejidatarios prevented themselves from becoming subjects controlled by the state, is also discussed by Krotz et al. He argues that the many illegal transactions with ejido land at the local level made ejidatarios averse to any new formal kind of organising coming from outside which would restrict their freedom (Krotz et al. 1985: 24). This fear of more control from above also becomes evident when ejidatarios are reluctant to have their land plots registered and do not want to provide data on the amount of land and cattle they possess, and maize they produce. They fear that information and registration will in the end lead to more control from above (for example, in the form of checks on land use and land transactions, and taxes).

The Difficulty of Autonomous Organisation

Although it is easily accepted that villagers are conscious of the risks involved in engaging the state bureaucratic machine, it is more difficult to see that villagers may be equally reluctant to become involved in 'local' or 'community-based' organisations. Yet, villagers may have good reasons to be reluctant about involvement in *any* type of more formal organisation. The point is that it seems impossible to think of any 'village' or 'community-based' organisation in which the state does not become involved in one way or the other. What is most striking 'is the degree to which the state has become implicated in the minute texture of everyday life' (Gupta 1995: 375). A strong presence of the state does not necessarily mean that there is much 'state control', but rather that its presence is felt in the way matters are formalised and the game is played (see Chapter 4). Yet this still means that *state law and bureaucracies influence local organising initiatives.*

There are different ways in which the state influences local forms of organising. For example, in the context of a state bureaucracy that has a history of establishing special contacts with influential well-placed people, it may be much wiser not to be organised in a formal 'local' or 'community-based' organisation. There is a high risk that the leaders or representatives of these organisations will establish personal relations with the state bureaucracy and 'there is in fact a danger that the elites may regroup and become re-empowered' by the creation of village development committees (Singh 1988: 44). In this atmosphere it also seems very reasonable to be reluctant to put your money and energy into a local cooperative. So, although many development theories stress the importance of 'building self-reliant village organisations' (Poulton 1988: 32), there are many situations in which it can be important for people to remain outside more formal kinds of organising, whether these are governmental, non-governmental, local, community-based or whatever.

Many people who have worked with peasant organisations in Mexico have explained the difficulties they encountered and many authors have tried to deal with the complexity of peasant organising in Mexico (Esteva 1987, Foley 1990). Esteva, who has considerable experience in working with peasants in Mexico, describes his frustrating experiences when he and others worked with ideas of empowerment of the peasants and local forms of organisation. On the basis of his experience Esteva has distanced himself from second-level organisations such as federations, unions, associations and political parties, with which he has had bitter experiences. Instead he tries to organise *issue* campaigns in concert with others through short meetings, well-defined in time and space, for the exchange of ideas and experiences, or for specific 'battles' that are shared (Esteva 1987: 148).

These experiences with local organising should be taken into account in the discussions about organising for development. Although in much of this literature a distinction is made between community-based organisations, non-governmental organisations and governmental agencies (Bebbington and Farrington 1993, Curtis 1991, Poulton and Harris 1988), in practice these differences are hard to maintain. For example, from a formal organisation perspective, the ejido is an organisation which is difficult to categorise. It is not a public sector institution, nor a private organisation. It is a form of locally based organisation imposed by the government, and subject to many laws and regulations. This ambivalence of the ejido, which is at once 'a state apparatus of political control and an organ of peasant representation' (Fox and Gordillo 1989: 131), has always played an important role in the debate concerning the ejido. Yet, the ejido is just one of many organisations and institutions which cannot easily be classified as governmental, non-governmental, local, etc. For that reason we should study the wider force fields in which organising takes place, and examine what relations with the state bureaucracy exist, rather than trying to distinguish (artificial) organisational categories.

THE MYTH OF THE 'MODERN', 'ACCOUNTABLE' ORGANISATION

When development workers or officials complain about 'disorganisation' or talk about 'a lack of organisation' at the local level they in fact refer to the absence of organising principles belonging to the ideological construct of the formal, 'modern' organisation with 'transparent' procedures and mechanisms of accountability. The idea that 'modern' forms of organising work in the interest of the collectivity and in this way can 'empower' the group is stimulated by the fact that many writers on organisation define organisations as groups of people who come together in pursuit of common goals. According to this line of thought it is argued that, by introducing organisations with procedures which secure accountability and democratic forms of decision-making, the whole group is empowered, as people with formal responsibilities can be effectively controlled and the decision-making remains with the majority.

Yet the reality of organising is different. Although we are usually encouraged to think about organisations as rational enterprises pursuing goals that aspire to satisfy the interests of all, there is much evidence to suggest that this view is more an ideology than a reality. In fact, this notion is based on a social systems perspective of organisations. Although the systems framework in organisational analysis was widely used in the 1970s and 1980s, many other perspectives have since been developed in organisational sociology which have been largely overlooked in the development literature. Yet, many authors have argued that organisations are often used as instruments of domination that further the selfish interests of elites at the expense of others. And there is often an element of domination in *all* organisations (Morgan 1986: 274–5).

Hence, collective and more formal organisations may also become important instruments of control and domination and do not necessarily lead to more power and freedom for the 'excluded' or the 'poor'. Furthermore, organisations can be empty shelters, which mask all kinds of power games. In fact, the idea of organisations as containers of action is a highly simplistic one.

Another problem is that in much development literature, organisations and institutions are treated as instruments of social change. In fact, the idea that new forms of organising can make a dramatic difference to the lives of the poor is based on the notion of social and legal engineering: the belief that by changing rules or introducing new forms of organisation one can change society. Yet, as Stiefel and Wolfe point out, 'processes of legal and institutional reform by themselves probably have little chance to sustain a democratic process and prevent new authoritarian structures from emerging' (Stiefel and Wolfe 1994: 200). As this book has shown, official rules and procedures may influence the development of organising practices in many different and often unpredictable ways. Although rules and formal structures may influence established practices they can never control or transform them in planned ways (see F. von Benda-Beckmann 1993). Processes of organisational reform by themselves have little chance of changing existing power relations and bringing more prosperity to the poor. This instrumental view of organisational reform, leads to a vicious circle within which ill-functioning organisations are made the scapegoat for the bad socio-economic conditions of the poor, and against which the propagation of new organisations is used as a magic charm (adaptation of F. von Benda-Beckmann 1993, 1994).

I contend that we should study the logic and value of existing forms of organising and look at the ways in which they are related to socio-political alignments. We have to study organising practices in their particular force fields and recognise a wide range of forms of control, accountability and organisation. In this book it has been shown that organising practices which do not follow the rules of 'modern' organisation have their own mechanisms of control and accountability. I concluded that the inadequacy or ineffectiveness of a decision-making body does not necessarily mean that there is a blatant abuse of power. An ejido commissioner who has much autonomy in his decisions and does not render accounts of what he does, is easily labelled from a modernist point of view as an exponent of a corrupt and non-transparent system. Yet in La Canoa the autonomy of the commissioner only concerns minor matters, and he does not have much influence over what is going on in important questions. Despite the absence of so-called transparent, democratic organising mechanisms, in the ejido La Canoa there is no question of easy abuses of power or nepotism. We find strong forms of ordering with respect to control over resources, and forms of accountability.

CONCLUSION: DECONSTRUCTING THE MYTHS IN THE DEVELOPMENT DEBATE

Local organisation is often presented as the solution to a wide range of developmental problems. In this same vein, development workers and government officials often label existing forms of organising as chaotic and corrupt. However, it can be argued that both the labelling of existing organising practices as 'disorganised', 'chaotic' and 'corrupt' and the widespread belief that 'modern', 'democratic' and 'collective' forms of organisation can improve the situation of poor peasants form part of broader discourses of development (cf. Apthorpe and Gasper 1996, Escobar 1995, Grillo and Stirrat 1997). In these discourses 'development narratives' are created, 'broad explanatory narratives that can be operationalised into standard approaches with widespread application' and that mobilise action (Roe 1991: 288). In effect, these simplifying stories have the general characteristic of de-politicising development issues and intervention itself (Cooke and Kothari 2001).

The de-politicising effects of discourses of participation and local organisation became very clear in the case of the programme of the Internal Ejido Rules in Mexico. In Mexico, officials used to depict ejidatarios as uneducated, lacking initiative and uncooperative. This figure of the 'distrustful, and distant' ejidatario deeply informs the thinking of bureaucrats and is reinforced by their experiences with ejidatarios in their daily work. Ejidatarios often do not show much interest in new government programmes or in the bureaucrats' explanation of them. Although this sceptical attitude is the outcome of ejidatarios' past experiences with government programmes, officials interpret this wait-and-see stance as a sign that ejidatarios do not take any interest in their own development. Hence, officials used to stress the need to raise the consciousness of the ejidatarios about their own situation and the importance of high levels of participation in programmes that personally concern them.

Salinas's propaganda that ejidatarios should become independent and self-reliant linked up with the officials' image of ejidatarios as ignorant and in need of empowerment. The new programmes for the ejido sector drew heavily on the discourses of consciousness-raising, education and local organisation. As we saw, this formed part of a broader institutional project in which a new agrarian institute, the PA, was created, alongside the SRA. The IER programme – in which ejidatarios had to show their own 'organising capacities' – was one of the programmes within this new intervention package. However, the IER programme obviously did not address the fact that the long history of state intervention in rural areas has shaped forms of governance in rather conflictive ways.

In La Canoa, the IER project had the effect that ejidatarios tried to resist as long as possible the interference of possibly 'corrupt' officials. They especially tried to keep the SRA at a distance when they noticed that some of these officials asked for money from other ejidos in the region in exchange for their assistance with the IER. In the end, this programme only led to the reshuffling of money within the agrarian bureaucracy and to institutional fights between different state agencies. As far as the organising practices in the ejido were concerned – the official aim of the IER project – it did not have any effect at all.

The case study also illustrates how people may take advantage of the unexpected and unintended opportunities created by a new government programme (Long 1984). It is obvious that state intervention exhibits its own dynamic, manifested in the transformation of programmes on the basis of power struggles within and between institutions and the interaction between functionaries and 'clients' (Arce 1993, de Vries 1997). It is a fallacy to believe that new laws or projects can have a dramatic and predictable effect. We could even argue that many organising practices develop as a side effect of formal laws and formal structures, which in effect are never applied as such.

Several people working on the theme of natural resource management have criticised the unrealistic images of community and local organisa-tions which dominate policy thinking in this field (Fairhead and Leach 1995, Leach et al. 1997, Mosse 1997). Fairhead and Leach, for example, show that environmental management often depends less on community-level authorities and socio-cultural organisations than on the sum of a much more diffuse set of relations: a constellation more than a structure (1995: 1027), or in my words, a force field. Furthermore, existing practices are not necessarily the result of 'organisational incapacities' but are more often the result of different elements in the wider field of power. What has happened in the case of La Canoa is due to the dynamics of a force field which developed over the years and which transcends the locality, even though officially the management rests with the ejido. Organising practices are shaped within force fields that, more often than not, are deterritorialised and composed of shifting sets of actors.

While discourses of formal organisation may be complicit with bureaucratic attempts to territorialise, and hence control, people's activities, villagers may prefer to embrace the opportunities created by increased globalisation and deterritorialisation. Before assuming that new forms of organisation can contribute to the solution of fundamental developmental problems we should first ask ourselves how existing organising forms are embedded in wider force fields, and how they relate to the state bureaucracy and a given culture of the state. Furthermore, we should be modest in our aims and accept that there is no way to 'control' the organising process, not even by an external 'specialist'. This conclusion about organisation for development can be summarised in five points:

- We often find non-formal kinds of organising practices, such as different personal networks (family, friendship, *compadrazgo*), group-formations, individual alliances, ad hoc constellations, and individual relations with officials or higher placed politicians. These kinds of organising may be of a loose and deterritorialised nature.
- When we study these apparently loosely structured organising practices in relation to specific problems or resources over a longer period of time, we discover certain forms of patterning and regularities. This patterning can refer to the way in which access to resources is arranged, but also to forms of accountability and control.
- These historically developed forms of patterning in organising practices have to be analysed in relation to the specific force fields in which organising occurs. For that reason, we have to distinguish the central resources at stake, the different groups with specific positions and interests, and the role of the law, official institutions and functionaries. We also have to realise that force fields generally transcend local and even national borders.
- More often than not the patterning of organising practices is of a decentred nature, which means that there is no single centre of control and that there is no single group or organisational body which controls the organising process.
- The notion of modern, democratic organisation, which stresses public accountability and transparency, is an ideological notion. Every type of organising creates power differences and fosters new (or old) forms of domination. In fact, the patterning of organising practices often develops as a side effect of formal organisations and legal regulations and takes unintended forms.

9 CORRUPTION, ORDER AND THE IDEA OF THE STATE

INTRODUCTION: POWER IN MULTIPLE FORCE FIELDS

This book began with the argument that anthropology should pay more attention to relations of power in general and to different dimensions of state power in particular. The in-depth study of the ejido La Canoa showed that organising practices develop within multiple force fields with differing dynamics, rather than within one overarching field. Force fields cohere around certain problems and resources and lead to forms of ordering in which socio-political categories with differing positions and interests define themselves. As organising practices tend to transcend boundaries in an increasingly 'deterritorialized' world (Appadurai 1997) it is not possible to 'freeze' force fields in terms of social or territorial boundaries. Force fields are always in flux.

The existence of multiple force fields explains that power relations are diversified and that, for example, the relation of the ejidatarios to the state cannot be reduced to a general vertical intermediation model with the *cacique* occupying a nodal point within the system. Around different resources and struggles, different divisions and power dynamics play a role. For instance, around the common lands, struggles developed in which ejidatarios are pitted against landless villagers, whereas around the 'lost land', ejidatarios are pitted against *pequeños propietarios*. In the case of inheritance questions divisions are based on age and gender differences within the family. These different force fields and modes of socio-political ordering have consequences for the resulting forms of governance and space for action for the different parties involved. In some force fields, people have much room for manoeuvre, while in others they have little individual influence. For example, around their arable plots the ejidatarios have developed a high degree of autonomy and keep the state bureaucracy at bay. Yet, around the 'lost land', they operate in a force field in which they are relatively powerless and are subject to the fantasies fostered by the state machine. The concept of force field helps us to analyse the weighting of different kinds of socio-political networks, the influence of law and procedures and the role of various discourses and of representations of power.

I have stressed throughout the book that the patterning which develops in organising practices and the accompanying forms of domination and struggle are related to active dialogues, self-reflection, irony and the production of multiple meanings through imagination and the work of interpretation. These reflections and dialogues around relations of power were explicitly discussed in the context of ejidatarios' domination over landless villagers, in the context of inheritance decisions in the family and in the context of the internal organisation and management in the ejido. Finally, the extraordinary kinds of imaginings surrounding the struggle for the 'lost land', were analysed. These dialogues reflect power relations and a continuous active engagement of social actors with the world around them (Pigg 1996, Tsing 1993). Yet, they are also a reflection of contradictions in the given discursive fields.

In my view, discourses are the product of processes of domination in society. They reflect the symbolic order and influence the formation of identities. However, because of the existence of multiple force fields, discourses are never totally consistent. Rather than being the executor of the symbolic order, the subject subjectivises himself by showing the inconsistencies of the symbolic order. This explains that subjects are shaped but not 'captured' within discursive formations. Discourses do not necessarily shape human minds and cognitive processes in a fixed way (see Bhabha 1991, Said 1978, Spivak 1987, Young 1995 for an interesting discussion on the effects of colonialism on the subjectivity of colonial subjects). Others have illustrated the hybridisation of authority and decentring of discourses from their position of power and authority (Bakhtin 1981). Hence, the use of powerful and influential discourses does not mean that they automatically shape people's consciousness. Instead, situated social actors, in their use of differing discourses, show the inconsistency of the symbolic order.

Of course, the existence of multiple fields of power impinging on different dimensions of our lives has always been a reality. But today, in a world where media and migration have a strong effect on the 'work of the imagination as a constitutive feature of modern subjectivity' (Appadurai 1997: 3), the existence of multiple force fields is even more evident. People live in a transnational world in which identity formation and socio-political processes can no longer be seen as automatically tied to certain localities or even nation-states. This is a widespread phenomenon and several authors have stressed that the deterritorialised and transnationalised world we are living in today not only forces us to look 'outwards', but also calls for different theoretical notions (Appadurai 1997, Gupta and Ferguson 1997a, Smith 1999). Thus I argue that the study of organising practices within multiple force fields provides an analytical strategy to study power relations and different dimensions of the state in these new socio-political settings.

FANTASY AND THE CULTURE OF THE STATE

As has been shown, peasants have a complicated and contradictory relation with the Mexican state. The state was their ally in the fight against the *hacendados* during the period of agrarian reform and it has also been the provider of all kinds of services (schools, water and electricity). But in other instances, the state is viewed as a corrupt and violent enemy, which is greatly feared and distrusted by the people. Hence, we have an image of the state as the protector and oppressor of the ejidatarios at the same time. Images of the state conjoin notions of evil with goodness. Obviously, this view of this state is no exception. For example, Reno, in his study of Sierra Leone, argues that, viewed from below, the state is seen as a distributor of benefits as well as an intruder. The state is simultaneously an oppressor and an ally; a source of much-needed goods, as well as of uncertainty and interference (1995: 13). Blom and Stepputat point out that, whereas certain forms of state inter-vention may be loathed and resisted, other forms of intervention may at the same time be intensely desired and asked for (2001: 9). This double feeling explains that the ejidatarios in Mexico may be supportive and enthusiastic towards the Mexican president at one moment, and cynical and distrustful about his speeches at another moment. Or they can laugh about themselves being deceived by the democratic and lib-eralising discourse of a president who later on proved to be one of the worst swindlers the country ever saw. The ejidatarios can be proud of being part of the project of the Mexican nation-state, but at the same time they can criticise powerholders for their corruption and for squeezing the peasants.

I have argued that the continuous theorising about power and politics in society not only concerns a rationalisation of actions but also an investment in the 'idea of the state'. These imaginings, which are con-stitutive of the culture of the state, are based upon a myriad of experiences and are mediated by a series of governmental techniques and by the media, education and movies. The culture of the state is central to the operation of the bureaucracy as a hope-generating machine. The hope-generating bureaucratic machine gives the message that everything is possible, that cases are never closed and that things will be different from now on. This permeates all aspects of life and triggers powerful responses. However, rather than producing a certain rationality and coherence, the bureaucratic machine generates enjoyments, pleasures, fears and expectations. Although people are never naive, during certain periods they can become inspired and enthusiastic about new programmes and new openings that are offered to them. One peculiarity of the Mexican bureaucracy is precisely its ability, at certain points and in certain circumstances, to overcome people's scepticism and, indeed, entice them to start fantasising again about new projects, hence recommencing a never-ending cycle of high expectations followed by disillusion and ironic laughter (cf. Beezley et al. 1994, Torres 1997).

Other studies have also analysed the role that conspiracies and incredible fantasies play in the wider field of power. For example, several studies in the field of witchcraft in Africa have analysed the role of desire in the shaping of collective fantasies in connection to relations of power. These studies analyse collective fantasies as products of the imagination which are always related to the realities of power, but in a loose and non-deterministic way (Thoden van Velzen and van Wetering 2001: 18). In contrast to conventional theories, in these studies witchcraft, incredible beliefs and conspiracy theories are not analysed as remnants of some traditional past, but as the way in which modernity manifests itself in Africa. They also stress moral ambiguities and the double-sided reaction of fear and fascination in relation to power and change (Geschiere 2001). However, where my approach differs from these perspectives is that I see conspiracies and imaginings as constitutive aspects of power relations rather than as epiphenomena of processes of social transformation or resistance to change.

The importance of conspiracy theories, fantasies and desires in the reproduction or contestation of regimes of power has important implications for the discussion on governmentality (Rose and Miller 1992, Rose 1999). Approaches on governmentality argue that power works through the constitution of defined subjectivities (such as citizens, civil servants) through discursive rituals and administrative practices. However, this study showed contexts where governmental techniques, though all-pervasive, are anything but effective in shaping modes of control and (self-)discipline. Furthermore, state discourses and techniques of intervention often generate side effects that are central to the reproduction of the bureaucratic system. Hence, while not really effective in controlling people, techniques of intervention are very effective in the reproduction of the hope-generating machine.

Interface situations (Long 1989) where ejidatarios and officials deal with each other foster these imaginings and the culture of the state. Together, ejidatarios and bureaucrats are implicated in the construction of the idea of the state through processes of rationalisation, speculation and the construction of fantasies, but also through processes of fetishisation, that is the attribution of special powers to objects such as maps and documents. In this complex of desire and fantasy, inscription is very important. People develop a fetishism around certain official documents, even when they cannot 'read' these documents according to official standards. In line with the work of Comaroff and Comaroff (1993) I call this the re-enchantment of governmental techniques. The same can be said of bureaucrats who tend to reify the law, in spite of 'knowing' that official procedures do not play a decisive role in the outcome of highly politicised land conflicts. In these processes, the 'idea of the state' is objectivised and inscribed in maps, documents and other legal texts. However, as was mentioned above, the strong influence of the culture of the state should not be equated with a strong state-apparatus. The study of La Canoa showed that while the culture of the state may be strongly felt in many aspects of life, the state bureaucracy has not had much control over local practices.

THE HOPE-GENERATING MACHINE AND ITS DIVIDING EFFECTS

State intervention in Mexico tends to have a divisive effect on the population, and to frustrate independent collective organising efforts 'from below'. There are several reasons for this situation. First, by privileging figures with good political networks, state intervention contributes to the creation of divisions. We saw in this book that personal relationships, rather than collective organising, have been central to obtaining village projects, jobs, access to credit, important information and so on. Yet these personal political networks create hard feelings among people who are 'less well connected' with political circles, and who therefore have less influence on, for example, the outcome of land conflicts or on village projects. There are also other reasons why the importance of personal networks has a divisive influence on collective projects from below. The leader of a group is never approached by the bureaucracy only as the representative of a group; he or she is also approached as a person with individual interests and 'political capital'. Through these personalised relationships and interests, the collective project often loses importance. Furthermore, the bureaucracy is overly dynamic and its composition is always changing. This causes much instability as when people in power change, different networks become effective.

For that reason, gossip, speculation, complaints about 'local' organisers and criticism of them, surround all government projects and government intervention. This strongly contributes to the situation of never knowing exactly what is going on, accompanied by the continuous quarrelling, rumours and distrust around projects. In this way we can conclude that state intervention itself tends to cause divisions and frustrate collective projects. Krotz points out that experiences with co-operatives in Mexico have shown that every intervention in a socially conflictual reality, such as rural Mexico, reveals, aggravates and creates conflicts (Krotz et al. 1985: 36). I would argue, however, that the cause does not lie in the conflictual nature of rural Mexican society as such, but in the disruptive nature of intervention itself and the particular ways in which 'local' people are approached by the bureaucratic machine.

The fostering of divisions by the bureaucratic machine became especially clear in the case of the 'lost land', when the ejidatarios had to deal with a continuous stream of contradictory messages from the state bureaucracy. One day they were told that the map was found and the next day that the map never existed. At one office they heard that an SRA surveyor would arrive in the ejido tomorrow, and on another day that the surveyor had disappeared because he was accused of corruption. As the ejidatarios work with several brokers and officials at the same time, it is never clear why certain things are finally achieved or sabotaged. If something does not work out well, there are many people who can be blamed for it. Sometimes the officials and intermediaries deliberately create divisions by saying that some ejidatarios are leaking information to the enemy, or they blame one of the ejidatarios for giving false information. Several brokers made clear that they only wanted to work with one specific person of the ejido. In this way, the fighters for the 'lost land' were entrapped in a world of speculation and conspiracy in which everybody blamed each other for things that went wrong.

Gledhill points out that the essence of the post-revolutionary experience in Mexico is precisely the removal of initiative and bargaining power from the base. Even developments in state policy towards the ejidos that might be considered 'improvements' in a narrowly material sense, are increasingly negative from this point of view (Gledhill 1991: 30). In this sense, from the agrarian reform onwards, top-down and politically motivated forms of state intervention have had a disruptive and dividing influence. Aitken also argues that 'the increased entrance of state institutions into local areas can create further fragmentation of communities as local disputes and problems can be mediated potentially through diverse patrons within the political system' (Aitken 1997: 292). It is precisely this type of intervention by the state apparatus and the fabulous hopes and fantasies generated by the bureaucratic machine, which frustrate collective local organising and explain the so-called lack of unity at the local level. In the light of the foregoing it is ironic that it is precisely in bureaucratic circles that so much emphasis is put on the need for ejidatarios to organise themselves. Many officials blame the ejidatarios for being divided among themselves and for not showing any interest in their own development. Paradoxically, while on the one hand, state intervention fosters division in ejidos and villages, on the other hand officials and development workers blame the ejidatarios for not being more united.

At this point I would like to add a personal note. I always felt very uncomfortable when officials asked me to suggest new government programmes for the ejido sector. After so many years of study, they felt that I should at least be able to formulate ideas for new development projects. However, I arrived at the conclusion that the problem was not a lack of good ideas or committed officials but the contradictory and divisive influence of the 'hope-generating machine'. How to explain to these committed people that any new government programme feeds on and fosters divisions and contradictions in society, thereby reproducing so-called traditional practices of clientelism and personalism? It was easier to explain to them that it is difficult to formulate general government programmes when the government's aims with regard to ejido lands are different from those of the ejidatarios. Many officials accepted the point that, while the success of state intervention is dependent on villagers' active and continuous involvement or 'participation', many ejidatarios deploy deterritorialised livelihood strategies in which they combine smallholder agriculture with income from migration to the United States.

CORRUPTION AND THE UNDERWORLD OF RITUALS

Many authors argue that the origin of corruption lies in the 'extreme personalisation of power relationships' (Bayart 1993). In many contexts, this is analysed in terms of the importance of patron–client relations and the close link between politics and the bureaucratic apparatus that frustrates the working of government institutions (Camp, 1996, Cornelius and Craig 1991, Grindle 1977). Several authors have endeavoured to come to grips with the conflicting principles, which determine the working of the bureaucracy, and of society in general. For example, Lomnitz-Adler (1992) talks about the coexistence of legal bureaucratic rationalism and personalism in the Mexican bureaucracy. Lomnitz-Adler argues that 'there has been tremendous tension between rational-bureaucratic practices and practices that are founded on other kinds of principles, such as friendship, kinship, and personal loyalty' (Lomnitz-Adler 1992: 297). In the same way, DaMatta (1991) argues that, in Brazil, two conflicting but complementary notions of the public self operate simultaneously: the notion of the individual and the notion of the person. The notion of the individual emphasises the universal application of the law to all subjects. On the other hand, the complementary notion of the person demands a singular application of the law, which should be bent especially for the person in question (DaMatta 1991: 180–2). Hence, 'the realm of individuals is to be found in this impersonal world of laws, decrees, and rules as they are applied and implemented in practice' (1991: 186). In contrast, in the realm of the person 'reciprocity, loyalty, charity, and goodness are basic values for which the core and focal point is a *system of persons*' (1991: 183). According to DaMatta, one notices in Brazilian society a complex dialectic between these two notions.

I argue that we need a view of corruption that goes beyond the dialectic between these two notions and which steps back from the view that the main problem of developing countries is their patrimonial or neo-patrimonial states. In this view, the public–private boundary, which is central to the concept of modern administration, is weak in developing countries and this is seen as the main cause of corruption (Theobald 1999: 492). Although bureaucratic practices are certainly influenced by personal relationships, much more is involved in practices and discourses commonly labelled as corruption. I also argue against the view that corruption is a dysfunctional aspect of state organisations or, in other words, a kind of disease that should be taken out of the bureaucratic apparatus. In fact, so-called corrupt practices form part of broader fields of power and are not limited to the bureaucracy. Conventional public–private and state–society dichotomies are of no use at all for the analysis of corruption and are often even complicit in sustaining existing relations of domination.

In order to arrive at a different approach of corruption, we should take into account dimensions of corrupt practices that have received little attention so far. These include, for example, the operational side, the performative side (Gupta 1995), the strong feelings of personal care for others in doing favours (Lomnitz-Adler 1992), and the enjoyment and pleasure in 'playing the game'. It is clear that 'personal connection with elite privilege may protect citizens against a state that does not protect

them in an institutional sense' (Reno 1995: 19). It should also be stressed
that personal relationships are not fixed or clear-cut and, in the bureaucratic negotiation process itself, an initially undifferentiated public gets
shaped into 'friends' and 'enemies' (Lomnitz-Adler 1999). For that
reason, people are always careful to establish friendly relationships with
officials, as one never knows how things will work out in the future.
Patience, politeness and knowing how to 'treat people well' are important
to keep you in the game (Lomnitz-Adler 1999). By paying more attention
to the operational, performative and spectacular sides of corruption (de
Vries 2002), it becomes clear that they form part of a culture of power
that goes far beyond the working of the bureaucracy and that cannot be
changed by the introduction of so-called 'democratic procedures' in the
bureaucracy.

This explains the contrasting attitudes of ejidatarios towards
corruption. The ejidatarios do not mind paying large sums of money as
long as they get what they want. In these cases they talk about
successful transactions and do not use the term corruption. On the other
hand, what frustrates them is that they often do not succeed in these
negotiations. In the case of the 'lost land' they paid large sums of money
but never got anything in return. They were lied to and deceived all the
time. The fact that they are fooled around with or are made to pay
excessive sums of money makes them feel stupid and in this context they
complain about the corruption of the government agencies and
shameless, corrupt officials. Hence, when they complain about
corruption they are not so much 'voicing their exclusion from
government services' but are rather expressing 'their frustration because
they lacked the cultural capital required to negotiate deftly for those
services' (Gupta 1995: 381).

The fact that corruption is part of a broader force field and cannot be
seen as separate from the formal bureaucratic scene, is illustrated by the
fact that more often than not state bureaucracies themselves are central
to the organisation of forbidden activities. These apparently contradictory and opposing phenomena of state law and evasion of state law are
interconnected. Officials can tolerate illegal actions or even play an active
part. As Heyman and Smart argue, state law inevitably creates its
counterparts, zones of ambiguity and outright illegality (1999: 1). They
are the unintended, yet inevitable, side effects of state involvement. By
creating this opposition between an intractable and traditional peripheral
rural society, which has to be modernised by a rational centre of power,
the necessary legitimacy is created for the interventions of the state. We
can take this a step further and follow Heyman (1998), who in his study

of undocumented immigrants at the Mexico–US border, points out that the state effects are not necessarily located in control and direct repression but in 'double-edged, successful, but entrapping conspiracies to violate the law' (1998: 158). Hence, contrary to conventional approaches to governmentality, violations of the law and corruption are seen as an effect of the state bureaucracy. They are rather the unintended, yet essential, side effect of state involvement.

Here I want to draw on the work of Žižek, who provides a very useful approach to these phenomena. According to Žižek, corruption is the shadow world that forms a central part of a regime of power (Žižek 1996). It is not the civilised public appearance of the state apparatus, but the underworld of unwritten rituals that is the actual lifeworld. Yet this underworld is only able to operate because of the existence of this image of the human civilised face, which creates the necessary sense of distance (1996: 101). In other words, regimes of power are, to a certain degree, always based on dirty, corrupt practices. Yet they can only maintain and reproduce themselves by publicly referring to the importance of the well-organised civilised state machine and the fight against corruption. Yet, we cannot stress enough that this shadow side is not exterior to the state machine, but constitutive of it. People are only able to participate in the benefits of the public official life if they follow the unwritten rules of the shadow realm. The penalty for breaking these unwritten, murky rules is much harsher than for breaking the public rules. It is not by breaking the official law that ejidatarios who sell their land end up having problems. Real problems are only caused if they refuse to follow the informal local customs for illegal land sales and if they do not know how to 'negotiate' these deals with the state officials. This explains the murky world of obscure rituals that forms the background of power. According to Žižek, the underside or obscure shadowy realm, is often permeated by enjoyment, structured in fantasies.

This is not to say that real scandals and corruption do not take place. There certainly always is an actual conspiracy or corruption scandal in which the state machine itself is involved. Yet, the obscurity and fantasies that surround corrupt practices effectively hinder the public revelation of the actual conspiracies and corruption cases (Žižek 1996: 120). According to Žižek, the real working of power 'resides in the very notion of conspiracy, in the notion of some mysterious agency that "pulls the strings" and effectively runs the show, that is to say, in the notion that, behind the visible, public power, there is another ... invisible ... power structure' (Žižek 1996: 96). Hence, the basis of the regime is the public belief in a mysterious agency that pulls the strings. The public reference made to a civilised society, the fight against corruption, and the belief in some kind of hidden master in what are, in reality, much more decentred practices of power (Abrams 1988, de Vries 2002, Rubin 1996), are complicit in maintaining regimes of power.

This means that, instead of undermining the public rule of law, corrupt practices and patron–client mechanisms support the civilised semblance of public power. In other words, the public authority can maintain a civilised, gentle appearance, while beneath it there is a shadowy realm in which the brutal exercise of power takes place. The one does not exist without the other. It is not corruption that weakens the civil public order. It is corruption linked to the notion of civil public order that forms the basis of power (see also Bayart 1993, Bayart et al. 1999).

This distance between the public, written law and its obscene counterpart leads – according to Žižek – to cynicism, or cynical distance, as the predominant form of ideological attitude of the late capitalist subject. Hence the cynical way in which officials and ejidatarios talk about society and stress how, in the end, everything is determined by 'money and relationships', is not a challenge to the system but, on the contrary, an ideological expression. By mocking the public law from the position of its obscene underside, the cynic leaves the public law intact (1996: 101). In this view, cynicism is the new ideological form that supports the regime.

Insofar as the enjoyment that permeates this underside is structured in fantasies, Žižek argues that one can also say that what the cynic leaves intact is the fantasy. Cynical distance and full reliance on fantasy are thus strictly co-dependent: 'the typical subject today is the one who, while displaying cynical distrust of any public ideology, indulges without restraint in paranoiac fantasies about conspiracies, threats, and excessive forms of enjoyment ...' (1996: 101). This is precisely what happens in Mexican society. People are highly distrustful of the state and cynical about the working of justice and the rules. At the same time, at all levels of society, people are continuously talking about conspiracies, murders and forms of enjoyment. They speculate about the phantasmatic logic of an invisible and for that very reason all-powerful Master. The fact that his very existence is doubted (people are not sure if he effectively exists or is just a mythical point of reference) adds to his power – 'I don't believe in God, but I'm nonetheless afraid of him' (Žižek 1996: 110).

Among officials we clearly notice this splitting of knowledge and belief: 'I know that the official rules are never applied in a straightforward way and that the bureaucracy is highly influenced by personal networks, yet I nonetheless believe that we should put pressure on the bureaucracy to follow the rules.' The belief concerns the public symbolic authority, while the knowledge concerns the working of power in the bureaucracy. This leads to a cynical distance that Žižek (1996) defines as the predominant form of ideological attitude of the late capitalist subject.

The foregoing means that the imagery of the struggle against corruption is complicit in maintaining the regime, rather than undermining it. The belief that corruption is a disease that can be cut out of the bureaucracy can work precisely as a reinforcement of existing regimes of power. In Chapter 7 it was shown how the governmental fight against corruption in Mexico had conservative consequences as the basis of power was not fundamentally addressed but only a 'rotten apple' in the system (in this case the SRA). In the same way, Reno shows for Sierra Leone that the 'irony of structural adjustment and its assumptions of state–society dichotomies is that they strengthen the very patrimonial features of African governance that the policies are meant to address' (1995: 12).

Many people would state that the desire for change, the generation of hope and the lack of transparent leadership are typical of Third World countries that have not yet reached a certain level of modernisation. In the same way, corruption and unaccountable leadership are said to be characteristic of the neo-patrimonial states of less developed countries. I do not agree with this view. As Bayart et al. point out:

it is not that the societies or the political systems of the sub-continent are more corrupt than others, as is so often believed. There is no reason to suppose that Japan, China, India, Russia, Turkey, Italy (or France for that matter) are any less tainted by this phenomenon. (1999: xvi)

In so-called developed states, we see the persistence of patronage and the importance of informal personal exchanges at all levels of formal structures (Theobald 1999: 497).

In fact, artificially splitting up the world into 'First', 'Second' and 'Third' world or into 'developed' and 'developing' countries conceals the global power processes at work (Hardt and Negri 2000). In my view, there is less difference in the nature of politics in different places than is generally assumed. Yet the type of dreams, fantasies and desires are different ones. For example, the image of the western world and the USA as being 'democratic' and 'free' countries organised on the basis of rational-legal principles, which help the rest of the world to become modern and democratic, can be seen as a western 'fantasy'. The context in which this fantasising occurs is a modern one. It cannot be dissociated from the process of globalisation of the planet, one of the key aspects of which is, at least for the time being, an unrestrained tendency towards economic liberalisation.

THE CONTINUING IMPORTANCE OF THE IDEA OF THE STATE

At this point it is important to pay some attention to recent changes in the Mexican political system. As was mentioned in previous chapters, the Mexican political system was, for a long time, dominated by the PRI (Partido Revolucionario Institucional) which has ruled since it was established in 1929. The general view is that the party nominated handpicked candidates, won by fraudulent elections and controlled the government bureaucracy by patronage relationships. From the mid-1980s, Mexico embraced neoliberal policies, including the North American Free Trade Agreement (NAFTA) and since the 1990s there have been reforms of the political system. In 1997 the PRI lost its majority at the national level. Although opposition parties have been gaining influence and in this sense the political system has opened up, the question remains whether this has also led to changes in practices of governance. While the changes in the electoral process and the growing importance of other political parties besides the PRI have received ample scholarly attention, the great majority of analyses have focused on electoral reform, parties and voter behaviour (Camp 1996, Cornelius et al. 1999, Dominguez and Poiré 1999). As Pansters points out, 'the relationship between the electoral process and the issue of political culture has hardly been examined' (Pansters 1997b: 30). Many authors seem to see the opening up of the party system as promising increasing democratisation in Mexico (Morris 1999). However, it is my argument that more competitive elections in themselves do not change political and bureaucratic practices. By analysing struggles and reconfigurations of groups in terms of such vague notions of 'democratisation' and the 'strengthening of civil society', we even run the risk of ignoring what is really at stake in terms of shifts of power relations within political elites. Electoral competition in itself does not displace elites as positions may easily circulate among different candidates. Furthermore, the close relations of both neoliberal politicians and bankers in Mexico to drugs trafficking and money-laundering make any conclusion about fundamental changes in the Mexican regime of power and 'growing democratisation' a naive one (Gledhill 1997). As Aitken points out, 'in a more general assessment of Mexico's "democratisation" a central question must be whether the change to a competitive party system has led to transformation in government practices and power relations at both national and local levels' (2000: 399). For the time being, however, there remains a strong interconnection between politics and the working of the bureaucracy in Mexico. People still receive benefits according to their party membership or in relation to the person in power over them. In this sense the power of patronage is still strong.

As was discussed in previous chapters, the Mexican Agrarian Law has also been radically changed in the 1990s. A heated debate arose when, in 1992, Article 27 of the Constitution was amended in accordance with current World Bank restructuring requirements. The reforms officially allow ejidatarios to rent, sell, sharecrop or mortgage their land parcels once their plots have been formally measured and registered. According to many authors, with the privatisation of the ejido, the state aimed to get rid of the small peasants and return to large landholdings that could compete with farmers in the United States and Canada under NAFTA. Academic interest shifted to state–civil society relations, popular movements and their changing role now that opposition parties are gaining influence. With respect to rural areas, the focus is on collective movements, indigenous struggles and new ways of expressing political consciousness. In the same way as in the past, little attention is paid to daily practices of people in relation to the state and to different dimensions of power.

Today, new forms of governance and rule are developing in which the sovereignty of the nation-state tends to be undermined, especially in the postcolonial world. As Hardt and Negri argue, in the global order 'sovereignty has taken a new form, composed of a series of national and supranational organisms united under a single logic of rule' (2000: xii). This new global form of sovereignty is what they call Empire. Empire establishes no territorial centre of power and does not rely on fixed boundaries or barriers. It is a decentred apparatus of rule (2000: xii). Within this regime of empire, nation-states lose influence to supra-national powers. They have to abide to international agreements and legal frameworks.

However, it is interesting that precisely at this time when the modernist/developmentalist functions of the nation-state are in question and the state has come to be represented as the cause of corruption and inefficiency in development circles, the state is playing a central role of developmental programmes of rule and governance (Blom and Stepputat 2001: 2). According to Blom and Stepputat, this paradox is based on the imagination of the state as an embodiment of sovereignty and a source of social order and stability (2001: 2). It is true that in many development programmes aimed at countering processes of lawlessness and moral decay, the state becomes the object of discourses of order. Also, in the popular imagination, the state should bring order and justice, defending the rules, and operate as the final arbiter (Abrams 1988). The state is addressed on its capacity to deliver on its promises of development. Hence, we still see the centrality given to the state as the ultimate recourse for accomplishing a state of order and countering moral decay. Blom (2001) in his analysis of violence in India's experience of modernity and capitalism talks in this respect of the importance of 'the imagination of the state as a distant but persistent guarantee of a certain social order, a measure of justice and protection from violence' (2001: 222). This, in fact, resembles Žižek's notion of the belief in 'a hidden Master who effectively keeps everything under control' (Žižek 1996: 97). These discourses of order are related to the creation of an imagery of a centre, coherence and control. In this transnational global world people direct themselves to the nation-state with questions of order. State power continues to be most important in the imagery of rule and governance. At the same time, people speculate about conspiracies, corruption scandals and the dirty workings of power. Hence, the idea of the state remains central as the object of fantasies and discourses of order.

NOTES

CHAPTER 1   AN ANTHROPOLOGY OF POWER AND THE STATE

1. The Mexican agrarian law has been changed several times this century. However, the main characteristics of the ejido regime were not changed between 1917 and 1992. In order not to cause confusion I use the term 'agrarian law' throughout the book and I refer to the Federal Agrarian Reform Law (FARL) of 1971 if I want to comment on specific articles of the agrarian law.
2. In order to avoid confusion I use the term Ministry of Agrarian Reform (SRA) whenever I refer to the institution that took care of ejido land affairs. For the majority of ejidatarios the name of the institution was of little importance, nor was the fact that it had become a ministry in 1974; it simply was the institution that interfered in ejido affairs.
3. The PRI, which ruled from 1929 till 1997, includes three main sectors: labour, peasant and popular, and many organisations are linked to one of these three sectors.
4. In anthropology the concept of the social field has a long history (Kapferer 1972, Long 1968, Mitchell 1969, Turner 1974). It has been used to show that 'individuals and groups do not operate in clearly defined institutional frameworks but rather construct fields of action which often cross-cut formal organisational boundaries and normative systems' (Long 1989: 252). In legal anthropology, the notion of field has been widely used for the analysis of established practices based on a combination of formal (legal) and informal (illegal) arrangements. For example, Moore analyses how, in the garment industry in New York, a semi-autonomous field develops with its own 'extralegal givings' and 'moral obligations' based on 'a series of binding customary rules' (Moore 1973: 62–79).

    Historians pay more attention to struggle and domination as central elements of the force field (see Jay 1993 on the work of Benjamin and Adorno; see also Roseberry 1994, Thompson 1978). Roseberry, for example, uses the concept 'field of force' to analyse 'the complex and dynamic relations between the dominant and popular, or between state formation and everyday forms of action' (Roseberry 1994: 358). However, most of these authors differ about what they see as the basis of power and domination and they are not all explicit about it.
5. Although these works make important contributions to the analysis of processes of state formation and state power, they can be criticised for the 'tendency to overemphasise the unity of the state, domination, and its consequences' (see Dean 1994: 151).
6. This research project was entitled 'Contrasting patterns of irrigation organisation, peasant strategies and planned intervention: comparative studies in western Mexico' and was directed by Norman Long.

CHAPTER 2   FACTIONALISM AND FAMILY AFTER THE AGRARIAN REFORM

1. In 1856 the Law of Alienation of Properties in Dead Hands (*Ley de Desamortización de Bienes de Manos Muertas*) was issued, which declared that all land belonging to civil or

ecclesiastic corporations would be expropriated and become the property of the people renting such land. Although the law offered the possibility for the Indian communities to ask for the protection of their rights within three months of the issuing of the law, most communities never made this formal request because of ignorance of the new law or lack of economic resources. Many people took advantage of this situation and appropriated most of the land of the Indian communities (see Reyes et al. 1974: 536–7).

2. An idea of land distribution at the beginning of the twentieth century can be gained from the following: in 1910 there were about 830 *hacendados* in Mexico who owned 97 per cent of the land, 410,300 farmers owned the remaining 3 per cent of the land, while 96.9 per cent of the heads of rural families owned no land. The *hacendados* often owned several haciendas and the largest among them owned millions of hectares (Zaragoza and Macías 1980: 2).

3. I elaborated 'maps of kinship' (genealogies of people) and 'maps of land transfers' (genealogies of land). I studied the land distribution at the start of the ejido and elaborated a genealogy of land plots from 1942 onwards. At that time the three stages in which the villagers received land had been finished and the ejido was 'completed'. The combination of these genealogies of land and people provided me with a general overview of land transactions in the ejido. Furthermore, it gave a good picture of the distribution of plots between different families in the village and how this changed over the years.

4. Three of the 97 ejidatarios do not possess an ejido plot but only a *coamil* in the commons.

5. Five García men bought private property land in Autlán in the past, and Ignacio Romero also recently bought private property land. Most of the García men have moved to Autlán.

6. Households with access to an ejido plot are those with (at least) one ejidatario or heir of a deceased ejidatario. Ejidatarios who live outside the village and who no longer have (part of) a household in the village are not counted among the 196 households.

7. Before 1946, births in La Canoa were registered in Autlán. Since the end of the 1980s, a growing number of women from La Canoa go to the clinic in Autlán to give birth and registration again takes place in Autlán. Therefore I take the period between 1946 and 1986 when births were registered in La Canoa.

CHAPTER 4   ILLEGALITY AND THE LAW

1. Gledhill (1991) presented the first detailed historical study of the history and transfer of ejido plots in an ejido in Michoacán.

2. This remained an awkward arrangement as the Agrarian Law stipulated that the heir had to be chosen from among the partner and children of an ejidatario. So, officially, inheritance by someone else would be illegal.

3. The new Agrarian Law of 1992 removes this part of the 'bargaining position' of officials, as it permits the renting out of ejido land.

CHAPTER 5   THE LOST LAND I: THE PRIEST AND THE LAWYER

1. I found one document in the archives of the Ministry of Agrarian Reform in which an SRA surveyor, who had started measuring work in La Canoa, was explicitly summoned by the head of the SRA in Guadalajara to stop the work immediately as serious problems were arising with private landowners in the region.

2. This murder led to the land sale described in Chapter 4.

CHAPTER 6 THE LOST LAND II: THE SURVEYORS

1. Several authors use the metaphor of the desiring-machine introduced by Deleuze and Guattari (1988). In his study on the working of the development bureaucracy in Lesotho, Ferguson points out that his use of the 'machine' metaphor is motivated not only 'by science-fictional analogy, but by a desire (following Foucault [1979, 1980] and Deleuze and Guattari [1988]) to capture something of the way that conceptual and discursive systems link up with social institutions and processes without even approximately determining the form or defining the logic of the outcome' (Ferguson 1990: 275). Ferguson defines the 'machine' as 'an anonymous set of interrelations that only ends up having a kind of retrospective coherence' (1990: 275). Goodchild (1996) discusses how knowledge, power and desire operate in Deleuze and Guattari's texts. He explains that, in their view, the machine is made up of thousands of uncoordinated actions and does not have a centre of control. The consistency and power of the abstract machine are desire; it is a 'desiring-machine' (Goodchild 1996: 50–1).
2. On another occasion, when Raúl and I were working in the local ejido archive, we found more than ten maps of the extension of the ejido. It seems this was the map they always received when they asked for the definitive map of the ejido.

CHAPTER 7 INSIDE THE 'HOPE-GENERATING' MACHINE

1. See Nuijten (1993) for a discussion of the public debate around the reform of Article 27 of the Mexican Constitution.
2. The aim is that the programme of PROCEDE will be applied to all ejidos. In this programme all ejido land and individual ejido plots will finally be measured and registered. Ejidatarios will then receive individual certificates for their plots. Once they have these certificates, the ejido can decide to transform the ejido domain into private land ownership (*pleno dominio*). If the majority of ejido plots have been measured, the ejido assembly can authorise the ejidatarios concerned to adopt full domain over their plots. If all ejido members decide to adopt full domain over their plots the ejido regime comes to an end. Only if 20 per cent of the ejidatarios (or at least 20 ejidatarios) decide to continue, they can continue as an ejido.
3. For an extensive description of this meeting, see Nuijten (1995).
4. Warman's most famous books are *Los campesinos: hijos predilectos del régimen* (1972) and *Y venimos a contradecir* (1976).
5. According to the new Agrarian Law, the PA is a decentralised agency of the Federal Public Administration falling under the SRA.

REFERENCES

Abrams, P. (1988) [1977] Notes on the difficulty of studying the state. *Journal of Historical Sociology* 1(1), pp. 58–89.

Aitken, R. (1997) Political culture and local identities in Michoacán. In W. Pansters (ed.) *Citizens of the pyramid; essays on Mexican political culture.* Amsterdam: Thela Publishers, Latin American Series. pp. 281–308.

Aitken, R. (2000) Mexico in perspective. *Bulletin of Latin American Research* 19, pp. 397–436.

Alasuutari, P. (1995) *Researching culture: qualitative method and cultural studies.* London: Sage.

Almond, G. and Verba, S. (eds) (1980) *The civic culture revisited.* Boston: Little, Brown Co.

Alonso, A. (1994) The politics of space, time and substance: state formation, nationalism, and ethnicity. *Annual Review of Anthropology* 23, pp. 379–405.

Appadurai, A. (1997) *Modernity at large: cultural dimensions of globalization.* Minneapolis: University of Minnesota Press.

Apthorpe, R. and Gasper, D. (1996) *Arguing development policy: frames and discourses.* London: Frank Cass and Co.

Arce, A. (1993) *Negotiating agricultural development: entanglements of bureaucrats and rural producers in Western Mexico.* Wageningse Sociologische Studies no. 34. Wageningen: Wageningen Agricultural University.

Arensberg, C. (1972) Culture as behavior: structure and emergence. *Annual Review of Anthropology* 1, pp. 1–26.

Bailey, F. (1969) *Strategems and spoils: a social anthropology of politics.* Oxford: Basil Blackwell.

Bakhtin, M. (1981) *The dialogical imagination: four essays,* trans. C. Emerson and M. Holquist. Austin: University of Texas Press.

Barth, F. (1993) *Balinese worlds.* Chicago: University of Chicago Press.

Bartra, R. (ed.) (1980a) [1975] *Caciquismo y poder politico en el México rural.* México: Siglo XXI.

Bartra, A. (1980b) Crisis agraria y movimiento campesino en los sesentas. *Cuadernos Agrarios* 10/1/.

Bayart, J. (1993) *The state in africa: the politcs of the belly.* London: Longman.

Bayart, J., Ellis, S. and Hibou, B. (1999) *African issues: the criminalization of the state in Africa.* Indianapolis: Indiana University Press.

Bebbington, A. and Farrington, J. (eds) (1993) *Reluctant partners: non governmental organizations, the state and sustainable agricultural development.* London: Routledge.

Beezley, W., Martin, C. and French, W. (eds) (1994) *Rituals of rule, rituals of resistance: public celebrations and popular culture in Mexico.* Wilmington, DE: Scholarly Resources.

Berkes, F. (1995) Community-based management and co-management as tools for empowerment. In N. Singh and V. Titi (eds) *Empowerment: towards sustainable development.* London: Zed Books, pp. 138–46.

Bhabha, H. (1991) The postcolonial critic. *Arena* 96, pp. 47–63.

Binford, L. (1985) Political conflict and land tenure in the Mexican Isthmus of Tehuantepec. *Journal of Latin American Studies* 17, pp. 179–200.

Bloch, M. (1971) The moral and tactical meaning of kinship terms. *Man* n.s. 6, pp. 79–87.

Bloch, M. (1975) *Political language and oratory in traditional society*. Cambridge: Cambridge University Press.

Blom, T. (2001) Governance and state mythologies in Mumbai. In T. Blom and F. Stepputat (eds) *States of imagination: ethnographic explorations of the post-colonial state*. Durham, NC: Duke University Press, pp. 221–54.

Blom, T. and Stepputat, F. (eds) (2001) *States of imagination: ethnographic explorations of the post-colonial state*. Durham, NC: Duke University Press.

Bourdieu, P. (1977) *Outline of a theory of practice*. Cambridge: Cambridge University Press.

Bourdieu, P. (2001) Habitus. In J. Hillier and E. Rooksby (eds) *Habitus: a sense of place*. Aldershot: Ashgate, pp. 27–36.

Bourdieu, P. and Wacquant, L. (1992) *An invitation to reflexive sociology*. Chicago: University of Chicago Press.

Buve, R. (1988) 'Neither Carranza nor Zapata!': the rise and fall of a peasant movement that tried to challenge both, Tlaxcala, 1910–19. In F. Katz (ed.) *Riot, rebellion and revolution: rural social conflict in Mexico*. Princeton, NJ: Princeton University Press.

Camp, R. (ed.) (1986) *Mexico's political stability: the next five years*. Boulder, CO: Westview Press.

Camp, R. (1996) *Politics in Mexico*. Oxford: Oxford University Press.

Carlos, M. (1992) Peasant leadership hierarchies: leadership behavior, power blocs, and conflict in Mexican regions. In E. Van Young (ed.) *Mexico's regions: comparative history and development*. La Jolla: Center for U.S.-Mexican Studies, University of California San Diego, pp. 91–114.

Cohen, A. (1994) *Self consciousness: and alternative anthropology of identity*. London and New York: Routledge.

Comaroff, J. and Comaroff, J. (eds) (1993) *Modernity and its malcontents: ritual and power in postcolonial Africa*. Chicago and London: University of Chicago Press.

Comaroff, J. and Roberts, S. (1981) *Rules and process: the cultural logic of dispute in an African context*. Chicago: University of Chicago Press.

Cooke, B. and Kothari, U. (eds) (2001) *Participation, the new tyranny?* London: Zed Press.

Cornelius, W. and Craig, A. (1980) Political culture in Mexico: continuities and revisionist interpretations. In G. Almond and S. Verba (eds) *The civic culture revisited*. Boston: Little, Brown Co.

Cornelius, W. and Craig, A. (1988) *Politics in Mexico; an introduction and overview*, revised edn. La Jolla: Center for U.S.-Mexican Studies, University of California San Diego.

Cornelius, W. and Craig, A. (1991) *The Mexican political system in transition*. La Jolla: Center for U.S.-Mexican Studies. University of California San Diego.

Cornelius, W., Eisenstadt, T. and Hindley, J. (eds) (1999) *Subnational politics and democratization in Mexico*. La Jolla: Center for U.S.-Mexican Studies, University of California San Diego.

Corrigan, P. and Sayer, D. (1985) *The great arch: English state formation as cultural revolution*. Oxford: Basil Blackwell.

Curtis, D. (1991) *Beyond government: organizations for common benefit*. London: Macmillan.

Czarniawska, B. (1997) *Narrating the organisation: dramas of institutional identity*. Chicago: University of Chicago Press.

DaMatta, R. (1991) *Carnivals, rogues, and heroes: an interpretation of the Brazilian dilemma*. London: University of Notre Dame Press.

De Vries, P. (1992) A research journey. In N. Long and A. Long (eds) *Battlefields of knowledge: the interlocking of theory and practice in social research and devlopment*. London: Routledge, pp. 47–84.

De Vries, P. (1997) *Unruly clients in the Atlantic zone of Costa Rica.* Amsterdam: CEDLA, Latin American Studies.

De Vries, P. (2002) Vanishing mediators: enjoyment as a political factor in Mexico. *American Ethnologist* 29(4), pp. 901–27.

Dean, M. (1994) *Critical and effective histories: Foucault's methods and historical sociology.* London and New York: Routledge.

Deleuze, G. and Guattari, F. (1988) [1980] *A thousand plateaus: capitalism and schizophrenia,* vol. II. London: Athlone.

Departamento de la Estadística Nacional (1921) *Censo General de Habitantes.* Mexico, DF: Departamento de la Estadística Nacional.

Departamento de Estadística Nacional (1926) *Censo General de Habitantes, 30 de noviembre de 1921, Estado de Jalisco.* Mexico, DF: Talleres Gráticos de la Nación.

Dirección General de Estadística (1952) *Séptimo Censo General de Población, 6 de junio de 1950.* Secretaría de Economía. Estado de Jalisco. Mexico, DF: Dirección General de Estadística.

Dirks, N., Eley, G. and Ortner, S. (eds) (1994) *Culture, power, history: a reader in contemporary social theory.* Princeton, NJ: Princeton University Press.

Dominguez, J. and Poiré, A. (eds) (1999) *Towards Mexico's democratization: parties, campaigns, elections and public opinion.* New York and London: Routledge.

Durkheim, E. (1965) [1912] *The elementary forms of religious life.* New York: The Free Press.

Escobar, A. (1995) *Encountering development: the making and unmaking of the Third World.* Princeton, NJ: Princeton University Press.

Esteva, G. (1980) *La batalla en el México rural.* México: Siglo XXI.

Esteva, G. (1987) Regenerating people's space. *Alternatives* 12, pp. 125–52.

Fairhead, J. and Leach, M. (1995) False forest history, complicit social analysis: rethinking some West African environmental narratives. *World Development* 23(6), pp. 1023–35.

Ferguson, J. (1990) *The anti-politics machine: development, depoliticization, and bureaucratic power in Lesotho.* Cambridge and New York: Cambridge University Press.

Foley, M. (1990) Organizing ideology, and moral suasion: political discourse and action in a Mexican town. *Society for Comparative Studies in Society and History,* 32, pp. 455–87.

Foucault, M. (1979) [1975] *Discipline and punish: the birth of the prison.* London: Penguin Books.

Foucault, M. (1980) *Power/knowledge: selected interviews and other writings, 1972–7.* New York: Pantheon Books.

Foweraker, J. (1994) Popular mobilization and popular culture in Mexico. paper presented at the XV Encuentro de la RNIU, 'Poder, Cultura y Pobreza', El Colegio de Michoacán, noviembre.

Fox, J. and Gordillo, G. (1989) Between state and market: the campesino's quest for autonomy. In W. Cornelius, J. Gentleman and P. Smith (eds) *Mexico's alternative political futures.* La Jolla: Center for U.S.-Mexican Studies, University of California San Diego, pp. 131–72.

Friedrich, P. (1986) *The princes of naranja: an essay in anthrohistorical method.* Austin: University of Texas Press.

Galanter, M. (1981) Justice in many rooms: courts, private ordering and indigenous law. *Journal of Legal Pluralism* 19, pp. 1–47.

Geschiere, P. (2001) Witchcraft and new forms of wealth: regional variations in south and west Cameroon. In P. Clough and J. Mitchell (eds) *Powers of good and evil: social transformation and popular belief.* New York: Berghahn Books, pp. 43–76.

Gilsenan, M. (1977) Against patron–client relations. In E. Gellner and J. Waterbury (eds) *Patron and clients in Mediterranean Societies.* London: Duckworth.

Gledhill, J. (1991) *Casi nada: a study of agrarian reform in the homeland of Cardenismo.* Austin: University of Texas Press.

Gledhill, J. (1994) *Power and its disguises: anthropological perspectives on politics.* London and Boulder, CO: Pluto Press.

Gledhill, J. (1995) *Neoliberalism, transnationalization and rural poverty: a case study of Michoacán, Mexico.* Boulder, CO: Westview Press.

Gledhill, J. (1997) Fantasy and reality in restructuring Mexico's land reform, paper presented at the annual Society for Latin American Studies meeting, St Andrews, Scotland. Electronic publication from the social anthropology web site of the University of Manchester, England.

Goldring, L. (1996) The changing configuration of property rights under ejidal reform. In L. Randall (ed.) *Reforming Mexico's agrarian reform.* Armonk, NY: M.E. Sharpe.

González, L. (1988) Lugares comunes acerca de lo rural. In J. Zepeda (ed.) *Las sociedades rurales hoy.* Zamora: El Colegio de Michoacán, CONACYT, pp. 51–61.

Goodchild, P. (1996) *Deleuze and Guattari: an introduction to the politics of desire.* London: Sage.

Gordillo, G. (1988) El leviatán rural y la nueva sociabilidad política. In J. Zepeda (ed.) *Las sociedades rurales hoy.* Zamora: El Colegio de Michoacán, CONACYT, pp. 223–54.

Gramsci, A. (1971) [1929–35] *Selections from the prison notebooks,* ed. and trans. Q. Hoare and G. Nowell-Smith. New York: International Publishers.

Grillo, R. and Stirrat, R. (eds) (1997) *Discourses of development: anthropological perspectives.* Oxford and New York: Berg.

Grindle, M. (1977) *Bureaucrats, politicians, and peasants in Mexico: a case study in public policy.* Berkeley and Los Angeles: University of California Press.

Grindle, M. (1995) Reforming land tenure in Mexico: peasants, the market, and the state. In R. Roett (ed.) *The challenge of institutional reform in Mexico.* Boulder, CO and London: Lynne Rienner Publishers, pp 39–56.

Gulliver, P. (1979) *Disputes and negotiations: a cross-cultural perspective.* New York: Academic Press.

Gupta, A. (1995) Blurred boundaries: the discourse of corruption, the culture of politics, and the imagined state. *American Ethnologist* 22(2), pp. 375–402.

Gupta, A. and Ferguson, J. (eds) (1997a) *Culture, power, place: explorations in critical anthropology.* Durham, NC and London: Duke University Press.

Gupta, A. and Ferguson, J. (eds) (1997b) *Anthropological locations: boundaries and grounds of a field science.* Berkeley, Los Angeles, London: University of California Press.

Hall, S. (1986) On postmodernism and articulation: an interview with Stuart Hall. *Journal of Communication Inquiry* 10(2), pp. 45–60.

Hansen, H.H. (1998) Governmental mismanagement and symbolic violence. *Bulletin of Latin American Research* 17(3), pp. 367–86.

Hardt, M. and Negri, A. (2000) *Empire.* Cambridge, MA: Harvard University Press.

Hardy, C. (1984) *El estado y los campesinos: la Confederación Nacional Campesina (CNC).* México: Editorial Nueva Imagen.

Harris, M. (1988) On charities and NGOs. In R. Poulton and M. Harris (eds) *Putting people first: voluntary organisations and Third World organisations.* London: Macmillan, pp. 1–10.

Harris, O. (ed.) (1996) *Inside and outside the law: anthropological studies of authority and ambiguity.* London: Routledge.

Heyman, McC. J. (1998) Immigration law enforcement and the superexploitation of undocumented aliens: the Mexico–United States border case. *Critique of Anthropology* 18, pp. 157–80.

Heyman, McC. J. (ed.) (1999) *States and illegal practices.* Oxford and New York: Berg.

Heyman, McC. J. and Smart, A. (1999) States and illegal practices: an overview. In J. McC. Heyman (ed.) *States and illegal practices.* Oxford and New York: Berg, pp. 1–24.

Hirschman, A. (1970) *Exit, voice and loyalty: responses to decline in firms, organization and states.* Cambridge, MA: Harvard University Press

Hobart, M. (ed.) (1993) *An anthropological critique of development: the growth of ignorance.* London and New York: Routledge.

Ibarra, J. (1989) *Propiedad agraria y sistema político en México.* Sonora: El Colegio de Sonora.

INEGI (1990) *Encuesta Nacional Agropecuaria Ejidal, 1988, Volume I: Resumen General.* Mexico, DF: INEGI.

INEGI (1991) *XI Censo General de Población y Vivienda, 1990: Jalisco Resultados definitivos. Datos por Localidad (Intergración Territorial)* Mexico, DF: INEGI.

Jay, M. (1993) *Force fields: between intellectual history and cultural critique.* New York and London: Routledge.

Jones, G. (1996) Dismantling the ejido. In R. Aitken, N. Craske, G. Jones and D. Stansfield (eds) *Dismantling the Mexican state?* London: Macmillan, pp. 188–203.

Joseph, G. and Nugent, D. (eds) (1994) *Everyday forms of state formation: revolution and the negotiation of rule in modern Mexico.* Durham, NC and London: Duke University Press.

Kapferer, B. (1972) *Strategy and transaction in an African factory.* Manchester: Manchester University Press.

Kearney, M. (1996) *Reconceptualizing the peasantry: anthropology in global perspective.* Boulder, CO and Oxford: Westview Press.

Knight, A. (1986) *The Mexican Revolution,* 2 vols. Cambridge: Cambridge University Press.

Knight, A. (1994) Weapons and arches in the Mexican revolutionary landscape. In: G. Joseph and D. Nugent (eds) *Everyday forms of state formation: revolution and the negotiation of rule in modern Mexico.* Durham, NC and London: Duke University Press, pp. 24–68.

Krotz, E. et al. (1985) *Cooperativas agrarias y conflictos políticos en el sur de Jalisco.* México: UAM Iztapalapa.

Law, J. (1992) Notes on the theory of the actor-network: ordering, strategy and hetero-geneity. *Systems Practice* 5(4), pp. 379–93.

Law, J. (1994a) *Organizing modernity.* Oxford: Basil Blackwell.

Law, J. (1994b) Organization, narrative and strategy. In J. Hassard and M. Parker (eds) *Towards a new theory of organizations.* London and New York: Routledge, pp. 248–68.

Leach M., Mearns, R. and Scoones, I. (1997) *Environmental entitlements: a framework for understanding the institutional dynamics of environmental change.* IDS Discussion paper 359. Brighton: IDS.

Lomnitz-Adler, C. (1992) *Exits from the labyrinth: culture and ideology in the Mexican national space.* Berkeley, Los Angeles and Oxford: University of California Press.

Lomnitz-Adler, C. (1999) Modes of citizenship in Mexico. *Public Culture* 11(1), pp. 269–93.

Long, N. (1968) *Social change and the individual: a study of social and religious responses to innovation in a Zambian rural community.* Manchester: Manchester University Press.

Long, N. (1984) Creating space for change: a perspective on the sociology of development. *Sociologia Ruralis* 24(3/4), pp. 168–84.

Long, N. (1988) Sociological perspectives on agrarian development and state intervention. In A. Hall and J. Midgley (eds) *Development policies: sociological perspectives.* Manchester: Manchester University Press, pp. 109–48.

Long, N. (ed.) (1989) *Encounters at the interface: a perspective on social discontinuities in rural development.* Wageningse Sociologische Studies no. 27. Wageningen: Wageningen Agricultural University.

Long, N. and van der Ploeg, J. (1989) Demythologizing planned intervention: an actor perspective. *Sociologia Ruralis* 29(3/4), pp. 226–49.

Massey, D., Alarcón, R., Durand, J. and González, H. (1987) *Return to Aztlán: the social process of international migration from Western Mexico.* Berkeley: University of California Press.

Meyer J. (1991) *La Revolución Mexicana.* México: Editorial Jus.

Mitchell, C. (1969) *Social networks in urban situations.* Manchester: Manchester University Press.

Mitchell, C. (1983) Case and situation analysis. *Sociological Review* n.s. 31(2), pp. 187–211.

Moore, S. (1973) Law and social change: the semi-autonomous social fields as an appropiate subject of study. *Law and Society Review* 7, pp. 719–46.

Morgan, G. (1986) *Images of organization*. Beverly Hills and London: Sage.

Morris, S.D. (1999) Corruption and the Mexican political system: continuity and change. *Third World Quarterly* 20(3), pp. 623–43.

Mosse, D. (1997) The ideology and politics of community participation: tank irrigation development in colonial and contemporary Tamil Nadu. In R. Grillo and R. Stirrat (eds) *Discourses of development: anthropological perspectives*. Oxford and New York: Berg, pp. 255–91.

Muría, J. (1982) *Historia de Jalisco, IV: desde la consolidación del Porfiriato hasta mediados del siglo XX*. Guadalajara: Gobierno del Estado de Jalisco.

Nader, L. (ed.) (1969) *Law in culture and society*. Chicago: Aldine.

Nagengast, C. (1994) Violence, terror and the crisis of the state. *Annual Review of Anthropology* 23, pp. 109–36.

Nuijten, M. (1992) Local organization as organizing practices: rethinking rural institutions. In N. Long and A. Long (eds) *Battlefields of knowledge: the interlocking of theory and practice in social research and development*. London and New York: Routledge, pp. 189–207.

Nuijten, M. (1993) De privatisering van de ejido in Mexico: het einde van de revolutionaire idealen? *Derde Wereld* 12(2), pp. 27–45.

Nuijten, M. (1995) Changing legislation and a new agrarian bureaucracy: shifting arenas of negotiation. S. Zendejas and P. de Vries (eds) *Rural transformations seen from below: regional and local perspectives from Western Mexico*. Transformation of Rural Mexico Series, no. 8. San Diego: Center for U.S.-Mexican Studies, University of California, Ejido Reform Research Project, pp. 49–67.

Nuijten, M. (1997) Agrarian reform and the ejido in Mexico: illegality within the framework of the law. *Law and Anthropology* 9, pp. 72–104.

Pansters, W. (ed.) (1997a) *Citizens of the pyramid: essays on Mexican political culture*. Amsterdam: Thela Publishers. Latin American Series.

Pansters, W. (1997b) Theorizing political culture in modern Mexico. In W. Pansters (ed.) *Citizens of the pyramid: essays on Mexican political culture*. Amsterdam: Thela Publishers, Latin American Series, pp. 1–40.

Parkin, D. (1984) Political language. *Annual Review of Anthropology* 13, pp. 345–65.

de la Peña, G. (1986) Poder local, poder regional: perspectivas socio-antropologicas. In J. Padua and Vanneph (eds) *Poder local, poder regional*. Mexico, DF: El Colegio de Mexico/ CEMCA.

Pigg, S. (1992) Inventing social categories through place: social representations and development in Nepal. *Comparative Studies of Society and History* 34, pp. 491–513.

Pigg, S. (1996) The credible and the credulous: the question of 'villagers' beliefs' in Nepal. *Cultural Anthropology* 11, pp. 160–202.

Pigg, S. (1997) 'Found in most traditional societies': traditional medical practitioners between culture and development. In F. Cooper and R. Packard (eds) *International development and the social sciences*. Berkeley: University of California Press, pp. 259–90.

Poulton, R. (1988) On theories and strategies. In R. Poulton and M. Harris (eds) *Putting people first: voluntary organisations and Third World organisations*. London: Macmillan, pp. 11–32.

Poulton, R. and Harris, M. (eds) (1988) *Putting people first: voluntary organisations and Third World organisations*. London: Macmillan.

Reed, M. (1992) *The sociology of organizations: themes, perspectives and prospects*. New York: Harvester Wheatsheaf.

Reno, W. (1995) Corruption and state politics in Sierra Leone. Cambridge: Cambridge University Press.

Reyes, S., Stavenhagen, R., Eckstein, S. and Ballesteros, J. (1974) *Estructura agraria y desarrollo agrícola en méxico: estudio sobre las relaciones entre la tenencia y el desarollo agrícola de México*. México: Fondo de Cultura Económica.

Rincón, R. (1980) *El ejido Mexicano*. México: Centro Nacional de Investigaciones Agrarias.

Roe, E. (1991) Development narratives, or making the best of blueprint development. *World Development* 19(4), pp. 287–300.

Rogers, A. and Vertovec, S. (eds) (1995) *The urban context: ethnicity, social networks and situational analysis*. Oxford: Berg.

Rosaldo, R. (1989) *Culture and truth: the remaking of social analysis*. Boston, MA: Beacon Press.

Rose, N. (1999) *Powers of freedom: reframing political thought*. Cambridge: Cambridge University Press.

Rose, N. and Miller, P. (1992) Political power beyond the state: problematics of government. *British Journal of Sociology* 43(2), pp. 173–205.

Roseberry, W. (1994) Hegemony and the language of contention. In G. Joseph and D. Nugent (eds) *Everyday forms of state formation: revolution and the negotiation of rule in Mexico*. Durham, NC and London: Duke University Press, pp. 355–66.

Rouse, R. (1989) Mexican migration to the United States: family relations in the development of a transnational migrant circuit. PhD diss., Department of Anthropology, Stanford University, California.

Rubin, J. (1996) Decentering the regime: culture and regional politics in Mexico. *Latin American Research Review* 31(3), pp. 85–126.

Sabean, D. (1984) *Power in the blood: popular culture and village discourse in early modern Germany*. Cambridge: Cambridge University Press.

Sabean, D. (1990) *Property, production, and family in Neckerhausen, 1700–1870*. Cambridge: Cambridge University Press.

Sabean, D. (1998) *Kinship in Neckerhausen, 1700–1870:* Cambridge: Cambridge University Press.

Said, E. (1978) *Orientalism: western representations of the other*. London: Routledge and Kegan Paul.

SARH (1985) *El programa de desarollo rural integral de la región Costa del Estado de Jalisco* (internal report). Guadalajara: SARH (Secretaría de Agricultura y Ricursos Hidraulicos).

Schryer, F. (1980) *The rancheros of Pisaflores: the history of a peasant bourgeoisie in eighteenth-century Mexico*. Toronto, Buffalo and London: University of Toronto Press.

Schryer, F. (1986) Peasants and the law: a history of land tenure and conflict in Huasteca. *Journal of Latin American Studies* 18, pp. 283–311.

Scott, J. (1985) *Weapons of the weak: everyday forms of peasant resistance*. New Haven, CT and London: Yale University Press.

Scott, J. (1994) Foreword. In G. Joseph and D. Nugent (eds) *Everyday forms of state formation: revolution and the negotiation of rule in modern Mexico*. Durham, NC and London: Duke University Press, pp. vii–xii.

Scott, J. (1998) *Seeing like a state: how certain schemes to improve the human condition have failed*. New Haven, CT: Yale University Press.

Silverman, D. (1993) *Interpreting qualitative data: methods for analysing talk, text and interaction*. London: Sage Publications.

Singh, R. (1988) How can we help the poorest of the poor? The impact of local elites in some NGO community development programmes in Nepal and Bangladesh. In R. Poulton and M. Harros (eds) *Putting people first: voluntary organizations and Third World organizations*. London: Macmillan, pp. 33–45.

Smith, G. (1991) The production of culture in local rebellion. In J. O'Brien and W. Roseberry (eds) *Golden ages, dark ages: imagining the past in anthropology and history*. Berkeley and Oxford: University of California Press, pp. 180–207.

Smith, G. (1996) Los contornos de la actividad colectiva: el rol de la organización y de la interpretación (traducción inglés), revised version of paper presented at coloqui, 'Las Disputas por el Mexico Rural: Transformaciones de Prácticas, Identidades y Proyectos', Colegio de Michoacán, November 1994.

Smith, G. (1999) *Confronting the present: towards a politically engaged anthropology.* Oxford: Berg.

Spivak, G. (1987) *In other worlds: essays in cultural politics.* New York: Methuen.

Starr, J. and Collier, J. (1989) *History and power in the study of law: new directions in legal anthropology.* Ithaca, NY and London: Cornell University Press.

Stephen, L. (1994) *Viva Zapata! Generation, gender and historical consciousness in the reception of ejido reform in Oaxaca.* La Jolla: Centre for U.S.-Mexican Studies, University of California San Diego.

Stephen L. (1997) Pro-Zapatista and pro-PRI: resolving the contradictions of Zapata in rural Oaxaca. *Latin American Research Review* 32(2), pp. 41–70.

Stiefel, M. and Wolfe, M. (1994) A voice for the excluded: popular participation in development, utopia or necessity. London and New Jersy: ZED Books in association with the UNRISD, Geneva.

Tapia, J. (ed.) (1992) *Intermediación social y procesos políticos en Michoacán.* Zamora: El Colegio de Michoacán.

Taussig, M. (1992) *The nervous system.* London: Routledge.

Theobald, R. (1999) So what really is the problem about corruption? *Third World Quarterly* 20(3), pp. 491–502.

Thoden van Velzen, B. and van Wetering, I. (2001) Dangerous creatures and the enchantment of modern life. In P. Clough and J. Mitchell (eds) *Powers of good and evil: social transformation and popular belief.* New York: Berghahn Books, pp. 17–42.

Thomas, N. (1994) *Colonialism's culture: anthropology, travel and government.* Princeton, NJ: Princeton University Press.

Thompson, E.P. (1978) Eighteenth-century English society: class struggle without class? *Social History* 3(2), pp. 133–65.

Torres, G. (1994) *La Refundación neoliberal del campesino Jaliscience y las estrategías de las organizaciones sociales,* paper presented at the XVI Coloquio at the Colegio de Michoacán, November.

Torres, G. (1997) *The force of irony: power in the everyday life of Mexican tomatoy workers.* Oxford: Berg.

Trouillot, M. (2001) The anthropology of the state in the age of globalization. *Current Anthropology* 42(1), pp. 125–38.

Tsing, A. (1993) *In the realm of the diamond queen: marginality in an out-of-the-way place.* Princeton, NJ: Princeton University Press.

Turner, V. (1974) *Dramas, fields, and metaphors: symbolic action in human society.* Ithaca, NY and London: Cornell University Press.

Tutino, John (1986) *From insurrection to revolution in Mexico: social bases of agrarian violence, 1750–1940.* Princeton, NJ and Oxford: Princeton University Press.

Uphoff, N. (1992) *Local institutions and participation for sustainable development.* West Hartford, CT: Kumarian Press.

van Velsen, J. (1967) The extended case-study method and situational analysis. In A. Epstein (ed.) *The craft of social anthropology.* London: Tavistock.

Verschoor, G. (1997) Tacos, tiendas and mezcal: an actor-network perspective on small-scale entrepreneurial projects in Western Mexico. PhD thesis. Wageningen: Wageningen University.

Vincent, J. (1990) *Anthropology and politics: visions, traditions and trends.* Tucson and London: Arizona University Press.

von Benda-Beckmann, F. (1992) Changing legal pluralism in Indonesia. *Tahun* 7, (Juli–August), pp. 1–23.

220 *Power, Community and the State*

von Benda-Beckmann, F. (1993) Scape-goat and magic charm: law in development theory and practice. In M. Hobart (ed.) *An anthropological critique of development: the growth of ignorance.* London and New York: Routledge, pp. 116–34.

von Benda-Beckmann, F. (1994) Good governance, law and social reality: problematic relationships. *Knowledge and Policy: The International Journal of Knowledge Transfer and Utilization* 7(3), pp. 55–67.

von Benda-Beckmann, F. and von Benda-Beckmann, K. (1998) A functional analysis of property rights, with special reference to Indonesia (internal paper). Wageningen University.

von Benda-Beckmann, F. and von Benda-Beckmann, K. (1999) A functional analysis of property rights, with special reference to Indonesia. In T. van Meijl and F. von Benda-Beckmann (eds) *Property rights and economic development: land and natural resources in Southeast Asia and Oceania.* London and New York: Kegan Paul International, pp. 15–56.

von Benda-Beckmann, F. and van der Velde, M. (eds) (1992) *Law as a resource in agrarian struggles.* Wageningse Sociologische Studies no. 33. Wageningen: Wageningen Agricultural University.

von Benda-Beckmann, K. (1981) Forum shopping and shopping forums: dispute settlement in a Minangkabau village in West Sumatra. *Journal of Legal Pluralism* 19, pp. 117–59.

Walton, J. (1992) Making the theoretical case. In H. Becker and C. Ragin (eds) *What is a case? Exploring the foundations of social inquiry.* Cambridge: Cambridge University Press, pp. 121–38.

Warman, A. (1972) *Los campesinos: hijos predilectos del régimen.* México: Editorial Nuestro Tiempo.

Warman, A. (1976) *Y venimos a contradecir: los campesinos de Morelos y el Estado Nacional.* México, DF: Ediciones de la Casa Chata.

Wiber, M. (1993) *Politics, property and law in the Philippine uplands.* Ontario: Wilfrid Laurier University Press.

Williams, R. (1977) *Marxism and literature.* Oxford: Oxford University Press.

Wolf, E. (1990) Facing power: old insights, new questions. *American Anthropologist* 92(3), pp. 586–96.

World Bank (1996) *The World Bank participation sourcebook.* Washington, DC: World Bank.

Young, R. (1995) *Colonial desire: hybridity in theory, culture and race.* London and New York: Routledge.

Zaragoza, L. and Macías, R. (1980) *El desarrollo agrario de México y su marco jurídico.* México: Centro Nacional de Investigaciones Agrarias.

Zárate, E. (1993) *Los señores de la Utopia: etnicidad política en una comunidad Phurhépecha.* Zamora and Guadalajara: El Colegio de Michoacán and CIESAS.

Zendejas, S. (1995) Appropriating governmental reforms: the ejido as an arena of confrontation and negotiation. In S. Zendejas and P. de Vries (eds) *Rural transformations seen from below: regional and local perspectives from western Mexico.* La Jolla: Center for U.S.-Mexican studies, University of California San Diego, pp. 23–48.

Zendejas, S. and Mummert, G., (1996) Beyond the agrarian question: the cultural politics of ejido natural resources. In W. Cornelius and D. Myhre (eds) *The transformation of rural Mexico: reforming the ejido sector.* La Jolla: Center for U.S.-Mexican Studies, University of California San Diego.

Zepeda, J. (ed.) (1988) *Las sociedades rurales hoy.* México: El Colegio de Michoacán.

Žižek, S. (1996) 'I hear you with my eyes': or, the invisble master. In R. Saleci and S. Žižek (eds) *Gaze and voice as love objects.* Durham, NC and London: Duke University Press, pp. 90–126.

INDEX

Compiled by Sue Carlton